Nationalism on the Iberian Peninsula During the Early 20th Century

Basque Politics Series No.21

Nationalism on the Iberian Peninsula During the Early 20th Century

CENTER FOR BASQUE STUDIES
UNIVERSITY OF NEVADA, RENO
2021

This book was published with generous financial support from the Basque Government.

Center for Basque Studies
University of Nevada, Reno
1664 North Virginia St,
Reno, Nevada 89557 usa
http://basque.unr.edu

Cover Design by Rebecca Lown

Library of Congress Cataloguing in Publication Data
Names: Alonso Olea, Eduardo J., author. | Cattini, Giovanni C., 1972-
   author. | Diéguez Cequiel, Uxío-Breogán, 1978- author.
Title: Nationalism on the Iberian Peninsula during the early 20th century.
Description: Reno : Center for Basque Studies Press, 2022. | Series: Basque
   politics series | Includes bibliographical references and index.
Identifiers: LCCN 2022004685 | ISBN 9781949805499 (paperback)
Subjects: LCSH: Nationalism--Spain--País Vasco--History. |
   Nationalism--Spain--Catalonia--History. | Nationalism--Spain--Galicia
   (Region)--History. | Spain--Politics and government--1886-1931. | País
   Vasco (Spain)--Politics and government--20th century. | Catalonia
   (Spain)--Politics and government--20th century. | Galicia (Spain :
   Region)--Politics and government--20th century.
Classification: LCC DP238 .N38 2022 | DDC 946/.074--dc23/eng/20220217
LC record available at https://lccn.loc.gov/2022004685

Printed in the United States of America

Contents

Introduction

The Italian historian Benedetto Croce effectively postulated that all history is, in effect, contemporary history as historians write from the perspective of the present and ask questions pertinent to their own times. Historians have unquestionably been one of the major intermediaries between society and the demands for knowledge of the past, and any period prior to the present has been analyzed from their present-day perspective. In this sense, the historiography about the various different concepts of nation and nationalisms in Spain allow us to analyze one of the principal problems that has characterized contemporary politics in the Spanish state. In this context, it should be remembered that historians who write the stories that configure state nationalism have the habit of presenting these national stories as a natural process, by which all people who are part of the state itself have to accept that identity and national history, projected by the institutions that make up the bureaucratic-political-administrative machinery of that state.

And it has always been like that; i.e., when Viriato fought the Romans, he had the clear conviction that he was resisting the invasion of Spain, with Madrid as its capital and defined borders with its neighbors, France and Portugal. In contrast, historians who work with (and even give validity or value to) the histories of stateless nations have greater difficulty in spreading their message: they must compete on unequal terms with the versions of history promoted by the state. Therefore, at the moment of truth, both those historians backed by the state, as well as the others, have become used to resorting to some

1

national imaginary or other which, often times, mixes the story of events (the historical reality) with resources more suited to the mythology associated with the unifying elements of the various nationalisms, especially when looking at extremely far-off times. In this sense, both Viriato and Zumalacárregui are equally distant in time.

The divergences between the different conceptions of understanding Spain (now not as a state but as a complex political situation throughout history) can be traced back to the nineteenth century; this was when a modern historiography began to crystallize in support of the projects to construct a liberal state in Spain and in many other places. If the study of history was professionalized as a social science, it is necessary to remember the importance of Modesto Lafuente's work, *Historia General de España* [General History of Spain], which appeared in thirty volumes between 1850 and 1867. The work offered a theological and idealized version of the history of Spanish unity: its interpretative methodology identified divine providence as the instrument which led to the reconquest of Spanish territory occupied by the Moors in the Middle Ages and the configuration of the Catholic Monarchs. With Ferdinand of Aragon and Isabella I of Castile, the transcendental plan for Spanish unity was fulfilled, its splendor reaching its apex across the Early Modern period. Lafuente added that the Spanish monarchy of the nineteenth century was heir to the constitutionalism of the Early Modern era and that, therefore, there was no need for revolutionary unrest as there was in France of 1789. Lafuente's theses were undeniably dominant in Spain, being backed by the institutions of the state. They were not the only ideas in existence, however. In Galicia, the Basque Country, and Catalonia there were versions of history that put forward the differential past of these territories. In Galicia, in the second half of the nineteenth century, there was growing support for a history of its own, pioneered by José Verea y Aguiar.[1] He was followed by authors including Martínez Padín, Benito Vicetto, and, lastly, Manuel M. Murguía, the historian who made the greatest contribution to the Galician national(ist) story. Murguía,[2] a driving force behind the Galician *Rexurdimento*, identified those specifically Galician traits— fierceness and indomitable spirit—as being rooted in the region's Celtic heritage. He defended the importance of the Galician language

as central to the vertebration of the national community, its decline
having started in the Lower Middle Ages as a result of the dominance
of Castilian and the oppression of the Galician nobility (as explained
in his five-volume *Historia de Galicia*, written between 1865 and 1913).

In the Basque Country, the tradition of cultivating Basques' own
history has resulted in a broad bibliography throughout the Early
Modern era (Andrés de Poza and Manuel de Larramendi were
authors who began to spread the idea of the Basque people as they
first arrived in the Iberian Peninsula and independent of all the later
invaders (Romans, Visigoths, Muslims . . .).[3]). During the first half of
the nineteenth century, there were important works by Juan Antonio
Zamácola,[4] Pedro Novia de Salcedo,[5] and Agustín Chaho;[6] they
shaped the historicist discourse on Basquism, founded in the establishment of their own laws (the *Fueros*) in the mythology of nobility and
Tubalism. From a certain perspective, the deep roots of the Basques,
the oldest people on the Peninsula, reached the extreme position of
citing them as the purest Spaniards. The mythology surrounding the
Fueros continued with undoubted success in works such as those of
Fidel de Sagarmínaga.[7] However, it should not be forgotten that it was
clear in certain circles that the *Fueros* were the oldest laws in Spain (if
the Basques are the oldest people, then their laws—the *Fueros*—must
be too) and that, furthermore, they had been accepted by successive
kings as good laws for the country.

In Catalonia, Próspero de Bofarull played a pioneering role in
Catalan historiography. As director of the general archive of the Crown
of Aragon, Bofarull was in charge of publishing ledgers and laws from
the old Catalan institutions. Thanks to this documentation, the archi-
vist vindicated those pages from Catalan history that had been silenced
by Spanish historiography. Catalonia had, throughout the medieval
period, undergone imperial growth. Furthermore, Bofarull related
the start of Catalan decline with the crowning of the Castilianised
Trastámara dynasty (dynasty started with the Galician Pedro Álvarez
Osorio, holder in 1445 of the *Condado de los Trastámara*) in the early
fifteenth century. His work passed down to new generations of historians such as Víctor Balaguer and Antoni de Bofarull, as well as to the
Romance poets of the *Renaixença* [Catalan Renaissance].

The historicist foundations for the Spanish national discourse, likewise those for Basque, Galician, and Catalan nationalism, focused on the same period of the nineteenth century. The difference resided in that the first was supported by the organizational strength of the state and the latter ones had to wait for the birth of a "regionalist" political movement which socialized the new creed in the corresponding territories. In Catalonia and the Basque Country, the first practical results of this strategy came in the early twentieth century when the nationalist movements made gains in the local and provincial elections (Sabino Arana, founder of the Basque Nationalist Party, was a provincial councillor in 1898), as well as in those elections for the Spanish Parliament. This fact brought with it the visualization of the problem of "peripheral" nationalism in Spanish political life. In fact, the first decades of the twentieth century were characterized precisely by the consolidation of the various national and/or nationalist historiographies that needed to respond to the petitions they received from different sectors of society. While they all shared the desire to highlight their scientific merits, it is difficult to separate the national historiography from the nationalist one, given that their perspectives crossed paths quite frequently.

With the aim of strengthening the entities dedicated to the study of the past at a state level, the *Junta de Ampliación de Estudios*, created in Madrid in 1907, was of particular importance. It backed the *Centro de Estudios Históricos* (1910) with the aim of researching Spanish history and culture, using the Castilian language as the national language, and leading to the creation of sections dedicated to, for example, "semiotic studies." However, no sections were dedicated to the analysis of the Galician, Basque, and Catalan languages and cultures, an indisputable demonstration of the idea of Spanish unity (excluding that which was not in Castilian), standardized on the foundations of Castilian with no wish to recognize plurality. On the other hand, in 1907, the *Diputación Provincial de Barcelona* created the *Institut d'Estudis Catalans* with the idea of recovering and homologating the importance of the Catalan language and culture in all aspects of scientific life with the creation of various sections. Thus, in 1911, the sections of archaeological history, science, and philology were created. In the Basque Country, the

Diputaciones of Araba, Bizkaia, Gipuzkoa, and Navarra created the *Sociedad de Estudios Vascos (Eusko Ikaskuntza)* in 1918, with similar aims as those of the *Institut d'Estudis Catalans*. On the contrary, in Galicia it was more difficult to create a similar body due to the lack of institutional support (and the absence of a national bourgeoisie). Even so, first, the *Real Academia Galega*, founded in 1906, and later the *Seminario de Estudos Galegos*, born in 1923, attempted to fill this void. This occurred with the ambition of producing sciences in the Galician language—the RAG provided written norms for this—with the extraordinary support and dissemination of the intellectual group *Nós* and their magazine, a true cultural platform for the renovation of the Galician culture which, from 1920 on, exercised its leadership and cultural hegemony until the fascist military coup and civil war of 1936.

The narration of Spanish history, after the civil war, was fossilized by the Franco dictatorship. It was only in the 1950s when this began to crack, and in the 1960s and 1970s, above all, when the histories of the various nationalities of the State could be published once more (with those working from exile being key to this). The arrival of democracy and the birth of a new Spain with its autonomies favored the cultivation of the local histories of the various "autonomous communities" and the critical study of Spanish nationalism and the nationalisms of the respective regions.

The coming to power of the People's Party in 1996 instigated a tendency that created—and creates—the need to alter the education system so as to transmit to Spanish society a national history, with unitary foundations and which rejects national plurality. Furthermore, when the People's Party also won the elections of 2000 with an absolute majority, a slow recentralization of the State began; this was interrupted by the electoral victory of the PSOE—Partido Socialista Obrero Español (Spanish Socialist Workers' Party)—in 2004, with the party remaining in power until 2011. Over the last twenty years, there has been a reaffirmation of the Spanish national history in response, a sometimes aggressive response, to what was considered "Catalan disobedience": the reformation of the Statute of Autonomy, approved in 2006, and which had its powers restricted by the Supreme Constitutional Court in 2010; and the emergence of a

Catalan independence movement that, as a result of frustrations with the Constitutional Court ruling and the effects of the economic crisis, has pivoted the entire state policy in an unambiguous way since the 2017 Catalan self-determination referendum.

In contrast to those researchers who wish to present the Spanish case as one of successful nation building, this work allows the reader to trace the plurality of the identities present in the Spanish state and to analyze some aspects that have characterized the political histories of Galicia, the Basque Country, and Catalonia, and their nationalist movements, in a chronology that spans from the late nineteenth century to the end of the Spanish Civil War and the start of exile.

In the Catalan case, we analyze the configuration of the birth of Catalan political nationalism, along with Catalan culture, symbolism, and ideological references over a period of forty years. In this timeframe, we study the variations and apparitions of a broad spectrum of nationalist organizations that range from the moderate liberal autonomist sectors of the early twentieth century, which included the *Liga Regionalista* of Enric Prat de la Riba and Francesc Cambó—who assumed all political prominence—to the independentist republicans, whose first party, *Estat Català*, was founded after World War I under the leadership of Francesc Macià. Macià himself sponsored the *Esquerra Republicana de Catalunya*, the hegemonic Catalan party during the Second Republic. It is important to note that the plurality of Catalan politics included various other organizations, including the *Unió Socialista* and the *Partit Català Proletari*, both in favor of Catalan self-determination. In this context, we reflect on the objectives attained by the Catalan nationalist movement: the pioneering form of self-government of the *Mancomunidad de Catalunya*, created in 1914, which was ended with the coup d'état of Primo de Rivera in 1923 (despite being formally dissolved in 1925); and the *Generalitat de Catalunya*, formed in 1931, which would be the autonomous instrument of self-government that remained in Catalonia until the end of the Civil War and which, with Francoism and the abolition of the Statute of Autonomy, survived in exile, despite enormous difficulties which included the capture of its president, Lluís Companys, by the German Gestapo. He was handed over to the Francoist authorities and killed by firing squad in Barcelona in October 1940.[8]

At the same time, we discuss the different international models that these Catalan political groups have used and analyze the alliances and cultural and political relationships that were developed from Barcelona to attract homologous movements in Galicia and the Basque Country to their cause. From the end of the nineteenth century and until the Civil War, this study analyzes how Catalonia has been a laboratory for such peninsular alliances, as demonstrated in the stipulation of the Tripartite Alliance of September 1923, signed in Barcelona in the wake of Primo de Rivera's coup d'état. In the years of the Second Republic, with autonomy already achieved, the Catalans ceded the limelight to the Galicians and Basques. Despite this, they also collaborated in the stipulation of the *Pacto de Compostela* of 1933 (immediately christened "Gal-Euz-Ca") and, finally, the Civil War would determine the necessary collaboration between the Basque and Catalan nationalists in defence of republican territories, while Galician nationalism remained trapped by the advance of rebel troops in their lands, confronted by an insufficiently strong resistance (which did, however, give rise to the first guerrilla groups). In exile, the three nationalist movements met up once more, giving rise to new phases in their political agreements and even to a certain amount of joint political action.

When one deals with nationalism in Spain, the Catalan movement always comes first, while the earliest and most multifaceted aspects of Basque nationalism come second. In this case, this is due to the will of one person: Sabino Arana (1864–1903). Thus, in the part that deals with Basque nationalism, our focus is not just on its evolution from World War I through to the Spanish Civil War; rather, we will look at it in the context of a dialogue—and on occasions as pure confrontation—with Spanish nationalism. We can see that many of the principal definers of *españolidad* [Spanishness], ever since the Generation of '98, are, in fact, Basques, or were raised in the Basque Country. And the effect of cohabiting/confronting should not be underestimated when looking at the development, at least partially, of what is the "essence of Spanishness," which, for some is precisely the same as the "essence of Basqueness."

While in the Basque case we talk about one person (Sabino Arana, "Angel or Devil," as he was called by José Luis de la Granja, one of the highest authorities on Basque nationalism), in the case of Galician nationalism the central figure was the meeting of various personages and their joint willpower, such as the creation of the first *Irmandade de Amigos da Fala* (Brotherhood of Friends of the Galician Language) in 1916 and the *Asamblea Nacionalista de Lugo* in 1918 (after Antón Vilar Ponte's rallying call). This assembly is considered as the formal and explicit birth of the Galician nationalist movement and a meeting that was fruitful in the theoretical production of Galicianism since the last third of the nineteenth century. It was headed at that far-off time by figures such as Manuel Murguía and Alfredo Brañas—organizationally crystallizing Galician nationalism at a national level at the *Asamblea de Lugo* (as the first general assembly of all the *Irmandades da Fala* that had been set up in two short years) with figures who would rejuvenate the Galician sovereignist discourse. This was the case with Antón and Ramón Vilar Ponte, Lois Porteiro, and Johán Vicente Viqueira. They created not only political organizations but also various publications and even high-culture institutions, as is the case with the *Seminario de Estudos Galegos* (1923). Galician nationalism was not exempt from internal diversity, problems, or social impact, as also happened with Basque and Catalan nationalism. (However, important differences emerged with regard to these; for example, Galician nationalism had no national bourgeoisie to support it—a social class that was sensu stricto—absent in Galiza.) This political movement would be capable of adapting with the times, as demonstrated during the Second Republic, giving rise to the *Partido Galeguista* (which had been on the cusp of calling itself the *Partido Nacionalista Galego*). This organization included figures of great importance during that period, such as Daniel R. Castelao and Alexandre Bóveda, giving rise to an important introduction and social support to Galician nationalism (Ánxel Casal holding the mayorship in Santiago de Compostela, for example A figure of great relevance in Galician sovereignty, as a printer and as a politician until his assassination in 1936). The organization also achieved a statute referendum on the eve, literally, of the July 1936 coup d'état, with a large majority of votes in favor (the statute would be approved in exile).

In conclusion, in the following chapters, from three different perspectives, we analyze relevant aspects of the nationalism movements in

Spain, not as cut off from each other but in a relationship between the three. Each was influenced, to a greater or lesser degree, by the others in a dialectic relationship that continues to this day, as evidenced by recent developments in Spanish politics.

—Barcelona, Bilbao, A Coruña, September 2021

Notes

1. Justo G. Beramendi, *De provincia a nación: historia do galeguismo político*. Vigo: Edicións Xerais de Galicia, 2008, ss. 74–169.
2. Uxío-Breogán Diéguez Cequiel, Lois Ríos, *A viaxe ás illas Blasket de Plácido Castro (1928)*, Compostela, Instituto Galego de Historia, 2020.
3. *De la Antigüedad y Universalidad del Bascuence en España*, Eugenio García de Honorato, Salamanca, 1728. *El impossible vencido. Arte de la lengua vascongada*, Antonio José Villagordo de Alcaraz, Salamanca, 1729.
4. *Historia de las Naciones Bascas de Una y Otra Parte del Pirineo Septentrional y Costas del Mar Cantábrico, Desde sus Primeros Pobladores Hasta Nuestros Días. Con la descripción, carácter, fueros, usos, costumbres y leyes de cada uno de los estados Bascos que hoy existen. Dividida en varias épocas*. Auch, 1818.
5. *Defensa Histórica, Legislativa y Económica del Señorío de Vizcaya y Provincias de Álava y de Guipuzcoa*. Librería Delmas e Hijo. Bilbao, 1851.
6. *Paroles d'un Biscaïen aux Libéraux de la Reine Christine*. Paris, 1834.
7. Fidel de Sagarminaga, *Memorias Históricas de Vizcaya*. Bilbao: Delmas, 1880. Fidel de Sagarminaga, *El Gobierno y el Régimen Foral del Señorío de Vizcaya Desde el Reinado de Felipe II Hasta la Mayor edad de Doña Isabel II*. 8 vols. Bilbao: José Astuy, 1891–1892.
8. Josep Maria Sole Sabaté. Lluís Companys. Biografia humana i política. 2 v. Barcelona: Enciclopèdia Catalana, 2006.

Basque Nationalism
and Spanish Nationalism

An Example of the Principle of Action/Reaction (1895–1923)

EDUARDO J. ALONSO OLEA[1]

*To every action there is always opposed an equal reaction:
or the mutual actions of two bodies upon each other
are always equal, and directed to contrary parts.*

—NEWTON'S THIRD LAW

Introduction

Nationalism is a key idea that, since its emergence in the nineteenth century, has been widely discussed and analyzed from very different perspectives and in different periods of time. It has experienced periods of growth and other periods when it was clearly in crisis, but it continues to be the object of continuous debate and investigation—its interest is not only historiographical, but also economic, social, and political. It continues to characterize political parties and positions, forms of life, and mentalities in all parts of the planet. In spite of being repeatedly declared dead and buried, discredited and guilty, accused of being obsolescent and antiquated, not only has it not disappeared from the political stage in Spain and many other places, but continues be to a factor that must be taken into account today. Even a "banal" version of nationalism has been discovered,[2] or used as a framework for analyzing the social;[3] in fact, banal nationalism has made its appearance even where it was supposedly not to be found, as in the case of Spanish nationalism, which has also recently been *discovered*.[4]

We are not going to make a general analysis of nationalism here, but instead we will focus on one concrete expression of the phenomenon: Basque nationalism between the late nineteenth and early twentieth centuries, and its dialectical relationship with Spanish nationalism within the Basque setting. As mentioned above, nationalism has been widely debated and researched, and Basque nationalism is no exception: from the first approaches made by Jean-Claude Larronde and Javier Corcuera,[5] up to the most recent works by other specialists such as Santiago de Pablo,[6] José Luis de la Granja,[7] Mikel Aizpuru[8] and Ludger Mees,[9] or the studies developed by the Sabino Arana Foundation.[10]

When dealing with peripheral nationalisms in Spain, it is Catalan nationalism that is usually mentioned first, as it was earlier and more multifaceted, with Basque nationalism in second place. The latter is held to have emerged thanks to the determination of one individual, Sabino Arana (1864–1903), but this is to ignore the existence in the Basque County up until 1877 of Representative Assemblies (*Juntas Generales*) and *foral* political governments that had a solid experience of self-government in all fields of Basque public administration.[11] To confirm this, it is sufficient to analyze their general budgets. Moreover, with respect to Basque nationalism, our approach not only analyzes its evolution from the first years of its existence as such up until the end of the restoration, but also views it in a context of dialogue—and at certain times of open confrontation—with Spanish nationalism. It can be seen how several of the individuals of the "Generation of '98" who played a key role in defining Spanish identity were in fact Basque, or, if born outside the Basque Country, were brought up there. And one should not underestimate the effects of coexistence/confrontation when observing the development—at least in part—of "the essence of Spanish identity," which in the opinion of some is precisely "Basque identity."[12]

Basque Nationalism: Its Origins
and Early Development—Sabino Arana

It is well known that Basque nationalism had a founder, its first visionary, an angel to some and a demon to others,[13] namely Sabino Arana y Goiri[14] (1865–1903). His political activity is considered to have begun in 1892 with the publication of his book *Bizcaya por su*

Independencia. Cuatro Glorias Patrias (Bizkaia for its independence. Four patriotic glories),[15] a legendary historical narrative about four battles waged by Bizkaians against troops from Léon or Castile: the battles of Arrigorriaga (888), Gordejuela (1355), Ochandiano (1355), and Munguía (1470).

He is considered to have made his first public political act in June 1893, when he gave a speech to a group of *fueristas euskalerriacos*[16] that had formed around Ramón de la Sota y Llano, in the course of which he employed the slogan *Jaungoikua eta Lagi-Zarra*[17] (JEL—God and the Old Law). He ended the speech with the slogan "Long live the independence of Bizkaia!" A few days later he published the first issue of the *Bizkaitarra* (Bilbao), the first Basque nationalist journal, in which he declared that he was "anti-liberal and anti-Spanish."

A little over one year later, in July 1894, the first nationalist center, the *Euskeldun Batzokija*, was opened in Bilbao, under the presidency of Sabino Arana. At these centers the ikurriña, the flag designed by his brother Luis, was hoisted for the first time. At the movement's first general assembly, its provisional regulations—originally drawn up four years previously—were approved, which included the program contained in the slogan JEL. In this process of giving structure to the movement, its first leadership body, the first *Bizkai Buru Batzarra* (Board of Directors), was organized in 1895 with Sabino Arana as president and his brother as vice president. Although this body was formed in clandestinity, this is considered to be the foundational moment of the Basque Nationalist Party.[18]

The publication of his articles in the *Bizkaitarra* quickly brought him into conflict with the law. In August 1894 Arana published an article ("*Un fino maketófilo*" [A fine love for foreigners]) that resulted in his being the object of a lawsuit, which reached court in August 1895. He was sentenced to one month and eleven days in prison and a fine of 125 pesetas for minor damages. On August 28 he entered prison for the first time, where he was to remain for four and a half months on this occasion. A few days later the *Bizkaitarra* published an article written by Engracio Aranzadi, nicknamed *Kizkitza*, under the pseudonym *Baso Jaun*, titled "*La invasión maketa en Gipuzkoa*" (The foreign invasion in Gipuzkoa), which resulted in a new complaint, two new trials (one civil and one military) against Arana as editor of the publication, as well *Kizkitza's* having to go into exile in Hendaye to avoid arrest.

The article must have exhausted the government's patience, since the first campaign against Basque nationalism began on September 13, 1895. The activities of the *Euskeldun Batzokija* were suspended, its central office was closed by government order, and its board of directors was tried and imprisoned; to which were added a fine and the trial of its 110 members. As Arana was still in prison, six members of the board were arrested, imprisoned, and held incommunicado. An arrest warrant was issued for the absent members and ten days later, after thirty-two issues, the *Bizkaitarra* was suspended by government order.

The government's reaction was, as can be seen, overwhelming. The appearance of the group led by Arana (consisting of a little over one hundred people) had, according to some of the media at that time, provoked hilarity rather than anything else.[19]

It seems that there was some sympathy for the group that had formed around Arana, but it was treated as a something of a joke. While it might have seemed a joke in 1892 and 1894, it should be recalled that the Cuban War was just beginning in 1895, and there was a clear suspicion that Arana's group was acting in connivance, or had the intention of weakening the Spanish position. In fact, the motives given for closing down the newspaper and the association itself were severe: "provoking rebellion" and "conspiracy to rebellion."

At the start of 1896, after his brother Luis had paid five thousand pesetas, Sabino Arana was released on bail. On leaving prison he dedicated his efforts above all to doing research on Euskera, although in July of that year, in his brother's absence, he formed a new board of directors for the *Euskeldun Batzokija* under the presidency of Ciriaco de Llodio. In any event, in Bilbao in November Arana was again put on trial for the crime of rebellion because of the publication of two articles by other authors in the *Bizkaitarra*, although he was acquitted by the popular jury.[20]

In the spring of 1897, Arana engaged in his well-known dispute with the Carlist journalist Eustaquio Echave-Sustaeta, in which he strongly criticized the Carlist program and gave an explanation of the historical-political meaning that the *Fueros*[21] held for nationalism.[22] The importance of this dispute is that it marked the shift from his initial *bizkaitarrismo,* or Bizkaian nationalism, to *euzkotarrismo* or Basque nationalism.

The year 1898 was key in the evolution and development of Basque nationalism. On April 24 of that year, with the outbreak of the war between Spain and the United States of America, participants in a demonstration organized by the liberal society *El Sitio* threw stones at the house of the Arana Gori brothers in Abando, forcing them to take refuge in the house of their friend Ángel Zabala in Gernika. Less than a month later his publishing company was shut down, although this was offset by the good news that the legal proceedings against *Euskeldun Batzokija* had been dismissed; and in the summer Sota's *fuerist* group, which had left the *Sociedad Euskalerria* of Bilbao, joined the PNV, in which it was to form an important moderate—not independentist—sector. This incorporation was essential for the electoral fortunes of Basque nationalism, given that Sota not only brought with him his political associates, but also and above all, his fortune, which while not yet immense was already substantial.[23]

The provincial election of 1898 showed how, with the injection of resources by Ramón de la Sota, a small party was able to start to win seats in the institutions. Conversely, the election also resulted in a reduction in the influence of the monarchist parties[24] that had dominated the Deputation up until then.[25]

TABLE 1. Results of the Provincial Election: District of Bilbao (November 11, 1898)

Name	Party	No. votes	% Votes cast
Enrique Aresti y Torre	Unión Liberal	4,823	40.86%
Sabino Arana y Goiri	Bizkaitarra	4,545	38.51%
Ildefonso Arrola y Bilbao	Carlist	4,353	36.88%
Casimiro Zunzunegui y Echevarría	Unión Liberal	4,316	36.57%
Atanasio Areyzaga y Orueta	Unión Liberal	3,496	29.62%
Marcelino Villar y Vera	Socialista	1,830	15.50%
José Aldaco y Ugarte	Socialista	1,820	15.42%
Manuel Orte Andrés	Socialista	1,788	15.15%

Source: Elaborated by the author using data proceeding from the electoral minutes. AFB. Administrativo. AJ01903/017. Elected candidates in italics.

The district of Bilbao was the most populous in the province, but what was worrying for the monarchist parties was the fact that Arana received 32% of the votes cast in Bilbao, 41% in Getxo, 49% in Deusto,

and 57% in Erandio. That is, the results he obtained were neither modest nor barely enough to win a place in the Deputation; instead he
achieved considerable electoral support.[26]

In any case, the main beneficiaries of the election were Víctor
Chávarri's conservatives, who managed to increase their number of
seats, while the liberals disappeared from the provincial Deputation.

Arana's activity in the Deputation was limited due to the problems he
faced—from 1902 onwards above all—and he was barely able to attend
the meetings of the Deputation. He complained that the circumstances
arising from his political activities and imprisonment prevented him
from fully exercising his role as a deputy.

He formulated his principal political initiative in 1898 when he proposed the formation of a "Basque-Navarrese Regional Council."[27] This
motion was rejected by the Deputation's Governing Committee, as were
other motions he presented, aimed at accelerating and facilitating the
monitoring of affairs proposed to the Deputation. He distinguished himself with his antiauthoritarian protests directed at the hegemonic party,
the *Unión Liberal*, formed of conservatives grouped around the figure
(and the fortune) of Victor Chávarri. While Arana's proposals and gestures
in the Deputation were not "revolutionary," they did upset some of his col-
leagues in the plenary sessions. In the municipal elections held on May 14,
1898, the PNV won five Councillors in Bilbao, another five in Bermeo, as
well as some in Mundaka and Arteaga (Bizkaia). It thus became clear that
Basque nationalism was not a marginal or transient force, but was instead
starting to establish a certain presence, at least in Bizkaia.[28]

Less than one month later, the first nationalist newspaper, *El Correo
Vasco*, went on sale. It was administered by Luis Arana and Sabino,
who acted as censor, lead writer, editor, and shareholder. Although
it experienced economic difficulties, Ramón de la Sota was the main
shareholder and it soon had over 1,000 subscribers.[29]

In 1898 harsh reality imposed itself. Spain had been unable to with-
stand the thrust of a new power, the United States of America, and con-
serve the remnants of its colonial empire. Spain's was not the only case,
as there were other disasters or near disasters for other powers (Fochoda
for France, the first Italian-Ethiopian war for Italy, or some years later,
the Russian-Japanese war), but it was clearly a disaster nonetheless. It

provoked different reactions, ranging from *regeneracionismo*,[30] which had clear antecedents at the start of the decade,[31] to the new proposals of what was later known as the "Generation of '98," young writers—or, like Unamuno, not so young—who sought new horizons that were not just aesthetic; while in a different setting, it helped provoke the development of what was soon to become the *Lliga* (League) in Catalonia.

The defeat at the hands of the United States and the loss of the last remnants of the formerly immense Spanish colonial empire can be viewed from a triple perspective with respect to its role in shaping Spanish nationalism:[32] the emotional impact of the complete, rapid, and conclusive military defeat at the hands of the North Americans; the clear need to mobilize all the national resources to remedy the state of prostration that had been decisive in bringing about that defeat; and, thirdly—and this is what interests us the most—the flowering of Catalan and Basque nationalisms, as genuine political movements and not merely literary or cultural ones.[33]

There were thus many facets to regenerationism, understood in a broad sense.[34] In the centralization/decentralization debate—which on close examination stretches down to the present day—these facets range from Luis Morote, who favored a decentralizing program, to a figure who was close to Basque politics, Joaquín Sánchez de Toca—conservative, minister, senator, president of the government, a major figure in the sugar sector, and a long etcetera,[35] who expressed himself clearly in 1899:[36]

> These regionalist ideals, precisely due to the vagueness with which they are formulated, constitute one of the most propitious substances for achieving—speaking serenely with good arguments—a useful filter of their ideologies. Proceeding in this way, it will not take long to see that quite a few of those who today declare themselves to be stubborn centralists are at bottom regionalists without knowing it. And just as many of those who now seem to be intransigent regionalists, as soon as they come to understand how they must work in the towns and places of their land in order to conduct regional life, will perhaps request greater protection from the central power than what the centralists themselves hold to be the predominance of the jurisdictions of the state.

The government of President Sagasta was blamed for losing the war, with the result that in March 1899 a "regenerationist"—at least in formal terms—government was formed under Francisco Silvela.[37] Among other measures[38] he confronted, Basque nationalism, which was now viewed as a clear danger. Accordingly, a Royal Decree of September 12, 1899, ordered the suspension of constitutional guarantees in Bizkaia, together with an undertaking to organize parliamentary support for this measure in the near future.[39] Rather than the decree itself, what is interesting is the brief but forceful exposition of motives, where it is recognized that until very recently it had been impossible to foresee that opinions would be expressed against the national spirit.[40]

The intention was to belittle, by means of superficial noise and scandal rather than substantial measures, these anti-patriotic manifestations that could be remedied by making slight adjustments to the penal legislation. But, in the meantime, the government could not permit such lamentable acts, with the result that, until the necessary reforms had been carried out, constitutional guarantees in Bizkaia were suspended.[41]

As a consequence of this decree, *El Correo Vasco* (September 15, 103 issues) was closed and the activities of the following were temporarily suspended: the Euskalduna club, the Basque Centre in Bilbao, the Batzoki in Bermeo, the Euskalduna Society in Baracaldo, and the Euskeria Choir of Bilbao. This suspension was to last until July 1900.

In 1901 Arana began to maintain relations with the recently created Regionalist League of Catalonia,[42] which was beginning to achieve an appreciable electoral success.[43] He thus moderated his initial refusal to accept that there was a relationship between the Catalan and Basque cases, an idea that he had expressed clearly in an article in the *Bizkaitarra* in 1894.[44]

But, as we have noted, he changed his position in 1901, at least sufficiently to build bridges towards the Catalans, recognizing Catalonia's right to be free of the same oppression suffered by the Basque Country.[45]

The issue continued to be a significant one, since in spite of the position of the more moderate *euskalerriacos* who were willing to really collaborate with the Catalans, the more recalcitrant Aranistas, such as José de Arriandiaga (*Joala*), continued to argue that it was incoherent to collaborate with the Catalans.[46]

To place the issue in a wider perspective, in general terms Basque nationalism barely took any notice of *Galleguismo*, which was still far from making an appearance in the Spanish political panorama. Conversely, it paid a lot of attention to Catalanism from 1901 onwards, which was followed by times, like World War I and the Second Republic, when it seemed it would be possible to obtain recognition for autonomy, the political goal of the more moderate sector of the PNV.

Also in 1901, an event took place in Bilbao that we believe was more transcendental than it is usually thought to have been. We are referring to the speech given by Miguel de Unamuno (1864–1936) on the occasion of the Floral Games taking place in Bilbao.[47] Unamuno had been an *euskalerriaco* in his youth and had known Arana for a long time. In fact, both had been candidates for the Chair in Euskera funded by the Deputation of Bizkaia in 1888,[48] a position that was finally awarded to Resurrección Mª de Azkue.

On August 26, 1901, Unamuno gave a speech on Euskera at the Floral Games of Bilbao, which gave rise to a protest from the Basque Centre and from Arana in his journal *Euzkadi*. Expressions like: "Suppress, before all else, that odious term *maketos*"[49] or "in Basque millenarianism there is no room for modern thought; Bilbao speaking Euskera is a contradiction in terms. And luck has given us an advantage over others, as this encloses us less inside our exclusive personality, with the risk of impoverishing it," caused a division of opinions in the auditorium.

But without any doubt his affirmation on the future of Euskera, which should be buried and studied as a philological relic, was more controversial.[50]

As noted, Unamuno was a longstanding acquaintance of Arana, and although he had nationalist friends he did not sympathize with their cause: "Poor fools. So pure, so noble, so enthusiastic, so saintly but so brutish," he wrote in 1908.

Further on, we will see more reflections exalting Spain proceeding from the regenerationist reaction, but, in Unamuno's case, he sometimes gives the impression that when dealing with Spain he was not as considerate towards some regions as others; for example, he underscored the defects of the Levantines and Andalusians that infected all of Spain.[51]

Unamuno was a writer, and in a certain way a "personality," who from the outset was not considered to be regionalist by some of those situated in the liberal variant of the Spanish nationalist tradition.[52] But he was a contradictory writer, highly emotional and even "telluric" at times, who in 1895 had already identified the essence of Spain—its "intrahistory"—with the soul of Castile[53] ("what is genuine, what is truly genuine, is the old Castilian lineage"[54]).

Certainly, he avoided the racial element and spoke more of "civilization,"[55] but he directly related Castile with its product, Spain— which Castile had forged and on which it had bestowed its greatest spiritual riches.[56]

In any case, as we noted, the contradictory figure of Unamuno greatly influenced the Generation of '98 and even subsequent thinking. He distanced himself from nationalism, constructing his anti-Basque nationalism as another of the pillars of the identity of Basque socialism,[57] and finally came to ridicule it. But he always held to a certain idea of Spain as an accumulation of cultures, some superior to others; and while in the case of Castile he admired its culture, this was not the case with other regions.

Societies and politics are not a succession of physical events, which is why the allusion to Isaac Newton's Third Law of Movement might seem exaggerated. However, what we wish to indicate by invoking it is that the processes involved in the formation of nationalisms are not watertight, but instead interact with each so that the advances and regressions of one explain, at least in part, the advances and regressions of the other.[58] We are not, of course, basing our argument on the existence of remote predetermined nationalisms. Instead, the processes of nation-building developed during the nineteenth and twentieth centuries in interacting—not exclusionary—processes, so that collective identities in different periods had a multiple character.[59]

To place the question in perspective, starting in the 1890s and coinciding with the appearance of Basque nationalism with Sabino Arana,[60] regenerationism emerged and then "irrupted" with the crisis of 1898, due to the defeat by the United States of America and the loss of Cuba. This was felt especially deeply in Bilbao, as several of the ships sunk in the battle had recently been launched at the Astilleros del Nervión.[61]

One of the watersheds of regenerationism[62] is clearly the Generation of '98, in which we find some authors of Basque origin, including Miguel de Unamuno from Bilbao, whom we have already considered, Pío Baroja from Donostia-San Sebastián—although he often insisted that there was no such thing as regenerationism[63]—and Ramiro de Maeztu from Araba. That is why the connection or the conflict between Basque nationalism and Spanish national regeneration affected them so directly.

On the other hand, it is true that Pío Baroja, who was much more skeptical than his generational comrades, did not adopt such a contrary position towards nationalism, or better put, was not so fanatical in his defense of the Spanish nation as they were.[64]

In these national debates, which were to find one of their most literal scenarios in World War I, Baroja, although he had expressed admiration for the French nation,[65] nevertheless drifted towards positions that were closer to Germanophilia.[66] This was in spite of his early opposition to Carlism.[67]

For Baroja, *Bizkaitarrismo* was a Latin and Semitic product that introduced a component of respect for the law in the Basques: "Traditionalism and love for the old laws is an essentially Jewish and Roman idea."[68] His statement, that nationalism could be summed up in a set of religious ideas closely linked to Jesuitism, is well known.[69] Such a derivation is not surprising if we bear in mind that Arana's education, and that many of the coreligionists and friends with whom he organized the initial activities of his party, had in common time they had spent in the Jesuit College in Urduña.[70]

But we will return to where we had left Arana as a provincial deputy. He was intensely active in 1901, although his economic standing was also affected by the stock market crash of that year,[71] which not only had a negative effect on his finances but also on those of his main source of funding, Ramón de la Sota. Thus, in March 1902, he was forced to close the journal *Euzkadi* due to a lack of resources with which to offset its substantial losses. On the other hand, Basque nationalism obtained an important result in the municipal elections (winning six new councillors in Bilbao).

He had further problems with the law as a result of his attempt to send a telegram to Theodore Roosevelt, the president of the United

States, congratulating him for granting independence to Cuba.[72] The text, however, which was probably never received in Washington because the local telegraph employee sent it straight to the civil governor of Bizkaia, was delivered in person by his brother Luis to the vice-consul of the United States in Bilbao, Carlos Jensen. A few days later Arana was put on trial and imprisoned in Larrínaga jail, where he spent over five months.

The following month, in June 1902, the nationalist councillors on Bilbao City Council were suspended by the civil governor, José de Echanove, because of the message of welcome they sent to the commander of the Argentinian training vessel, *Presidente Sarmiento*; this was a move that increased the pressure on Basque nationalism due to its independentism. This can be considered the starting point of Arana's well-known "*españolista* evolution,"[73] in which he introduced a new element, the renunciation of independence, in favor of broad autonomy—an early symptom of which might have been his motion in the Deputation in 1898—although in jail he wrote a text titled "*Mi pensamiento*" (My thought), in which he notes that his hidden goal is "the independence of Euzkadi under the protection of England."[74]

In any case, the first public manifestation of the *españolista* evolution was published in *La Patria* with the title—but without Arana's signature—of "*Grave y trascendental*" (Serious and transcendental), and a few days later, in an interview given to *La Gaceta del Norte* and published in *La Patria*,[75] Arana argued for "the most radical autonomy possible within the unity of the Spanish state" as the goal of the *Liga de Vascos Españolistas* (League of Basque *Españolistas*—henceforth the League), the new party he founded to replace the PNV. This turn was supported by the *euskalerriaco* sector in an editorial in *Euskalduna*, the mouthpiece of this sector.[76]

In November, in the midst of the party's reorganization in keeping with the new aim of the League, Arana was tried and acquitted by a popular jury, thus recovering his freedom. Nonetheless, the prosecutor appealed against the ruling and, to avoid returning to jail, Arana moved to San Juan de Luz, but his case was again dismissed and he was able to return and took up residence in Pedernales-Sukarrieta. However, he was already suffering from Addison's disease, which would result in his death.

In the provincial election of March 1903, the nationalist candidates Pedro Chalbaud and Ángel Zabala were elected for the districts of Bilbao and Gernika, respectively. Although the monarchist parties continued to have absolute control over the Bizkaia Deputation (they had sixteen out of twenty deputies), Basque nationalism increased its presence from one deputy (Arana) to two. On a different front, in the legislative election held the following month, in April, Arana reached an agreement with the catholic José María de Urquijo, founder of the catholic newspaper *La Gaceta del Norte*, to form a common front against the *Piña*,[77] a group that was now breaking up following the death of its prime mover, Víctor Chávarri. In return for Catholic support in the provincial election, Urquijo and the independent Catholic, the Marquis of Acillona, won the seats for Bilbao and Markina, respectively.[78] In the district of Gernika, Sota was defeated due to the irregularities committed by the monarchist parties.

On September 30, 1903, Sabino Arana named Ángel Zabala[79] (*Kondano*) to succeed him as president of the PNV. On November 25, 1903, at the age of 38, he died in Pedernales-Sukarrieta, and both *Kondano* and his brother Luis Arana laid the *Españolista* evolution to rest alongside him.

In 1903 Basque nationalism, which had barely been in existence for ten years, entered a new stage. Before addressing this, it is interesting to consider the effects or reflections that Arana's work and ideas had on his milieu. We have seen how he came under attack from Unamuno, who since the time of the examination did not hold Arana in high personal esteem. Additionally, he diagnosed that some of the elements of Aranist nationalism were more closely linked to reaction than to the "new times" that had been brought on by industrialization and, above all, the intense mining activity that Bilbao and its tidal river had experienced since the end of the Carlist War. One of these elements was without doubt the rejection of foreigners, so-called "*antimaketismo.*"[80]

We should not be deceived by these observations. The main motive for rejection—and not only of what was foreign—was the religious element, which was so important in Arana's thought, and appeared within the confrontations between clericals and anti-clericals in Bilbao at that time and later, which even resulted in bloodshed on the streets of the city.[81] In the nationalist imaginary, ideology and religion are mixed in vocabulary, rites, symbols, etc., in order to defend Basque identity—morality, the salvation of the soul—from Spanish identity—perversion, contamination . . . which would lead to spiritual perdition.[82]

Besides the government's reaction, in the directly repressive sense we have seen at key moments in Sabino Arana's biography, there were other reactions to Arana's new ideas.[83] In reality, many of these reactions can be related to the regenerationist movement and were not concerned specifically with Arana—although, as we have seen, those of Unamuno were—but instead with the general question of the regeneration of Spain and the idea of Spain.

In fact, and this is one of the hypotheses we will be examining, one of the elements strengthening this regenerationism and giving greater precision to the nature of Spain was the emergence and ideological configuration of Basque nationalism (and, of course, Catalan nationalism)—the idea that there was interaction between them.

Basque Nationalism after Arana

As we have seen, the person Arana appointed to be his "successor" was not his brother Luis, but Ángel Zabala (*Kondaño*) instead. There were soon disagreements between the latter two, but what they did agree on was putting an end to his *Españolista* evolution. However, not everything then became a question of independentism; what was generated instead was a pragmatic program that moderated the nationalist vote and made it more attractive.

Thus, by 1906 Basque nationalism accepted something that, while not ideal, was no longer viewed so negatively—even though Sabino Arana had disliked it: the Economic Agreement. In 1894, Arana had clearly expressed his position, literally describing as "traitors" those who that year were negotiating—with clear advantages—the renewal of the Economic Agreement[84] and asking for favors at the court, for which they could count *in extremis* on senator Víctor Chávarri, whom Arana described as a "scoundrel."[85]

However, by 1906 the panorama had changed substantially. At that time another process of negotiating the Economic Agreement was underway, giving rise to a resurgence of the desire for a return to the *Fueros*, above all in Gipuzkoa;[86] this sentiment was less successful in Bizkaia and Araba, but nonetheless conditioned elections during those years.

This provides the context in which the change of position by nationalism in this respect should be interpreted. Indeed, the adoption of the pragmatic program was decisive in *Kondano*'s decision to abandon the party's leadership. Conversely, the party's moderation not only made electoral success possible, but under the Maura government in 1907, resulted in the appointment[87] of the first nationalist mayor of Bilbao, Gregorio Ibarreche,[88] who replaced the liberal Gregorio Balparda. Whether or not this was a coincidence, it was from this point on that Balparda began to distance himself considerably from Basque nationalism.

In 1903 more than 30% of the councillors on the City Council of Bilbao were nationalists. By 1909, nationalism continued to be hegemonic—together with socialists and republicans—on the City Council, while the monarchist parties now had only a residual influence.

Balparda's reaction to the nationalist surge that had cost him the mayoralty (with the inestimable help of Maura, of course) provides one of the clearest examples of liberal antinationalist thinking. The basis of Balparda's attack on nationalism was not Euskera, as in the case of Unamuno, but instead the weakness of its juridical and historical thought. In this respect he coined certain ideas that would later be taken up by the socialists.

Gregorio Balparda,[89] a prestigious lawyer, son of an outstanding liberal as he himself was, concentrated on demolishing the central idea of Basque nationalism: that the old *Fueros* had been codes of sovereignty. He first elaborated his ideas in reaction to the manifesto of the Elgoibar Assembly of 1908,[90] and later gave them a more decisive and systematic form following his direct electoral confrontation with nationalism in the elections of 1918 and 1919, in which Balparda lost the first and won the second in the district of Balmaseda.[91]

By 1908, having been ousted from the mayoralty by Ibarreche, Balparda began his work as an anti-Basque nationalist polemicist. At different talks given in the *El Sitio* Society and in the Academy of Law and other Social Sciences, in Bilbao, he enlarged his criticisms of Basque nationalism.[92] He began with the judicial aspect. Rather than relate the *Fuero* of Bizkaia to a code of sovereignty, as nationalism had done, he held it up as a clear demonstration of exemplary *foral* freedom, which was always linked to the kingdom of Castile, of which Bizkaia formed a part. Religion was another aspect that Balparda emphasized in order to underscore the inconsistency of Arana's arguments. He insisted on the resistance of the *foral* institutions, which refused to bow down to the wishes of the church. From Balparda's perspective, this made the separation between the *Fueros* and religion absolutely clear. Some months later he published another pamphlet, this time directly aimed at *bizkaitarrismo*, in which he emphasized the shortcomings in the juridical and historical understanding—in this he agreed with Unamuno—of the founder of nationalism, which meant that Arana's ideas were destined, in Balparda's opinion, to be manipulated by others.[93]

But his most direct criticisms were aimed at Sabino Arana, whom he accused of using insulting language at a time—1898—of special difficulty for Spain.[94]

Within this broad attack on Basque nationalism, he also criticized Catalan nationalism, although he drew an important distinction between the two. While there was no justification for Catalan nationalism, Basque nationalism was simply ridiculous. The former had certain, much more solid cultural foundations in comparison with the latter, which was founded by one individual, Arana, who had no intellectual training.[95]

Many of Balparda's criticisms were to become commonplace in anti-Basque nationalist thinking from then onwards—not only in the liberal camp but also in the socialist one, as we will see in the debates of 1918 and 1919.

The Basque Nationalist Party set the goal of independence to one side in order to concentrate on achieving the suppression of the Law of 1839. The pragmatic line thus imposed itself on the orthodox line, a change that was accompanied by electoral successes. From 1913 onwards, the party began to be called *Comunión Nacionalista Vasca* (Basque Nationalist Communion) in order to distance itself even further from political radicalism. The differences between the pragmatists and the orthodox became more pronounced with the interventions by the youths from the *Eusko Gaztedi Batza* (Association of Basque Youth) and by Eli Gallastegi and Eguileor, who called for a change in the party's program and a return to separatism. All these differences

culminated in the expulsion of the orthodox militants from the organization and their refounding of the Basque Nationalist Party (*Aberri*)
on the basis of separatist postulates.[96]

Basque nationalism's fundamental electoral foothold was undoubtedly
its pragmatism, but other strengths included its Catholicism and the fact
that the majority of its candidates were individuals with personal fortunes
to finance their candidacies (Pedro Chalbaud and Ramón de la Sota were
important entrepreneurs, Ibarreche was a prestigious architect...). In short,
these were "people of order," whom the Aranists were unable to remove
from the party because they had the economic means together with influence on the juridical bodies to be able to carry out their political activities.

The Basque Nationalist Communion had no problem in allying
itself with other right-wing political parties when this was necessary in
elections. The party's electoral behavior varied from province to province and from election to election, but in general, where nationalism
had more influence, fewer coalitions were formed.

On November 30, 1913, in the Trueba Theatre in Bilbao, one of
the most important conservatives, Ángel Ossorio y Gallardo, gave an
eagerly awaited speech. He was the leader of conservatism in Zaragoza
and Huesca. He had resigned from his posts shortly after Eduardo
Dato had been entrusted with forming a government by Alfonso XIII
the previous October 27, in this way displacing the head of the conservatives, Antonio Maura. The evening before his arrival in Bilbao
by train, there were shouts of support for Maura, but also shouts of
support for the Republic, for Ferrer, and calls for Maura's death, while
fighting broke out between supporters and opponents.[97]

Maura had withdrawn from politics temporarily, but his supporters
promoted a movement in his favor. In the case of Bilbao, one of those
who collaborated in organizing the event at the Trueba Theatre was
Ramón Bergé, an important shipowner and ship insurer; additionally, he
was the son of one of the founders of the Conservative Party in Bizkaia, a
business partner and friend of Antonio Maura.[98] It was no accident that
the meeting was held in Bilbao as Bergé and a large part of the conservatives sided with Maura, and the younger members above all declared
themselves to be "Maurists,"[99] even when the Mallorcan politician was
in temporary retirement and giving no indication of his intentions.

Maurism was a confused movement that oscillated between the old Conservative Party that it aimed to surpass—participating in elections like the rest, with the same combination of propaganda and electoral fraud—and a new form of practicing politics, involving new forms of association and propaganda, such as taking recourse to violence. One of the fundamental points of the new movement was the exaltation of a new Spanish sentiment, a nationalism that bore more resemblance to the integral form of this ideology—which had already appeared in France with Maurras—than to the Spanish liberal tradition. In fact, in the speech he gave in Bilbao, Ossorio stressed that Maurism was a movement that should keep watch over the vigor of the Spanish fatherland.[100]

With time this nationalism developed into right-wing Maurism, an organic traditional formulation, very close to the integral nationalism of Charles Maurras. In short, many of those young Maurists finally ended up in the ranks of authoritarian, antiliberal groups and in some cases even fascist ones. And some of them had been born or brought up in Bilbao, such as José Félix de Lequerica, Fernando Ybarra, and Sánchez Mazas. Rivalry with Basque nationalism was one of the reasons for their radicalization, which was accentuated by the advances made by Basque nationalism during the years of the Great War.

The Action/Reaction Principle: Basque Nationalism vs. Spanish Nationalism

In 1914 another, even more distorting element was added to the turbulent Spanish political panorama. This was World War I, which broke out in August that year and in which Spain remained neutral. But it had important consequences for the politics and economics of the time.

The first consequence was the polarization between pro-allied and pro-German sentiment, with Basque nationalism favoring the former while Carlism inclined towards the latter.[101] During the first months of the war, a turbulent situation in Bilbao caused by the bankruptcy of the Crédito de la Unión Minera bank took several months to resolve, and the main bank in the city, the Banco de Bilbao, needed to guarantee its operations with the fortunes of its main directors.

The following year, 1915, a provincial election was held and the result was especially controversial, above all in the district of Bilbao.

The socialists and nationalists were victorious. However, the monarchist majority in the Deputation, using the scandals and violence that had occurred during the elections as an argument, managed to have the results for the Bilbao district (which had elected two republican-socialists and two nationalists) annulled, with the result that there continued to be a monarchist majority on the provincial Deputation (seven conservatives out of sixteen deputies).

On March 11, 1917, a new partial provincial election was held to renew the districts of Durango, Balmaseda, Markina, and Bilbao. Although this should, in theory, have consisted of electing new deputies for the first three districts, there was also an election in Bilbao, since the previous election in 1915 had been annulled, making it necessary to complete the number of provincial deputies by raising it to twenty.

In the two years that had elapsed between 1915 and 1917, when the fields of Europe continued to be stained with blood, many things changed in Bizkaian politics. The monarchist parties continued to be beset with the problems that had caused the Maurists to break away in 1913, and some of the Bizkaian Maurists continued to have considerable political influence. The liberals were unable to organize a strong electoral candidacy, and the conservatives were still affected by the breakup of the *Piña*. In the field of the republican-socialist union things were no better, as shown by the expulsion of Facundo Perezagua because of his confrontation with Prieto. Symptomatic of the weakness of the union was the fact that, while in Bilbao, republicans and socialists stood together in elections, in Balmaseda each fielded its own candidacy.

Facing the disunity of the monarchist parties (conservatives—who were in their turn divided: Maurists and liberals) and the republican-socialists, the nationalists reached an understanding with the Carlists for the districts of Markina, Durango, and Bilbao. They fielded joint candidacies for the occasion.[102] In light of the electoral results they scored a resounding success. Only in Balmaseda—a district controlled for many decades by the Chávarri family—were the conservatives able to partly check the nationalist advance, and even so Ramón de la Sota y Aburto—son of Ramón de la Sota y Llano—won the seat reserved for the minority in the district.

This result played a decisive role in producing a previously unheard of circumstance. This was the first—and last—time that the nationalists managed to wrest the presidency of the provincial Deputation of Bizkaia from the monarchist parties.

TABLE 2. Constitution of the Deputation, May 4, 1917

Name	Affiliation	Post	District	
Bilbao Lopátegui, José Ramón	Nationalist		Bilbao	Incoming*
Torre Carricarte, Mariano	Nationalist		Bilbao	Incoming
Urrutia Ibarra, Luis	Nationalist	Vice-president	Bilbao	Incoming
Fatrás Neira, Vicente	Republican		Bilbao	Incoming
Bilbao Eguía, Hilario	Jaimista		Durango	Incoming
Eguileor Orueta, Manuel	Nationalist	Secretary	Durango	Incoming
Elguezabal Urrengoechea, Cosme	Nationalist		Durango	Incoming
Rotaeche Llamas, Ramón María	Nationalist		Durango	Incoming
Enderica Hormaeche, José María	Conservative		Gernika	Continues
Goicoechea Ateca, Lorenzo	Conservative		Gernika	Continues
Nardiz Zubía, Álvaro	Conservador		Gernika	Continues
Alzaga Apraiz, Juan	Nationalist		Gernika	Continues
Garay Lesunaga, José María	Jaimista		Markina	Incoming
Landaburu Madaria, Félix	Nationalist	Secretary	Markina	Incoming
Urrengoechea Aguirre, Luis	Nationalist		Markina	Incoming
Zubicaray Badiola, Fernando	Nationalist		Markina	Incoming
Tierra Echanonjáuregui, Juan Francisco	Conservative		Balmaseda	Incoming
Ybarra Elcano, Vicente	Conservative		Balmaseda	Incoming
Pisón Quintana, Alejandro	Liberal		Balmaseda	Incoming
Sota y Aburto, Ramón de la	Nationalist	President	Balmaseda	Incoming

* In provincial elections half of the districts were renewed every two years; thus, there were deputies elected in 1915 (those for the district of Gernika), who continued in 1917 until 1919. The four elected for Bilbao in 1915 had not been declared, so the Deputation had been left with 16 provincial deputies. Thus in 1917, in addition to electing the deputies in the districts requiring renewal, it was necessary to elect the deputies for the district of Bilbao so that the Deputation would again be formed of twenty members.
Source: Elaborated by the author on the basis of the minutes of the Provincial Deputation of Bizkaia (4-5-1917), A.D.F.B. Section Administrative, J-00333/001.

As can be seen in Table 2, in the election of 1917 as many as ten nationalists entered the Deputation, and together with their deputy from the previous period they achieved a majority that enabled Ramón de la Sota y Aburto to be elected president of the Deputation and Luis Urrutia as vice president.

The changes implied by this new majority in the management of the province were of greater significance in some aspects than others. In the fiscal field there were no great novelties, except that provincial taxes on certain consumer products considered to be of basic need, such as oil, were now eliminated. Conversely, they introduced a budgetary reorganization that was to persist; namely, a change in budget classification that clarified its structure and fit in better with the special powers of the Deputation. It should be borne in mind that income from the Triano mining railway or outlays like the *Miñones* (the provincial police dependent on the Deputation) did not fit into the obligatory template approved by the Government Ministry.[103] In other fields, such as culture, we find new practices, such as, for example, sending out notices in Euskera[104]—when the Deputation had never before used Euskera as an administrative language—or encouraging new cultural platforms like the *Sociedad de Estudios Vascos-Eusko Ikaskuntza* (Basque Studies Society) in 1918. One accusation leveled at the nationalist administration was that it was using the budget to employ its sympathizers, causing a double effect: on the one hand, contracting superfluous or barely qualified personnel, while at the same time increasing the number of retirements (since one way of making the contracting of new personnel necessary was by retiring existing staff), which meant a further outlay for the Deputation.[105] An examination of the documentation indicates that in fact a few employees—later dismissed because they were nationalists—were contracted at the time, but this was by no means a significant number and was far from what happened under the II Republic. Finally, another cause for reproach was the increase in outlays during these two years, which is true, although not by as much as stated because it was also influenced by the high inflation caused by the world war and the government's practice of monetizing the deficit.[106]

In short, initiatives were indeed made that modernized the management of the Deputation, but not many changes were introduced. That is not to say that the Deputation was inoperative. Quite the contrary, as it headed a movement in favor of autonomy.

The nationalist victory in 1917 determined a new political direction—in combination with the political and social convulsions of that year and the next, when World War I ended—not towards the restoration of the *Fueros*, but going beyond that, towards autonomy.

The conservatives under the presidency of Dato returned to office in June 1917 and, facing the threat of social revolution, constitutional guarantees were suspended and press censorship was imposed. In Catalonia, the reaction was to convene an assembly of parliamentarians for July 19 that would deal with the system's "taboo" issues: the organization of the state, autonomy, the armed forces, etc.[107]

In the Basque Country, bearing in mind the composition of the Deputations (with nationalist control in that of Bizkaia and Carlist control in the other two), it is not surprising that there was a movement of solidarity with the Catalan initiatives, already shown during Cambó's visit to Bilbao and Donostia-San Sebastián at the start of that year.[108]

On the eve of the Barcelona Assembly the Basque Deputations, on the proposal of the Bizkaian Deputation, met to consider how to ask the "Public Powers for greater autonomy for the Basque-Navarrese region."[109]

On July 16, 1917, the Basque Deputations held a plenary meeting in Vitoria. They were joined, by special and personal invitation, by the Navarrese Deputies Antonio Baztán, Francisco Martínez, and Javier Sanz. After the opening greetings, Carmelo Echegaray—chronicler of the provinces—read out a draft agreement,[110] which noted the opportunity for requesting greater autonomy at a time when winds of change were also blowing in other parts of the country—such as Catalonia—especially since the "Basque provinces had the most sacred and imprescriptible historical rights in their favour."[111]

Two agreements were proposed and unanimously approved. The first requested from the public powers—within the bounds of national unity—"a broad autonomy that is in keeping with the constant aspirations of the Country" for both the Deputations and the Municipal

Councils.[112] The second agreed to entrust the presidents of the three Deputations with convening the representatives in the Spanish Parliament in the near future and delivering the agreement to them.

In synthesis, the message sent to the government effectively stated that their economic and administrative regime was safeguarded with the Economic Agreement, "but that autonomy is not sufficient for developing the activity and effort of the inhabitants of this land. For that reason, the Deputations, without for one moment abandoning the historical rights that have been invoked in all periods by the corporations that speak in the name of Bizkaia, Gipuzkoa and Araba, consider that it is necessary for them to widen the autonomy that they enjoy, because the delays in processing the issue in the Public Offices and the influence that the changes in general policy are having in the administrative sphere constitute an obstacle to the progress of the general interests." This autonomy would not of course diminish the essential attributes of the state: Foreign Relations, War and the Navy, Customs Posts, Post and Telegraphs, Weights and Measures, Currency and Public Debt. Meanwhile, Education at all levels, Charitable Works, Public Works and Hydraulic Services, Agriculture, Industry, and Trade, "and others that there is no need to specify, and that in no way are contrary to the sovereignty of the state,"[113] would be managed by the Deputations.

For these reasons the government was asked to adopt, or propose in the Spanish Parliament following an audience with the Deputations, the regulations relevant to their aspirations for greater autonomy. These could be summarized in a general regulation that would more or less state that "reserving to itself everything concerned with Foreign Relations, War and the Navy, Public Debt, Customs Posts, Currency, Weights and Measures and Post, the state leaves to the country itself, represented by its *foral* organizations, the management of all the other public services."[114]

This plenary meeting of the Deputations was followed with great expectation, and they received telegrams of support from numerous Municipal Councils.[115] The City Council of Bilbao subscribed to the agreements of Vitoria at the request of the deputies for the Bilbao district, but this was after Sota had assured them that the Deputation would concede autonomy to the Municipal Councils, to which end he would convene the necessary meeting. The agreement established the principle of national unity, thus eliminating resistance from the socialist councillors Merodio and Carretero. The Municipal Councils gave their approval to the initiatives of the Deputation, with only one vote against, once it had given them guarantees that it would, in turn, concede that same autonomy to the Municipal Councils of the province.[116] An expression of support for these requests for autonomy arrived from Barcelona, where the Assembly of Spanish Senators and Deputies held its first meeting on July 19, 1917. On the proposal of Aniceto Llorente, who was from Araba but was republican deputy for Valencia, the assembly sent "a warm greeting to the Basque Deputations for their agreement to call for the implantation of the autonomous regime in the Spanish Nation."[117] In answer to this greeting, the City Council of Bilbao agreed in early August 1917 to support the resolutions adopted at the Assembly of parliamentarians held in Barcelona on July 19, 1917, in relation to municipal autonomy.[118]

The Vitoria agreements had the rare virtue of being to nearly everyone's liking, although they fell well short of meeting the ideals of all the groups. The allusion to the unity of the Spanish nation dispelled suspicions of separatism, the promise of municipal autonomy was music to the ears of the Municipal Councils, and the reference to "historic rights" pleased the staunchest *foralists*. As the Carlist Hilario Bilbao declared in Vitoria, "the accepted formula was not the ideal of all those present, but it was a formula that moved towards that ideal."[119]

Honoring the promise made by Sota, the Bizkaian Deputation convened the Municipal Councils of the province to an assembly to be held on August 9 to hear their opinion on the autonomy initiative.[120] The same was done with the former deputies of the province,[121] who were convened on August 7 to help in a committee appointed by the Deputation to address the complex issue of autonomy.

At the meeting on August 7, Ramón de la Sota informed the former deputies of his activities and initiatives. He made it clear that the latter were not aimed at aggravating the crisis of the state, but at solving it by contributing new ideas on government, "namely, a totally new government ideology."[122] He pointed out that the message agreed upon in Vitoria was necessarily generic in character, since it was intended to provide support for the attempt to obtain the government's agreement with the Deputations, leaving the concrete petitions of each of the latter for later.

Sota stressed that it was not a question of requesting anything for the Deputations, but for the country, in such a way that "if the freedom to govern ourselves that we are requesting is not granted, it is certain that the Deputation in its current form will disappear and those that replace them will be the direct and legitimate representation of the people." He also insisted that the message signified compromise since it did not provide full satisfaction to many, but that everybody had made concessions to reach a broad agreement.[123]

Ramón Madariaga, who together with Indalecio Prieto could be considered a representative of the left, emphasized two aspects: firstly, that the meaning of "broad autonomy" should be specified in detail; and secondly, an explanation of how it should be achieved was needed. "One is the restoration of the state of law prior to a certain date: with respect to this there is a diversity of opinions. The other, consists in taking the present situation as a starting point and trying to improve it, with the result that our state of law should be consolidated and perfected, always to the general benefit of the country."[124]

That is, *foral* reintegration understood as a return to 1876 (or 1839) was not being considered, but instead, starting out "from that new law, which began to take effect from the year 1841 or 1842 and that was then improved considerably in the time of Egaña in the 1850s and later with the Economic Agreements, has been fully developed and established. That law is only partly written down and for that very reason it is necessary to it [to] return to it again and improve, perfect and consolidate it."[125] And even this, Madariaga declared, would only be accepted on two conditions: the first, that the same regime would be made extensive to the rest of Spain, and the second, that there would be respect for the "innate immanent rights of the personality, the faculties and attributes of the human personality, which in no way can we consent to their being trampled on, either by the State, the Province or the Municipality."[126]

José J. Ampuero, in the name of the traditionalists, fully supported the message and work of the Deputation. He supported *foral* reintegration, prior to 1839, although he accepted that it should be reformed to adapt it to the circumstances of the present time and, in his capacity as deputy to the Spanish Parliament for Durango, he put himself at the disposal of the Deputation for whatever it might require, both in and out of parliament.

Indalecio Prieto was the next to speak. He spoke in harsh terms about "the sad spectacle of the decomposition of the Spanish state, whose ruling bodies are completely corrupted."[127] From this perspective, any attempt at regeneration originating in "the strong regions, with their own life," seemed to him laudable, which is why the resurgence of the *foral* aspiration seemed reasonable to him. "With respect to the meaning of coupling the enormously democratic, profoundly liberal spirit of the *Fueros* to the complexities of modern social life, the Deputation can count not only on my personal blessing and approval, but also on the enthusiastic participation of the people who are militants in the political camp to which I belong."[128] According to Prieto the problem was a tactical one. If historical dates started to be evoked when formulating their aspirations, it would be better to resist their demands, "and that is why I believe it is better to demand greater autonomy for the country, as the President said, with whose skills I was unacquainted until now, and which I sincerely recognise."[129] He therefore proposed taking advantage of the *foral* tradition to obtain greater autonomy, even at the risk of other regions not obtaining it. But this autonomy should have regulations to avoid the danger of despotism. "If the Deputations try to directly recreate the General Assemblies, care must be taken to return to the primitive sources of sovereignty of those bodies, to what in this sense we could call the germ of the Basque *Fueros*, to the popular sovereignty from which the Basque institutions emerged."[130] In sum, Prieto supported the activities in favor of autonomy while avoiding details that might harm unanimity, but municipal autonomy had to be put into practice, and there should be no return to old formulations that denied popular sovereignty.

The nationalist Pedro Chalbaud agreed with Prieto on almost everything. He proposed making a formal protest against the Law of

July 21, 1876, to safeguard "all the historical rights"; but to proceed no further because there should not be talk "beyond the part that unites us . . . and there are not going to be *foral* bodies, nor is the *Fuero* going to be adopted; instead it seems simpler to adhere to the agreements of Vitoria and in this sense the most complete faculties possible should be requested."[131]

The most controversial issues were avoided and therefore no great arguments arose. There was no clear specification of what was understood by autonomy, nor was emphasis placed on complete *foral* reintegration. Thus, motives for confrontation were largely reduced.

Two days later, the meeting between the assembly of representatives of the Municipal Councils and the commissioners from the Deputation was held in Gernika.[132] In spite of the assembly's only having a deliberative character, two agreements were reached. The first contained a solemn protest against the laws that had abolished the *Fueros* in the past, while the second expressed the unanimous support of the municipalities for the efforts of the Deputation.

Following these meetings between the Deputations and their respective municipalities, different contacts were held between the Deputations and between the latter and the parliamentarians in Madrid.

Following these provincial meetings, different contacts were held between the Deputations and between the latter and the parliamentarians in Madrid. While on other occasions there had been almost total agreement between the Deputations and parliamentarians, on these occasions there was no unanimity.[133] But the Deputations did not let that stop them. They finally prepared a message to the government in which they set out their demands for autonomy.

In October, it appears that they visited the King, who expressed his agreement with the requests of the Deputations, although no documentary evidence of this survives.[134] We do not know whether it was prior to or following this interview that Ladislao de Zavala asked the president of the government, Eduardo Dato—who was a deputy for Vitoria—for an audience in order to hand him the message.[135] However, it was necessary to postpone the delivery of the message due to the fall of Dato's government in November 1917,[136] and another date had to be set with Dato's replacement.

The new president, Manuel García Prieto, arranged an appointment with them for December 17. Ladislao de Zavala, president of the Deputation of Gipuzkoa, read the message to the president, who replied with very polite words, and the duly delivered text thus joined the infinite number of papers and files that disappeared into the entrails of the Ministries.[137]

The government of García Prieto only lasted until March, when he was replaced by Maura, who headed a government that included the leading figures of the main parties (Dato, Maura, Romanones).[138] Maura's assuming of the presidency of the Council of Ministers is an unmistakable symptom of the delicate situation in which the monarchy found itself. But it was believed to be the only means of regeneration.[139] And the Basque Deputations aligned themselves with this attempt.

> It seems that Spain wants to proceed to a spiritual liquidation. In it, with all the mistakes and insane notions that one might point to, on one side were the Catalan parliamentarians, the Military Boards, the *Basque Deputations*, the producers of Córdoba, the municipalities of Coruña and Salamanca, all with hopes of regeneration; and on the other, the King, the monarchist parties, the trust, the oligarchy, quietism, poverty.[140]

Thus far no reference had been made to a political and administrative unity that would differ in any way from the provinces governed by their Deputations, which in this case were *foral*. This reintegration, in the broad frameworks within which it was proposed, would not alter the economic relations between the Deputations and the government, since a clear statement of the usefulness of the Economic Agreement was made. The most controversial points of a return to the *Fueros* had not of course been cleared up: the system for electing the Representative Assemblies and the *foral* Deputations.

Nationalism's change towards pragmatism, which moderated its declarations, its control of the Bizkaian Deputation, the agreement with the socialists (who agreed in general terms on municipal autonomy) once the unity of Spain had been recognized, was a humiliation for those who had traditionally controlled the Bizkaian Deputation. It was therefore not surprising that the monarchist parties in Bizkaia became alarmed at the perspective of losing control of a key institution for determining provincial development—in addition to their gaining a reputation of being opposed to the *Fueros*. It is not only the political aspects of this question—which are important—that should be considered, but also the economic ones. The Deputations at this time were holding talks with the central treasury on the application of a reform of the tax on company profits, which excluded foreign companies from the Economic Agreement with the result that they could not be taxed by the Basque Deputations. In this aspect all of the parties agreed upon defending the Economic Agreement.[141]

We should not only focus on events in the narrow framework of the Basque Country—if we have been referring especially to events in Bizkaia, this is because of nationalism's important position in that province, which in a certain way marked the line to be followed by the other two Deputations. Instead, these events must be viewed in combination with the consequences of the world war and the problems that nationalism was causing to several of the belligerent powers, especially Irish nationalism. Indeed, the "leap" from *foral* reintegration to autonomy was not taking place in a vacuum, but coincided with Catalan aspirations, where the constitution of the Mancomunidad in 1914 had not brought a definitive resolution to the Catalan question. Much less did it represent a model for the Basque Deputations which, from the outset, had decided this was not a course to follow, as the Economic Agreement already had a much wider range of competences.[142]

The Basque Deputations closely studied the Royal Decree authorizing the provincial Deputations to request the formation of a Community of Deputations, and also its application in the Catalan case.[143] The main problem with the concept was undoubtedly that there was no specification with respect to competences. The Communities of Municipalities did not involve any cession of competences by the state, but instead authorized the Deputations to form communities to better organize and provide services. It did allow for more competences to be requested, but this required the approval of the Spanish Parliament. The Catalan Deputations accepted the decree and were the only ones to organize a community. The Deputations of the Basque Country made a clear diagnosis from the start: the decree could not be compared with the Economic Agreement, which gave a much wider margin of maneuver than that provided by the timid measure of forming a community.

As we noted, the international context also brought novelties. Since 1912, Great Britain had been involved in the process of granting autonomy to Ireland (home rule), but this process was abruptly halted with the outbreak of the armed conflict as the war took up all of the government's efforts. But in 1916 the Easter Rising took place, which was harshly supressed by the British Army. This gave rise to an intense debate within Basque nationalism between the radical and moderate currents, which resulted in Luis de Arana abandoning the leadership of the party at the start of the year. The Easter Rising was also used by other political parties to attack nationalism, enabling "Basque traditionalists and conservatives to delve into the contradictions of Basque Nationalist Communion, which was in theory Anglophile and in favor of the Entente."[144]

Therefore, in the years between 1916 and 1919, political tensions rose in a context that included: the Russian Revolution—which made clear that the much-feared revolution was not only possible but had in fact overthrown the autocratic regime of the Czars; the final months of the First World War, which brought the end of three empires (German, Austro-Hungarian, and Ottoman); and the crisis of the restoration system in Spain, which was unable to resolve the steep rise in prices, the demands for Catalan autonomy, and the demands of the armed forces. In the narrow field of Basque politics, the interests of the political parties and some individuals coincided on some points but not on others: depending on where the debate was centered, there were short-term alliances—or estrangements. This was at a time when public opinion was becoming an increasingly important factor, at least in certain places like Bilbao, when it came to forming significant majorities on certain issues: autonomy, religion . . .

Put synthetically, with room for evident nuances, in those years it can be said that the main political groups—not necessarily parties[145]— could be aligned with respect to certain issues, as follows:

	Conservatives	Liberals	Carlists	Nationalists	Republicans	Socialists
Anti-monarchist		X		X	X	X
Catholics	X	/	X	X		
Right-wing	X		X	X		
Civil rights		X			X	X
Foralists	X	X	X	X	X	
Left-wing		/			X	X
National unity	X	X	X		X	X

It is not easy to give a univocal meaning to these terms. For example, in this period *foralism* was already a very vague term. For some it meant a return to the purity of the *Fueros* prior to 1839; this was questioned by others who, like Balparda, argued that, following 1837, the provinces were already assimilated; while for others the term meant maintaining—or even widening—the Economic Agreement. Therefore, nearly all the groups expressed support for the Economic Agreement, which they liked to a greater or lesser degree, with the exception of some socialists. The latter linked it to the Deputations' use of the power to set certain taxes, placing the fiscal burden on consumer taxes to the detriment of the working masses, while property (urban, industrial, or capital) was taxed less, or even exempted.[146] The fiscal issue was not alien to the debates on autonomy at that time. It should be recalled that in 1916 the Alba reform was proposed, which as noted above was one of the factors that provoked the "*traída de catalanes*" (the invitation to the Catalans), in which Cambó had played a leading role. To a certain point this had been of concern to the Deputations, insofar as it could affect the concerted quota—set ten years previously until the year 1926—which is why autonomy might come to provide a supplementary guarantee to the Economic Agreement and the fiscal status quo.

In February 1918, in keeping with the nationalist policy of participation, the nationalists stood in the general election. It seems that Sota took advantage of his presidency of the Deputation in order to benefit the nationalists at the expense of the monarchists.[147] Whatever the case, the fact is that the nationalists achieved significant success in the election in Bizkaia, where they obtained five deputies[148] and three senators (Chalbaud, Horn, and Campion).[149]

On February 24, 1918, as we noted, an election was held that brought a resounding victory to nationalism:

Basque Nationalism and Spanish Nationalism

TABLE 3. Candidates Elected for the Districts of the Basque Country in the Election for the Congress and the Senate in 1918.

Name	Province	District	Electoral platform
Urquijo Ussía, Luis Cayetano	Araba	Amurrio	Urquijista
Artiñano Galdácano, Gervasio.	Araba	Laguardia	Independent Catholic
Dato Iradier, Eduardo	Araba	Vitoria	Conservative
Sota Llano, Ramón de la.	Bizkaia	Balmaseda	PNV
Zaballa Loizaga, Alejandro.	Bizkaia	Barakaldo	PNV
Prieto Tuero, Indalecio	Bizkaia	Bilbao	PSOE
Rotaeche Velasco, Ignacio.	Bizkaia	Durango	PNV
Ortueta Azcuenaga, Anacleto.	Bizkaia	Gernika	PNV
Arroyo Olave, Antonio.	Bizkaia	Markina	PNV
Senante Martínez, Manuel	Gipuzkoa	Azpeitia	Ultra-conservative
Eizaguirre Ayestarán, José.	Gipuzkoa	Bergara	PNV
Azqueta Monasterio, Horacio.	Gipuzkoa	Donostia-San Sebastián	Liberal
Bilbao Eguía, Esteban	Gipuzkoa	Tolosa	Carlist
Arteaga Echagüe, Joaquín	Gipuzkoa	Zumaia	Catholic
Domínguez Arévalo, Tomás	Na	Agoitz	Jaimista
Llorens Fernández De Córdova, Joaquín	Na	Estella-Lizarra	Carlist
Pradera Larrumbe, Juan Víctor	Na	Pamplona	Carlist
Aranzadi Irujo, Manuel.	Na	Pamplona	PNV
Leyún Villanueva, Celedonio.	Na	Pamplona	Conservative
Mencos Bernaldo De Quirós, Joaquín I.	Na	Tafalla	Conservative
Méndez Vigo Méndez Vigo, José María	Na	Tudela	Conservative

Senators elected* for the Basque Country.

Name	Province	Electoral platform
Urquijo Ussía, Juan Manuel	Araba	Urquijista
González De Echávarri Vivanco, José María.	Araba	Conservative
Unceta Berriozabal, José María.	Araba	Carlist
Urquijo Ussía, Estanislao	Araba	Urquijista
Horn Y Mendia De Areilza.	Bizkaia	PNV
Campión Jaimebón, Arturo	Bizkaia	PNV
Chalbaud Errazquin, Pedro.	Bizkaia	Independent Catholic
Murua Rodríguez Paterna, Antonio María.	Gipuzkoa	Ultra-conservative
Arana Belaústegui, Teodoro	Gipuzkoa	Carlist
Seoane Ferrer, Ramón	Gipuzkoa	Liberal
Elío Magallón, Luis	Na	Conservative
Sanz Escartín, Romualdo Cesáreo	Na	Carlist
Gayarre Arregui, Valentín	Na	Liberal

* Besides those elected, there were another nine Senators, Senators for life (7) and Senators by right (2), either born in or with connections to the Basque Country. All were monarchists (Liberals, 2, Conservatives, 6, and *Urquijista*, 1). Estanislao Urquijo—the Marquis de Urquijo—following his election to the Senate, was promoted to the rank of Grandee of Spain; he was therefore automatically entitled to be a Senator by right, which meant that a partial election had to be held, won by his brother Juan Manuel. As a result, this meant in this legislative period Araba had four Senators, when in fact three corresponded to the province.

The nationalists' victory in the Congress was accompanied by their winning all three seats in the Senate with the election of Arturo Campion, Pedro Chalbaud, and José Horn.

Although in Araba, the Marquis of Amurrio—logically an *Urquijista*—had won in the district of Amurrio and Eduardo Dato (conservative) in the district of Vitoria, the traditionalist Artiñano had won in the district of Laguardia.

These results occurred in a parliament, where there was a clear split among the monarchist parties that had broad dissident minorities in their ranks. As a result the governability of the country became increasingly difficult, which is shown by the next election taking place in June 1919.

This change in the provincial representation in the Spanish Parliament closed a parenthesis in the Deputations' activities aimed at advancing their project for *foral* reintegration. On March 20, representatives of the three Basque Deputations met. They unanimously agreed that a meeting should be called in Madrid with the Basque representatives to give them an amendment to present in the Spanish Parliament.[150]

However, when everything appeared to be proceeding smoothly, the moment came for the nationalists to intervene in the Spanish Parliament. The nationalists who had brought with them a moderate program found themselves frontally opposed not only by the monarchist parties, but also by Prieto (it seems that the earlier guarantees were not enough for him), and they stood together in defense of national unity. The atmosphere grew heated in the discussion on the Balmaseda Bill presented by Pradera and Balparda.

The election of Ramón de la Sota for the district of Balmaseda was discussed in the Supreme Court, which issued a report on the claims presented by the defeated candidate, Gregorio Balparda.[151] He opposed the former's election because of coercion and the purchase of votes, in addition to his incompatibility for the post of deputy as he was president of the Board of Works of the Port. The Supreme Court found nothing probative in those accusations, nor did it consider Ramón de la Sota's post at the port to be incompatible. But the attacks on Ramón de la Sota grew more intense during the debate on April 5. In fact, when he first took the floor to speak against him, Víctor Pradera (Carlist Deputy for Pamplona) declared that de la Sota was not entitled to occupy his seat, but not for legal reasons, which he did not discuss, but because he had disowned the Spanish fatherland.[152]

Víctor Pradera was an outspoken critic of both Catalan and Basque nationalism. A former student of Juan Vázquez de Mella,[153] to whom he was now politically close, he proposed an organic idea of the nation with certain essential elements: including the traditional monarchy, and the church and the *foral* regime, which in his case was not understood as a basis for sovereignty.[154]

The president allowed the defeated candidate, Gregorio Balparda, to put the case for his election. He once again attacked de la Sota y Llano, on this occasion for his activities in the provincial Deputation, whose president was his son, Ramón de la Sota y Aburto.[155]

Although Balparda[156] did make some allusion to the concrete motives for annulling de la Sota's election as a deputy—above all since being a deputy was incompatible with his position as president of the Board of Works of the Port—he insisted on his negative political evaluation that de la Sota was calling for the destruction of the state. The deputy for the district of Markina, the nationalist Antonio Arroyo, rejected Balparda's attacks, arguing that they were not discussing the legal reasons for contesting the seat, but that he was instead putting Sota's political ideas on trial. And if this was the line of argument, he did not understand why the Catalan deputies—who were just as nationalist as the Basques—were attending the plenary session, which they had been doing for many years.[157] The debate was conducted in a harsh tone at times. There were occasional interruptions by other deputies, amongst them Prieto, who declared that the blame for the development of nationalism "lies with you"—in clear reference to the monarchist parties or to some Catalans, like Felip Rodés, who replied that Prieto was completely departing from the issue at hand. This debate, beyond the fact that Sota was accepted as a deputy, shows the growing tension between the nationalists and at least some of the Carlists and liberals.

As a result of all this, the presentation of the message to the Spanish Parliament was put on hold. It appears that the Deputations themselves secretly agreed to this, with the result that when the Spanish Parliament suspended its activities in the summer, no progress had been made.[158]

What had happened since December 1917—when it had seemed that there was so much unanimity about requesting autonomy—such that a few months later there were so many problems with the issue? Neither the socialists nor the monarchist parties were particularly willing to follow the course of autonomy. Without doubt, the electoral results had been a clear victory for nationalism, which is why the monarchist parties, in particular, became increasingly distrustful of the ambiguous demands for autonomy.

The socialists, with Prieto as their spokesperson, entered the debate on the *españolista* course.[159] The debate on autonomy that took place between 1917 and 1919 was the first occasion during which Spanish socialism had to address the regional question. Indalecio Prieto was the first Spanish socialist who, recognizing the existence of what he called the "Basque problem," urged that it should be resolved by managing the "*foral* question" and/or "Basque question" using the legal system of the Spanish nation. Thus, these arguments were not aired the first time by Prieto when he was in office during the II Republic, but were as early as April 17, 1918, in the Congress of Deputies, and he was to repeat them from then onwards until the end of his life.[160]

In that speech in the Congress of Deputies[161] he reiterated the socialist view that Basque nationalism was a Catholic, racist, and separatist movement.

As Antonio Rivera[162] observes, while his speech on April 17 at the Congress of Deputies was not entirely original, it was certainly important as it was the first occasion on which Carlists, Basque nationalists, the government, a Catalanist minister, and the socialist-republican position, expressed by Prieto himself, all faced each other in the parliamentary chamber. In reality, Prieto's position was already known to the country, given that he had insisted on characterizing Basque nationalism as fundamentalist and secessionist.[163] As a liberal he had no problem with restoring the *foral* spirit, but it had to be adapted to the circumstances of the time. In a certain way he took up the argument of Balparda, stressing that it was precisely the weight of nationalism's narrow Catholicism that ran counter to a *Fuero* filled with preventive clauses against ecclesiastical power. As Balparda had done, he attacked the government insofar as nationalism had prospered due to the inability of the Basque monarchists to assimilate "the true spirit of the country."

Indalecio Prieto held a clearly negative opinion of Basque nationalism, although it is logical that different alternatives and nuances can be found over the course of a political career spanning more than fifty years.[164] In fact, in 1919 a nationalist newspaper published an article titled "*Españolismo* in the Basque Country is Indalecio Prieto Tuero,"[165] but at the same time, as noted above, he recognized that there was a territorial problem that required a solution. These arguments, together with his political practice, enabled him to win and subsequently hold a seat for Bilbao from 1918 onwards, facing the other two sides of the triangle: Basque nationalism and the Spanish right-wing.[166]

In September 1918, the Congress of Basque Studies was held in Oñate,[167] which served to demonstrate the underlying appetite for autonomy—and not only among nationalists—on the condition that this was achieved by means of collaboration, not confrontation, among the political parties.[168]

In November 1918, with the end of the hostilities of World War I, the collapse of the Austro-Hungarian Empire, the fall of Maura, and with Cambó as Minister of Development, events accelerated in such a way as to encourage aspirations for autonomy, and not only among the Basques.

It should be recalled that in the final years of the war and the first months of peace, the application of the "Wilson Doctrine,"—recognizing the right to self-determination in facing the breakup of the old multinational empires, held significance. Even in other geographical situations, such as Ireland, which reactivated the demand for autonomy, and Galicia, where its importance spread, were notable.[169]

At that time, the national and international situation was considered to be highly favorable for achieving the goal of autonomy by
both Catalans and Basques. Support was even sought abroad.[170] On
November 6, in a very heated debate, the nationalist deputies presented a bill that involved repealing the Law of 1839.[171] One week later
the Catalans made their own request for autonomy. The resignation
of Maura on November 9 exemplified the tense political atmosphere
of the time. The Marquis of Alhucemas, Manuel García Prieto, was
entrusted with forming a new government. While Europe sighed with
relief at the cessation of hostilities in the fields of Belgium and the
defeat of Germany, the tensions in Spanish politics did not cease.

In the debate on the nationalist proposal[172] held one month later,
Romanones insisted that the proposal should not be considered. He
had said this in the commission as a minister in García Prieto's government, and he restated his opinion as president of the Council of
Ministers, a post he held from December 5 onwards.[173] Nonetheless,
he gave his assurance that a solution to the issue would be sought in
a wider framework—that of autonomy—and that it fell to the government to set in motion the preparatory work for this, which would later
be presented to the Congress.

Sota, as events were developing rapidly in Madrid, proposed that a
conference should be held with the other two Deputations in Vitoria,
as had occurred on November 19.[174] This was followed one month later
by a meeting with the Municipal Councils, which had received a promise of greater autonomy.

The growing tension over the question of autonomy came into the
open at the Assembly of Municipal Councils of Bizkaia on December
15, where there was a noisy confrontation between, on one side, the
socialists and the monarchist parties, and the rest of those attending
on the other. The nationalist mayor of Bilbao, Mario de Arana, insisted
on the repeal of the Law of 1839, while Balparda, employing old arguments, held that its first article benefited them because it recognized
the *Fueros*, while the Law of 24 June 1876 (sic) was really abolitionist.
He stated that he would not accept anything that did not include an
explicit declaration of national unity. As the commotion grew worse,
the monarchist politicians chose to leave the room; feelings were

clearly running high since, after the meeting had ended in the City Hall, the brawl continued in the city itself, and there was even an attack on the office of the Maurist newspaper *El Pueblo Vasco*.[175]

As a result of these events, the Minister of Governance agreed to suspend Arana as mayor of Bilbao; and the examining magistrate issued an indictment against Arana, the provincial Deputy Luis de Urrengoechea, and Tomás Charte.[176]

Similar events in Barcelona and a demonstration against autonomy in Madrid resulted in the suspension of the Spanish Parliament. In order to leave the dead end in which the restoration system found itself—not only because of the aspirations for autonomy, but also due to pressure from the armed forces and social conflicts, together with the crisis of the monarchist parties—Romanones, who had been president of the government since December 5, issued a Royal Decree by which an extra-parliamentary commission was formed to draw up a bill on autonomy to be presented to the parliament.

This commission, which was formed on December 27 and consisted of thirty-three personalities[177]—although some declined to participate (Dato, Vázquez de Mella, the Catalans, and the left), in its turn appointed a committee, formed of Sánchez de Toca, Maura, Tirso Rodrigáñez, Niceto Alcalá-Zamora, and Joaquín Ruiz Jimenez, which was entrusted with drawing up the text on municipal autonomy and another on Catalan autonomy.[178] A subcommittee was also appointed, made up of José de Orueta, Manuel Senante, and Chalbaud, to draw up a Basque statute.[179] Orueta, appointed by Romanones, immediately offered his services to the Deputations to work in their favor whenever possible.[180]

The subcommittee drew up a project for autonomy, paying heed to the Deputations of Gipuzkoa and Bizkaia.[181] In the subcommittee Orueta, Senante, and Chalbaud followed the line of the message from one year before, which had insisted on *foral* reinstatement. This would be articulated by repealing the laws of September 18, 1837, and October 25, 1839, and in general any laws or regulations that altered the system and the workings of the Basque Municipal Councils and Deputations, thus reinstating their powers within the unity of the nation.[182] As a result, the *foral* bodies would be restored (article 2), adapted in consultation with the government to the present situation. Until the

Representative Assemblies were constituted, the Deputations would have the power to define their workings.

In the second section, in light of the foreseeable rejection of the ideal situation, namely *foral* reinstatement, and after making provision for the appropriate protest, the foundations were laid for a solution based on autonomy. In three months (extendable to six months) the Municipal Councils of the three provinces would meet to agree on the constitution of the *foral* bodies, whether adapted or new. The powers of the province would extend to the municipal regime, Education at all levels, Public Works, the Merchant Marine (except for registering ships under the Spanish flag), Regulation of Wealth, Charity, Health and Hygiene, Regulation of Gambling, Fine Arts, Public Order, Statistics and Prisons; with the freedom to appoint or dismiss personnel and regulate municipal affairs. Each province would have the power to establish public and private law; Spanish and Euskera would have a co-official character. The provinces would pay contributions for Customs Posts, Tobacco, Post and Telegraphy, Monopolies, Lotteries, and Military Quotas. Each province would pay a quota to the state, in proportion to its population, with an automatic basis of proportionality to be applied in each annual budget of the state's incomes[183] (article 7). With respect to military service, recruitment would be by province, where the recruits would be trained and serve, except in the case of war.

In spite of the high expectations that had been generated, "the result was depressing."[184] The text of the subcommittee was presented as a dissenting proposal (*voto particular*), and the plenary of the extra-parliamentary commission instead used another text presented by Alba as a basis. This contained the aspiration to return to the *foral* institutions (Representative Assemblies and Deputations), but it would be the Municipal Councils that would determine their regime, constitution, and workings. The government would have a supervisory role.[185]

In the text that was finally submitted, besides equating the juridical situation in Navarre and the Basque provinces, only those attributions that were held by the other provinces were recognized, and finally, the initiative in the whole process was given to the Municipal Councils.[186] Under such conditions it is not surprising that the Deputations protested.

The pronouncement of the Commission of the Congress responsible for drawing up the proposal concerning the organization of municipal and regional autonomy included some of the committee's ideas. Nonetheless, it did not satisfy the Basque members at all, who insisted on presenting it as a dissenting proposal (*voto particular*).[187]

All the hopes raised by the project were dashed. The self-exclusion of the Catalans, who refused to collaborate as the Basques had done but instead presented their own Catalan Statute, and above all the worsening of the social crisis, meant that the government redirected its attention to the wave of strikes in Catalonia and the question of public order in general. And with the closure of the Spanish Parliament in late February the issue of autonomy was left unresolved. With the end of the strike at the Canadiense, Romanones resigned, which signaled the failure of the campaign for autonomy.

The replacement of Romanones by Maura on April 15, 1919, with a government that consisted of "theatricality and the frenzied right-wing,"[188] put an end to "the only serious attempt made by the regime to find an autonomous solution to the Spanish regional problem."[189]

The fact that Maura's government only lasted for three months did not prevent nationalism from losing ground in this brief period of time, and with it the movement in favor of autonomy as well. With the change in the composition of the Deputations the monarchists recovered control of the Deputation of Bizkaia, while the other "sister Deputations" continued to pursue a *foralist* line.

In spite of this failure of the undertaking to obtain autonomy, the project to create an institution common to the three—or four—Deputations continued to be an alternative, but one with diminishing fortunes and a limited public echo.

What is the explanation for such tenacity with respect to the municipal basis of autonomy? This was because in liberal thinking decentralization tended to be situated at the municipal level, much less at the provincial level and even less so at the regional level. There was suspicion that "new tyrants" would emerge—new political bosses in the provinces or regions who would replace state centralism with other centralisms.[190] But it was also because the monarchist parties controlled a large proportion of the municipalities, with the exception of localities like Bilbao or Barakaldo. Their network of political clients was more extensive than those of the nationalists or the socialists, especially in some municipalities in the district of Balmaseda or in rural parts of Bizkaia like the districts of Markina and Durango.

We have already seen that at certain times, such as in 1907, when Antonio Maura was the champion of administrative reform, and initially his tendency claimed to support autonomy—above all at the municipal level. But by 1919 his position had changed radically. In the notes for his speech on autonomy, Maura had written, "*Prohibit the verb FEDERATE and its derivatives.*"[191] This means that he ruled out going beyond simple administrative decentralization and argued for a deepening of municipal autonomy, in some ways in line with his attempt to reform the local administration between 1907 and 1909.[192]

The subcommittee's project for a statute included an article that was intended to safeguard self-government and make it effective: "The central administration will not intervene in any way in the exercise of the autonomous functions that are mentioned in this article." It also established a new philosophy for the public treasury that would replace the system of agreements with a single, overall quota.

In his notes on the project Antonio Maura wrote that "the design and literal terms of article 3 are unacceptable, and also inappropriate to the sensible state of the issue." He considered that financing should be subjected to the regulations envisaged for the rest of the regions. In his opinion, "the current economic agreements are increasingly unsustainable, and should there be any aspiration to persist in them, this would make an agreement extremely difficult."[193] In the other sections, the concessions made in the proposed statute for Catalonia were the point of reference.

The Deputation of Bizkaia, under the presidency of Ramón de la Sota y Aburto, abandoned its project for an organic statute in favor of a statute inspired by the *Fueros*. This was in order to ingratiate itself with the *foralist* and ultraconservative Carlists of Gipuzkoa, for whom defense of the catholic faith was a priority in the face of the project for autonomy. Finally, the monarchist *Urquijistas* of Araba presented their own project.[194]

Maurism, which as we saw had emerged in late 1913, positioned itself in favor of the central European empires, as did Carlism under

Vázquez de Mella, as opposed to the pro-allied position of Basque nationalism, which followed the pro-British line of its founder and the economic interests of its main financier, Sota.[195] But without doubt the confrontation with the monarchist right-wing radicalized the positions of both sides. Consequently, there were writers and politicians who evolved towards positions that were clearly authoritarian and clearly *Españolista*.

This was the case of Maurists like Lequerica, Sánchez Mazas, or the Ybarra brothers in this highly effervescent cultural environment. It is not surprising that the years between 1917 and 1922 saw the publication of the most innovative cultural undertaking of the time, the journal *Hermes*, the result of an initiative by a Basque nationalist, Jesús de Sarría. However, its first editorial council included José Félix de Lequerica, which marked an attempt to bring the two positions closer together.

Lequerica (1890–1963) belonged to a family of Bilbao merchants,[196] and was an active member of the *Lion D'Or* conversation group in Bilbao. This group was a good reflection of the cultural fervor in the city since its members included Pedro Eguillor, the poet Ramón de Basterra, Rafael Sánchez Mazas, Joaquín Zuazagoitia, and Pedro Mourlane Michelena. Pedro Eguillor, a champion of Spanish unity, was a leading figure in this group although he wrote very little, and a plaque in his memory was even placed in the café itself. In this *Noucentista* milieu they spoke about Sorel, Barrés, and Charles Maurras. This is reflected in Lequerica's articles published in the Ybarra brothers' newspaper, *El Pueblo Vasco*, and the café was clearly a center of Spanish monarchism and antinationalism.

In Lequerica's case these flirtations with, or approaches to, Basque nationalism through the *Hermes* milieu should not deceive us. In political terms he was a very ambitious figure, as well as a relatively successful entrepreneur.[197] In 1915 he stood for the first time in an election for the Bilbao City Council and was defeated by the nationalist Eguileor and the Republican Ernesto Ercoreca. In 1918 he stood as a Maurist candidate in Bergara, where the nationalist José Eizaguirre Ayestarán was elected. That same year he stood for Congress, in this case for the district of Barakaldo, where the previous results for the seat had been annulled, and he was again defeated by another nationalist, Domingo

Epalza López de Lerena.[198] Finally, in 1919 he managed to get himself elected as a *cunero*,[199] also through Maura's mediation, winning the seat for the district of Illescas in Toledo, which he held until 1923. In 1921, in reward for his loyalty, Maura appointed him as head of the civil administration and undersecretary of the presidency of the Council of Ministers in his last government.

Rafael Sánchez Mazas (1894–1966) was another member of Lequerica's conversation group. He was born in Madrid, but his father died during his childhood and his mother moved to Bilbao, from where her mother's family proceeded and where he was brought up. As well as literary and journalistic activity, he also managed family business interests like Santa Ana de Bolueta, where he formed part of the council together with *Txomin* Epalza between 1916 and 1919. In spite of their political differences, they both supported giving a grant—on the initiative of Sánchez Mazas—for the creation of a popular library in the premises that the company owned on Ripa Street. In 1921 Sánchez Mazas went to Italy as a correspondent for the newspaper *ABC*, and there he witnessed the coming and development of fascism, which was why in 1933, when he collaborated in the formation of the Spanish Falange, he was very well-informed about the nature of fascism.

In this evolution, some of the regenerationsists also moved towards aggrandizing Spain, like Azorín and José Mª Salaverria, who in spite of being born in Madrid, was from a Gipuzkoan family and had been brought up in Donostia-San Sebastián. He worked as a journalist since he could not make a living from his literary vocation. It was in the years of World War I that he confirmed his political evolution with the publication of *La afirmación Española* (The Spanish Affirmation)[200] in 1917. This marked the start of his ultranationalist campaign "because he was no longer convinced by Unamuno's revolution of consciences, nor by the conservative policy of Maura and La Cierva, supported by Azorín, nor by Maeztu's reformist regenerationism, nor by Baroja's scepticism, nor by socialism or any other solution that emerged from within the liberal system. He therefore began to reaffirm his call for an absolute power that would crush the parliamentary system in order to install an absolutist monarchy or an enlightened dictatorship."[201]

His article of August 1923 is well known. In this he pointed to the stagnation of Spanish political thinking, which he said had not progressed since before the World War I :

> The world thinks with freedom and in a very revolutionary way and, as easily as it banishes renowned dances, with the same assurance with which it installs the jazz band and the dances of the Yankee negroes, it renounces the liberal doctrine of the previous century and enthrones nationalism, militarism in France and fascism with all its consequences in Italy.[202]

This new fashion could be traced back to the wartime years, in the sense that this was when Salaverría began to publicly air his views on Spanish nationality. He was a somewhat strange author in this context due to his lack of interest in the religious element. His time spent in Argentina led him to relate his vision more closely to history and the great figures who had forged Spain, like the Spanish conquerors of America, whom he saw not as evangelists but as the builders of an empire.[203]

The failure of the autonomist project was accompanied by the "return to reality" signified by the new provincial and general elections of 1919. In the former case adjustments were made so that it was easier for the monarchist camp, now organized in the Monarchist Action League, to control the results.[204] This produced the fusion of the districts of Markina and Durango, while Bilbao was split between the Centre and the Ensanche.[205] Although nationalism continued to be a relevant political force, it lost its majority and Ramón de la Sota ceased to be president of the Deputation. The Monarchist Action League won six provincial deputies, which together with three conservatives and one liberal meant that the nationalists were left with eight seats in the Bizkaian Deputation.

The basis for the nationalist defeat was the agreement for the general election made by the republicans, the socialists, and the recently created Monarchist Action League. In this agreement the monarchists did not put forward a candidate in Bilbao, leaving the way open for Prieto to renew his seat, since he was able to face the nationalist Chalbaud unhindered. On the other hand, the socialists gave a free hand to the monarchists in the other districts. The result was lethal for nationalist aspirations. Although they won in their districts, their victories were later annulled.

In the case of the general election of 1919 a similar process occurred.

TABLE 4. Deputies Elected in the General Elections of 1919 and 1920 in the Districts of Bizkaia.

Elections of 1919		
Bilbao	Prieto, Indalecio	Socialist
Balmaseda	Balparda, Gregorio	Liberal
Gemika	Arana, Mario de	Nationalist
Durango	Anulled (Rotaeche, Ignacio)	Nationalist
Markina	Anulled (Arroyo, Antonio)	Nationalist
Barakaldo	Anulled (Epalza, Domingo)	Nationalist
Elections of 1920		
Bilbao	Prieto, Indalecio	Socialist
Balmaseda	Balparda, Gregorio	Liberal
Gemika	Nardiz, Venancio	Conservative
Durango	Chávarri Anduiza, Víctor	Conservative
Markina	Aznar, Alberto	Conservative
Barakaldo	Goyoaga, José Luis	Conservative

The liberal Gregorio Balparda, defeated by Sota in the Balmaseda district in 1918, emerged victorious on this occasion, while Prieto continued to hold his seat in the district of Bilbao. The only remaining nationalist was Mario de Arana, as the elections in the other three districts were annulled. In the election of 1920—the quick succession of elections clearly shows the system's instability—the members of the League won the entire representation with the exception of Bilbao, where Prieto held his seat.[206]

In the Senate, while in 1919 Horn and Chalbaud had held their seats with the *Jaimista* Esteban Bilbao—elected as the third senator for Bilbao—in 1920 the Monarchist Action League once again made a clean sweep: Luis de Salazar, Cosme Palacio, and Manuel Lezama Leguizamón.

While the monarchist parties formed an alliance and their anti-nationalist front was well organized in 1920, the nationalists, following their first split in 1916, suffered a second split led by Eli Gallastegi. This was yet another of several divisions and regroupings that nationalism experienced between its emergence and the civil war.[207]

On the eve of the dictatorship of Primo de Rivera it seemed that the waters had become calm, with the monarchist parties controlling both Deputations and the parliamentary representation. But the restoration system, under attack from different fronts for many years, finally came to an end in September 1923 at the hands of Miguel Primo de Rivera, the captain general of Catalonia. This was not a chance circumstance, thus inaugurating a political system of exception.

In short, we find a varied range of positions opposing nationalism, which were later to focus on defending the Spanish nation. One clear case is that of the Ybarra brothers, Fernando (1875–1936) and Gabriel (1877–1951),[208] leaders of Bizkaian conservatism and later linked to Maurism, who not only organized a party but also a newspaper (*El Pueblo Vasco*) as a platform for spreading their ideas. Fernando adopted a much more radical position in the period of the Republic, in the party *Renovación Española* (Spanish Renovation), and was one of the main figures who financed the coup of July 18, 1936. Gabriel, who unlike Fernando did survive the civil war, maintained an editorial line that was pro-Catholic and antinationalist.[209]

The son of Gabriel, Javier Ybarra y Bergé, deliberately highlighted the growing conflict between the monarchist parties—mainly the conservatives, but also liberals like Balparda—and the nationalists in his historiographical work, *Política Nacional en Vizcaya*.[210]

The Second Republic

Another period of strong tensions, and not only in the territorial dimension, was without doubt the II Republic. In the well-known oscillations of Basque nationalism, in this case between Catholicism and autonomy, it initially opted for the former (without deviating from the latter), which was the motive for promoting the so-called Statute of Estella-Lizarra. This was fiercely attacked by figures like Indalecio Prieto, who spoke of a "Gibraltar of the Vatican". The process of approving the so-called Statute of the Managers [*Estatuto de las Gestoras*] advanced slowly, by successive steps, from 1932 onwards—until it was attained in October 1936 in a very special situation and with a different content due to the Civil War.

For obvious reasons of space, we will not make a complete review of the extensive process of obtaining autonomy in 1936, but we will refer to its main aspects, concentrating not so much on the process itself as on the influence that the tension between Spanish and Basque nationalism had on it.

Following the first failure of 1917–1919, new and clear perspectives were opened up with the Second Republic. In fact, in 1930 the party had been reunified (*Comunión* and *Partido Nacionalista Vasco (PNV)*) following the *Aberri* split of 1921. The appearance of *Acción Nacionalista Vasca* [ANV—Basque Nationalist Action] that same year meant a new fracture. In spite of a more favorable situation in the context of the State, with the new Republic being more permeable *a priori* to the desires for autonomy, the fact that the PNV had allies like the Carlists meant that its attempts to obtain autonomy did not make any real advances. Its ambiguous position regarding the republic/monarchy debate, which was something coherent in a conservative, nationalist and ultra-Catholic party like the PNV of 1931,[211] meant that its demands were not well received in Madrid.

Therefore, the Basque statutory process was highly problematic: due firstly to the Statute's very definition, and secondly to the process of obtaining acceptance from other political forces in Madrid. As we have observed, the alliance of the PNV with the *Comunión Tradicionalista Carlista* in the religious aspect, something that clearly united them, was in contradiction with Carlism's limited inclination towards autonomism—its interest did not extend beyond its strategy of obtaining a type of extra-territoriality in religious matters, a clerical, conservative and anti-republican counter-power.[212] It is clear that with allies such as these, a statutory project was doomed to be short-lived in the context of the parties that led the first Biennium (1931–1933).

It was thanks to an initiative by Indalecio Prieto that the constitutional route towards Basque autonomy was taken. This involved a decree[213] that awarded the statutory initiative to the managers of the deputations (it remained to be seen whether this would take the form of a single statute or provincial statutes).

On June 19, 1932, an Assembly of Municipal Councils took place in Pamplona that signaled Navarre's self-marginalization from the Basque statutory process. This had the clear advantage of allowing the PNV to distance itself from the Carlists, necessary allies on some issues but highly awkward ones on others. It had become increasingly clear that the two parties had different motives. While the Basque nationalists wanted an autonomy statute, the Carlists quite simply wanted to eliminate the Republic.[214] This separation by the Navarrese led the PNV to alter its perspective in a few days; it continued to hold to the idea of obtaining a statute, albeit without Navarre, but on condition that the possibility of this province's later incorporation was recognized.

In the summer of 1933 an agreement amongst different nationalist groups materialized in which each attempted to gain certain advantages. The Basque and Galician nationalists needed the help of the Catalans to put pressure on the Republican government in order to speed up the process of transacting their respective autonomy statutes. But the Generalitat also needed allies if it was not to be left isolated in the evolving framework of republican politics, in which the more centralist right-wing was gaining weight. In this context, and after overcoming several problems arising from political jealousies among the different parties, in the summer of 1933 the *Galeuzca* pact[215] was signed, which on this occasion did bring together all of the nationalists of the three countries (GALiza, EUZkadi, and CAtalunya).

Also in that summer of 1933, after more than a year of waiting, a statutory project—with Navarre eliminated from its text—was presented at an Assembly of Municipal Councils of Araba, Gipuzkoa, and Bizkaia held in Vitoria, which gave rise to a new and bitter debate. The right-wing forces adopted an openly contrary position—not only to autonomy in itself, but to everything that the republican regime was attempting to do— while the nationalists received support from the autonomist left-wing forces, but not the entire left.

The results of the Assembly revealed what was to come: clear support for autonomy in Bizkaia and Gipuzkoa, and less enthusiastic support in Alava; the latter province was the nucleus of the Carlist opposition, which was to continue doing everything in its power to obstruct the statutory process.

Having completed the formal procedure of the Assembly of Municipal Councils, a committee was appointed, controlled by the left, to prepare the referendum and submit the text of the Statute for its approval in parliament. But just when it seemed that the way was clear for the process in Madrid, events took place that slowed it down even further: the fall of Azaña's government and the dissolution of the Cortes, with the resulting call for a general election on November 19, 1933. The referendum on the Basque statute had already been called for November 5; hence the debate on autonomy became directly related to the struggle for power.

The referendum produced clear results, or ones that at least seemed to be clear. In Bizkaia and Gipuzkoa it won broad support in votes, nonetheless in Alava over 10% of the votes were negative and, worse still, there was a significant abstention. This was one of the arguments used by the Carlists, led by José Luis Oriol, for continuously placing every type of obstacle in the path of the statutory process.

TABLE 5. Results of the Referendum on the Autonomy Statute for the Basque Country in 1933.

	Alava	Gipuzkoa	Bizkaia	Total
Electoral census	56,056	166,635	267,466	490,157
Voters	32,710	151,613	241,629	425,952
% of Voters	58.35%	90.98%	90.34%	86.9%
Votes "For"	26,015	149,177	236,564	411,756
% "For"	46.4%	89.52%	88.44%	96.7%
Votes "Against"	6,695	2,436	5,065	14,196
% "Against"	11.94%	1.46%	1.89%	3.3%
Abstention	16,651	12,586	20,772	50,009
% Abstention	29.7%	7.6%	7.8%	10.2%

Source: https://www.euskadi.eus/web01-a2haukon/es/contenidos/informacion/ w_em _ref_result_circunsp_ 1933/es_def/index.shtml

In the Basque Country the results of the election—held a few days later—signified a clear victory for nationalism, which won twelve seats, while the left suffered a huge defeat, losing seven seats and holding only two in Bilbao, those of Indalecio Prieto and Manuel Azaña, who stood as a *cunero* since the impending collapse had been perceived.[216] In overall terms this was a clear disaster for the left with the result that the right-wing majority in the Cortes could now undermine the statutory process. The nationalists had won the election but lost the Statute.[217]

At the end of 1933 the bill on the statute reached the Cortes where there was a clear center-right majority. During the long parliamentary process it not only encountered open obstruction by the traditionalist deputy from Alava, José Luis Oriol Urigüen, but he was also aided in a self-interested way by other left-wing deputies.

The great social and political instability of 1934 meant that the distance between the PNV and the right-wing forces increased (and, in parallel, its distance from the left diminished). In spite of the fact that Basque nationalism remained apart from the revolutionary movement of October 1934, the government accused it of connivance, with the result that it was once again subjected to persecution. This hastened the encounter between Basque nationalism and the left.

In December 1935 the confrontation with the Spanish nationalist forces found parliamentary expression in the debate on the proposal by Renovación Española to declare Basque nationalism illegal due to its complicity and participation in the revolution of 1934. The origin of the debate was a motion[218] in which José Calvo Sotelo, Andrés Amado, José Mª Pemán, and José Mª Albiñana (27 far-right deputies in total) condemned the speeches made by several deputies at a nationalist meeting in San Sebastian (at the Uremea fronton) on November 24. It demanded that the government take "energetic measures to put an end to the scandalous campaign against Spanish unity that is being developed in the Basque-Navarre region."[219] Before the debate started, the nationalist deputy José Horn[220] requested that different articles from the Constitution and the Rules of the Chamber be read out. In general these articles defended the freedom of parliamentarians to express their opinions in public and, equally, allowed for the three arraigned deputies to take the floor in self-defense. This was refused by the speaker (who was none other than the old liberal Santiago Alba).

In defense of his proposal, Calvo Sotelo emphasized the deeply-felt Catholicism of the deceived mass of nationalist sympathizers and also the paradox that one part of the "Basque plutocracy" (in allusion to Ramón de la Sota, *Txomin* Epalza, or Pedro Chalbaud) was participating in this separatist idea, in spite of benefitting greatly in its business deals due to customs protection and even to "economic tax privileges"—in clear reference to the Economic Agreement. In Calvo Sotelo's opinion, the ideas of Arana, besides being based on the idea that, for the Basques, there was only one homeland, Euzkadi, consisted in "a savage, sickly hatred, in a repulsive hatred of Spain, not of the Spanish State."[221] In sum, "Basque nationalism, as believed, defined, and preached by Sabino Arana, is a feeling of Basque independence based on hatred of the Spaniards and Spanish nationality, on hatred of the history of Spain."[222]

Turning to the issue at hand, the meeting at the Uremea fronton, Calva Sotelo stressed that Arana's principles had been updated and adapted to the new circumstances, so that in reality regionalism, or statutism, was a farce, "fiction, hypocrisy (. . .) What do you want the statute for? This was stated by Mr. Irujo at the Uremea meeting: 'To follow the course of Cuba[223] and the Philippines; to follow the course of the peoples who have emancipated themselves, who have become independent.'"[224] While he accepted that there were Basques who believed that the path opened up by the Pact of San Sebastian aimed at achieving the statute within the unity of Spain, Calvo Sotelo argued that was not the case with the nationalists, who wanted it as a step towards total independence. He therefore called on the government to take measures. He accepted that some had already been taken, but these were not strong enough. For that reason he declared:[225]

> I consider that every organization of a nationalist type that attacks the sacred essences of the Homeland, as this one does, should be banned completely. There are no longer any intermediate formulas; this is such a serious issue that it stands above inter-party disputes.

He continued by uttering one of his best-known phrases ("I would prefer a red Spain to a broken Spain"), underscoring that in reality, although many issues separated them from the left-wing forces (monarchy/republic, Christian/atheist Spain) what united them was without doubt the idea that Spain had to be one and indivisible; and, conversely, that the supposed Catholicism of the nationalists was not so in reality, given that it was subordinated to their faith in independence. His speech ended with the reiterated demand for the government to adopt a clear position by banning flags, colors, and anthems other than the Spanish ones; and for it to take the clear decision to declare the statutory process dead, at least as it was presented by the nationalist deputies, with its pronounced anti-Spanish tone.

In the debate, Telesforo Monzón opened his reply with quotations from outstanding ultraconservatives, Carlists, republicans, and conservatives (Juan de Olazábal y Ramery, Alejandro Pidal y Mon, Francisco Pi y Margall, and Joaquín Sánchez de Toca) that emphasized, in the context of the *Foral* crisis, the rupture of the pact that had exonerated the Basque Country from certain obligations, in this he was following the line of argument used by Juan Tellitu 50 years before.[226] Up to this point the occasional protest was made, but what really infuriated a great many deputies was Monzón's clear allusion to the request for autonomy that had been made by Cuba, Puerto Rico, and the Philippines, which were now independent; as did his assertion that "a time will come when the autonomy you are offering to our people will no longer be satisfactory. When all of the Basques demand more than autonomy from you, that is when you will be prepared to offer us a little bit; but that might be too late, as it was in Cuba (. . .) We are moving towards a strengthening of our Basque personality (. . .) What course should we take? That depends more on you than on us."[227]

These words resulted in the interruption of the session and the intervention of the president of the government, Joaquín Chapaprieta, who threatened to "take note" of the words of "those gentlemen". Aguirre requested the floor and was much more restrained in his words, but he insisted that if things ended badly, responsibility would lie with the Cortes. Irujo raised the tone by claiming that it was the mistakes of the past that had resulted in the colonial losses and he also said, "It's not enough for you to have killed off the monarchy through your clumsiness; you also want to put an end to the Republic and to liberty."[228]

The debate brought about little more than a huge patriotic and pro-Spanish reaction from the right-wing and radical deputies; but the government was in its death throes (with the Radical Party involved in two big corruption scandals). With the result that when in January 1936 Alcalá-Zamora called an election for February 16, there was only one clear option facing Basque nationalism: to support the group that would facilitate access to autonomy. That the right was not going to do so had been apparent since 1933, so only the left remained.

The PNV stood on its own in the election, but it wagered on a victory of the left in Spain. Its number of votes fell (by 30,000) as did its number of seats (from twelve to nine); but what mattered was the clear victory[229] of the left; so that advancing the Statute depended on reaching an understanding with the Popular Front. Thus, its deputies voted in favor of dismissing president Alcalá-Zamora and voted in favor of the government of Azaña, who they also supported one month later in his election as president of the Republic.

The new Statutes Committee, formed in mid-April 1936, had Indalecio Prieto as its president and José Antonio Aguirre as its secretary. On this occasion Prieto got along perfectly with Aguirre and prevented the attempts by the right to revive the dilatory strategy of the previous Biennium. The Committee advanced in its work and Prieto became "the man of the Statute" inasmuch as he kept his electoral promise that "the autonomy of the Basque Country, reflected in its Statute, has to be the work of the left-wing forces that make up the Popular Front."[230] It was thus the tandem formed by Prieto and Aguirre that made it possible to accelerate the process of approving the new Statute, which was briefer and had fewer details, thus limiting the motives for disagreement.

In the relationship between Aguirre and Prieto[231] we can see how the relationship between Basque nationalism and socialism evolved; from being bitter enemies in 1931, they became political adversaries between 1931 and 1933 while a new statutory project was elaborated; but in the summer of 1934 an initial rapprochement took place and in the Spring of 1936 they reached agreement on the approval of a Statute. In fact, literally on the threshold of June 18, agreement was reached on the final aspect of the debate in the Committee, namely the delicate issue of the autonomous treasury.

With the coup d'etat of July 18[232] and the start of the Civil War, faced with the dilemma of either Catholicism or the Statute, Aguirre and Irujo opted for the latter and an alliance was thus formed in September-October 1936 against the right-wing and the military rebels. The good personal relationship between Aguirre and Prieto was once again essential for reaching this political understanding, with the result that the Statute came into effect and the first Basque government was formed with the Civil War already underway.[233] The text that was finally approved was much briefer, almost unrecognizable, and difficult to connect with the earlier projects, but the state of war not only explains the haste involved, but also the use the Basque government made of its competences, acting far beyond what would have corresponded to it in a normal situation, due to the virtual disappearance of the republican State.

In short, what proved decisive in the game in pursuit of autonomy was the determination of Aguirre and Prieto who, while they did not share the same goals, both had their hands forced by the strong Spanish reaction. As we saw in the bitter debate of December 1935, the right made it clear that it was never going to accept an Autonomy Statute due to its fear, whether well-founded or not, that this would be the antechamber to independence, and this finally obliged Basque nationalism to align itself with the left. Of course, another factor to keep in mind was the reunification of Basque nationalism itself, which recovered—with the exception of the small party *Acción Nacionalista Vasca*[234]—its unity and cohesion.[235] The successive *set-backs* suffered during the right-wing Biennium, which produced a clear understanding that not only would a Statute not be obtained but that the exercise of competences linked to the Economic Agreement would be continuously hindered by the government,[236] obliged Basque nationalism to reach agreements with republicans and the left, in both the Basque Country and beyond. This is where the "black beast", Prieto's nickname, entered the game. In the Cortes in 1918, he had resolutely opposed autonomy, but in 1936 he had no choice but to reach an agreement with the nationalists if he was to attract them to his side,[237] literally speaking.

Other Basque nationalists, facing the dilemma of Catholicism or the Statute, opted for the former, and there were some who entered Bilbao on June 19, 1937 with the Navarre Brigades. At the same time, also on the side of the victors, there were those, such as the Ybarra family mentioned above, who supported the formation of the *Liga de Acción Monárquica* [Monarchist Action League], participated in the *Liga Patriótica Española* [Spanish Patriotic League] of 1919[238] and then in *Renovación Española* or in the Falange. The latter organization was founded—and this was no accident—by José Antonio Primo de Rivera with invaluable help from Sánchez Mazas and Mourlane, who passed from a certain recognition of Spanish regional variety to defending much more centralist positions for the sake of the struggle against separatisms; this was José Mª Areilza's case as well.[239] As a result when Bilbao fell into the hands of the Francoist troops in June 1937, the new regime did not bother to repeal the Basque Statute (while it did so in the Catalan case). In addition, it eliminated the Economic Agreement with Bizkaia and Gipuzkoa,[240] with the justification that they had repaid the benefits that this privilege had brought them with treason, while the Economic Agreement was maintained in Alava, as was the Economic Covenant in Navarre.

Conclusions

We have reviewed the origins of Basque nationalism, and the legal problems faced by Sabino Arana, its founder, when nationalism had ceased to be treated as a joke. We have seen its highpoint between 1917 and 1919, when its electoral victory enabled it to control the Bizkaian Deputation. These were convulsive years, with new nation-states taking shape, many of them emerging from the breakup of empires, but some, like Ireland, from an empire that had been victorious in the war. In that international context, the restoration was incapable of providing an answer to many of the new problems it faced (the social question, the territorial question, the religious question . . .). In those tumultuous times, the Bizkaian Deputation and the nationalists who controlled it took part in the same movement in favor of an autonomy statute as the Catalan nationalists. However, in spite of the initial and apparent unanimity in support of their demands, the process encountered problems, due to the resistance of the successive governments and the reorganization of the monarchist right-wing parties that did everything in their power to sabotage the process, together with the scant collaboration—following some apparently promising contacts with Prieto—of the socialists and republicans.

We have considered the conflict between nationalism and other forces in the electoral field, and also in the doctrinal field insofar as the emergence and development of Basque—and Catalan—nationalism caused a reaction that gave shape to different ideas about Spain. In several cases, it was writers born or brought up in the Basque Country who raised their voices against nationalism, generating opinion and political principles that, together with other writers, gave form to a generic "*españolismo.*" This was no accident. The political struggle between them, the creation of print media on both sides, had one of its centers in the Basque Country, above all Bizkaia. In this dispute, the individuals who Sánchez Mazas called "the Bizkaian legion" gained prominence in their reaffirmation of a united Spain.

Two questions can be posed: Why, if the defense of the *Fueros* was so unanimous—whatever this might have meant for each side—was internal unity not achieved? Secondly, was there a real collaboration between Basques and Catalans at different times, such as in 1917–1919, to obtain autonomy?

There was one factor that for many years bound Basque public opinion together. This was the defense of the *Fueros*—we once again stress that this was interpreted by each group as it wished—with the result that no party could call itself anti-*foral* and expect to receive broad public support. (Criticising the *Fueros* is a different question: for more than a century Basque socialism has been criticizing the application of the Economic Agreement, to the benefit of entrepreneurs and the detriment of workers.) Proof of this is that only a small minority wanted to bring the tax system in the Basque provinces into line with the rest of Spain.[241] It is thus not surprising that monarchists, nationalists, republicans, and even socialists did not oppose the *foral* idea *a priori*; the question was how to fill it with content.

The other question is also interesting. It is true that at certain times there was collaboration, above all between the extreme positions of the two nationalisms, but it must be borne in mind that the starting point was different in the two cases. Indeed, a differentiated situation already existed in the Basque Country, the Economic Agreement and its derivations, which allowed the Deputations to exercise broad competences, which did not only concern fiscal matters. Nothing similar existed in Catalonia, which is why from the Basque perspective any change to the situation had to entail an improvement; nor could the competences that they already possessed be lost or even be put at risk. From 1914 onwards the Mancomunidad might have meant an important advance for the Catalans, but for the Basques it bore no comparison with what could already be done in connection with the Economic Agreement; thus, the consequences of the failure were different in both cases. Maintaining the *status quo* was not detrimental for the Basques, but was clearly so for the Catalans.

In short, then and also now—the emergence of Vox[242] is good proof of this—the development of peripheral nationalism stimulated Spanish nationalism and, inversely, the development of the latter gave a boost to the former. As Vox's meager results in the Basque Country show, there is a circle of mutual influence. In sum, this is the process by which the two nationalisms develop.

Bibliography

Acosta López, Alejandro. "Aliadófilos y germanófilos en el pensamiento español durante la Primera Guerra Mundial. Balance historiográfico de una Guerra Civil de palabras." *Studia historica. Historia contemporánea* n°. 35 (2017): 339–67.

Agirreazkuenaga J. *The Making of the Basque Question: Experiencing Self-Government, 1793–1877.* Reno: Center for Basque Studies-University of Nevada, 2011. pp. 311

Agirreazkuenaga, Joseba. "El tránsito del discurso foral al autonomista: El 'vasco-catalanismo' de 1917." In *Conciliar la diversidad pasado y presente de la vertebración de España : VII y VIII Seminarios Ernest LLuch,* edited by J., Astigarraga and C, Arrieta J., 113–40 Bilbao: UPV-EHU, 2009.

Agirreazkuenaga, Joseba, ed. *La articulación político-institucional de Vasconia: Actas de las "Conferencias" firmadas por los representantes de Alava, Bizkaia, Gipuzkoa y eventualmente de Navarra (1775–1936).* 2 vols. Bilbao: Diputaciones Forales de Bizkaia, Gipuzkoa y Alava, 1995.

Agirreazkuenaga, Joseba, (dir.). *Bilbao desde sus alcaldes: Diccionario biográfico de los alcaldes de Bilbao y gestión municipal, en tiempos de revolución democrática y social. 1902–1937.* Bilbao: Ayuntamiento de Bilbao, 2003.

Agirreazkuenaga, Joseba, Alonso Olea, Eduardo J., ed. *Historia de la Diputación Foral de Bizkaia. 1500–2014.* Bilbao: Diputación Foral de Bizkaia, 2014.

Agirreazkuenaga, Joseba, et al. *Diccionario biográfico de Parlamentarios de Vasconia (1876–1939)*. Vitoria: Eusko Legebiltzarra-Parlamento Vasco, 2007.

Agirreazkuenaga Zigorraga, Joseba. "La transición por la 'Constitución Vascongada' (1852): De la 'Constitución Foral' (1808) al 'Estatuto de la autonomía de las regiones de Araba, Guipuzcoa y Vizcaya' (1919)." In *I Seminari Catalunya-Euskadi. La Institucionalització política: de les Constitutions històriques als Estatus d'Autonomia (1808–2005)*, 19–42. Barcelona: Generalitat de Catalunya-Museu d'Historia de Catalunya, 2007.

Aizpuru Murua, Mikel Xabier. *El Partido Nacionalista Vasco en Guipúzcoa (1893–1923): orígenes, organización y actuación política*. Bilbao: Universidad del País Vasco/Euskal Herriko Unibertsitatea, Servicio de Publicaciones, 2000.

Alonso Olea, Eduardo J. *Casilda de Iturrizar Urquijo. Viuda de Epalza (1818–1900). Una biografía*. Bilbao: Fundación Bilbao 700- III Millennium Fundazioa, 2019.

Alonso Olea, Eduardo J. *Víctor Chávarri (1854–1900). Una biografía*. Donostia-San Sebastián: Eusko Ikaskuntza-Ayuntamiento de Portugalete, 2005.

Alonso Olea, Eduardo J. "Concierto Económico y fiscalidad privilegiada: el uso del «paraíso fiscal» vizcaíno. 1878–1937." In *Economía y empresa en el norte de España (Una aproximación histórica)*, edited by Martin Aceña, Pablo, Garate Ojanguren, Montserrat. Donostia-San Sebastián: Diputación Foral de Gipuzkoa-U.P.V., 1994.

Alonso Olea, Eduardo J. *Continuidades y discontinuidades de la administración provincial en el País Vasco. 1839–1978. Una «esencia» de los Derechos Históricos*. Oñati: IVAP, 1999.

Alonso Olea, Eduardo J. "De lo privado a lo público. La protección sobre accidentes de trabajo en Vizcaya durante el siglo XX." In *Estado, protesta y movimientos sociales*, edited by Ortiz de Orruño, J. Mª, Castillo, S., 159–64. Bilbao: UPV-EHU/Asociación de Historia Social, 1998.

Alonso Olea, Eduardo J. *El Concierto Económico (1878–1937). Orígenes y formación de un Derecho histórico*. Oñate: Instituto Vasco de Administración Pública, 1995.

Alonso Olea, Eduardo J. "La fiscalidad empresarial en Vizcaya 1914–1935. Un beneficio del Concierto Económico." *Hacienda Pública Española* nº. 2-3/1997 (1997): 3–26.

Alonso Olea, Eduardo J. "La recaudación de Impuestos Especiales. Vizcaya (1876–1937)." *Zergak. Gaceta Tributaria del País Vasco* nº. 1-1998 (1998): 67–97.

Alonso Olea, Eduardo J. "Los conflictos fiscales entre las Diputaciones vascongadas y el Ministerio de Hacienda. (1876–1937)." *Forum Fiscal de Bizkaia* nº. Marzo-1997 (1997).

Alonso Olea, Eduardo J. "Los proyectos de reinstauración de las asambleas representativas por las Diputaciones provinciales (1876–1937)." In *Contributions to European Parliamentary History. Studies presented to the International Commission for the History of Representative and Parliamentary Institutions*, edited by J. Agirreazkuenaga, M. Urquijo, 459–81. Bilbao: Juntas Generales de Bizkaia, 1999.

Alonso Olea, Eduardo J. "Para repensar el Concierto Económico: de 'migaja' a Derecho Histórico." *Historia Contemporánea* n°. 13 (1996).

Alonso Olea, Eduardo J. "Primeros Juegos Florales de Bilbao de agosto de 1901. Premios y premiados." *Bidebarrieta. Anuario de Humanidades y Ciencias Sociales de Bilbao* n°. XI (2002): 39–57.

Alonso Olea, Eduardo J. "Fueros, fiscalidad y la España asimétrica." In *Naciones y Estado. La cuestión española*, edited by Archiles, Ferran, and SAZ, Ismael, 271–96. Valencia: Publicacions de la Universitat de Valencia, 2014.

Alonso Olea, Eduardo J., Erro Gasca, Carmen, Arana Pérez, Ignacio. *Santa Ana de Bolueta, 1841–2016. Renovación y supervivencia en la siderurgia vizcaína.* 2 ed. Bilbao: Santa Ana de Bolueta, 2016.

Alvarez Junco, José (coord.). *Las historia de España. Visiones del pasado y construcción de identidad.* Edited by Fontana, Josep, Villares, Ramón. Vol. 12, Historia de España. Madrid: Crítica-Marcial Pons, 2013.

Antxustegi Igartua, Esteban. *El debate nacionalista. Sabino Arana y sus herederos.* Murcia: Universidad de Murcia, 2007.

Arana Perez, Ignacio. "Aproximación al fracaso de un ambicioso proyecto empresarial. Astilleros del Nervión." In *Symbolae Ludovico Mitxelena Septuagenario Oblatae.* Vitoria: Fac. Filología, Historia y Geografía, 1985.

Arana Perez, Ignacio. *El monarquismo en Vizcaya durante la crisis del reinado de Alfonso XIII (1917–1931).* Pamplona: Eunsa, 1982.

Arana Perez, Ignacio. "Las iniciativas autonómicas en el siglo XX (II)." *Muga* n°. 59 (1987).

Arana Y Goiri, Sabino. *Vizcaya por su independencia.* Bilbao: Imp. Amorrortu, 1892.

Archilés Cardona, Ferran, y Quiroga, Alejandro. *Ondear la nación. Nacionalismo banal en España.* Granada: Comares, 2018.

Balparda y de las Herrerias, Gregorio. *La Tradición de Vizcaya y el bizcaitarrismo.* Bilbao: Casa de Misericordia, 1908.

Balparda y de las Herrerias, Gregorio de. "El bizcaitarrísmo." *Nuestro Tiempo* n°. 123 (1909): 294–323.

Balparda y de las Herrerias, Gregorio de. *Errores del nacionalismo vasco.* Madrid: Juan Pueyo, 1918.

Balparda y de las Herrerias, Gregorio de. *Historia crítica de Vizcaya y de sus fueros.* 3 vols. Madrid: Artes de la Ilustración, 1924.

Baroja, Pío. *Las horas solitarias. (Notas de un aprendiz de psicólogo).* Madrid: Ediciones 98, 1917.

Baroja, Pío. *Obras Completas.* Edited by Mainer, José Carlos, 25 vols. Barcelona: Opera Mundi, 1998.

Bello Portu, Javier. "Pío Baroja, artífice, colaborador e impulsor de la generación del 98." *Bidebarrieta* n°. 4 (1999): 31–38.

Bilbao Notario, Miren. "Jose María Salaverría: España en su pensamiento político, 1873–1940." Universidad de Deusto, 2001.

Billing, Michael. *Nacionalismo banal.* Madrid: Capitan Swing, 2014.

Blas Guerrero, Andrés de. *Sobre el nacionalísmo español.* Madrid: Centro de Estudios Políticos y Constitucionales, 1989.

Camino, Iñigo. *Nacionalistas (1903–1930).* Bilbao: Alderdi, 1985.

Cangas De Icaza, Javier. *Gregorio de Balparda. (Forja y destino de un liberal).* Bilbao: Laida, 1990.

Carr, Raymond. *España: 1808–1975.* 4 ed. Barcelona: Ariel, 1988.

Castells Arteche, Luis. *Los Conciertos Económicos. La Liga Foral Autonomista. 1904–1906.* Donostia-San Sebastián: Haranburu, 1980.

Castells Arteche, Luis, and Gracia Cárcamo, Juan Antonio. "La nación española en la perspectiva vasca." In *Historia de la nación y del nacionalismo español,* edited by Morales Moya, Antonio, Fusi, Juan Pablo, and Blas Guerrero, Andrés de, 973–97. Barcelona: Galaxia Gutenberg, 2013.

Clavero, Bartolomé. "Anatomía de España: Derechos hispanos y derecho español entre Fueros y Códigos." *Per la storia del pensiero giuridico moderno* 2, n°. 34/35 (1989).

Clavero, Bartolomé. *Fueros vascos. Historia en tiempo de constitución.* Barcelona: Ariel, 1985.

Corcuera Atienza, Javier. *Orígenes, ideología y organización del nacionalismo vasco. 1876–1904.* Madrid: Siglo XXI, 1979.

Chacón Delgado, Pedro José. "El regeneracionismo de 1898: historiografía y nacionalismo español." Dpto, Historia del Pensamiento político. Universidad del País Vasco/Euskal Herrriko Unibertsitatea, 2003.

De Blas Guerrero, Andrés de. "Regeneracionismo español y cuestión nacional." In *Historia de la nación y del nacionalismo español,* edited by Morales Moya, A., Fusi Aizpurua, J.P., and De Blas Guerrero, A. de. Barcelona: Galaxia Gutemberg, 2013.

Echegaray, Carmelo de. *Cartas a D. Serapio de Múgica. (1899–1925).* Donostia-San Sebastián: Grupo Doctor Camino de Historia Donostiarra, 1987.

Estornes Zubizarreta, Idoia. *La construcción de una nacionalidad vasca: el autonomismo de Eusko Ikaskuntza (1918–1931).* Donostia-San Sebastián: Eusko Ikaskuntza- Sociedad de Estudios Vascos, 1990.

Fernández Sebastián, Javier. "Antecedentes: fuerismo, carlismo y nacionalismo." In *Los nacionalistas : historia del nacionalismo vasco, 1876–1960,* 17–51. Vitoria: Fundación Sancho el Sabio, 1995.

Fernandez Soldevilla, Gaizka. "De Aberri a ETA, pasando por Venezuela. Rupturas y continuidades en el nacionalismo vasco radical (1921–1977)." *Bulletin d 'Histoire Contemporaine de l 'Espagne* n°. 51 (2015): 219–64.

Ford, Richard. *Manual para viajeros por el País Vasco y Navarra y lectores en casa.* Madrid: Turner, 1981.

Fuentes Quintana, Enrique. *Las reformas tributarias en España. Teoría, historia y propuestas.* Barcelona: Crítica, 1990.

Fusi, Juan Pablo. "Los nacionalismos y el Estado español." *Cuadernos de historia contemporánea* n°. 22 (2000): 21–52.

García De Juan, Miguel Ángel. "Pío Baroja y su germanofilia en la conflictiva segunda década del siglo XX." *Revista de Literatura* LXXVII, n°. 154 (2015): 399–422.

Garcia Delgado, José Luis (Dir.), Cabrera Calvo-Sotelo, Mercedes, Comin Comin, Francisco. *Santiago Alba. Un programa de reforma económica en la España del primer tercio del siglo XX.* Madrid: Instituto de Estudios Fiscales, 1989.

Gascue, Francisco. *El Fuerismo histórico y el Fuerismo progresivo en Guipúzcoa.* San Sebastian: Tip. La Voz de Guipúzcoa, 1909.

González Cuevas, Pedro Carlos. *Acción Española: teología política y nacionalismo autoritario en España (1913–1936).* Madrid: Tecnos, 1998.

González Cuevas, Pedro Carlos. "Tradicionalismo, catolicismo y nacionalismo: la extrema derecha durante el régimen de la Restauración (1898–1930)." *Ayer* n°. 71 (2008): 25–52.

González Hernández, Maria Jesús. *Ciudadanía y acción. El conservadurismo maurista, 1907–1923.* Madrid: Siglo XX, 1990.

González-Allende, Iker. "From the self to the nation: willpower in José María Salaverría." *Romance notes* 49, n°. 1 (2009): 61–69.

Granja, José Luis de la, and Sala Gonzáléz, Luis. *Vidas crizadas. Prieto y Aguirre. Los padres fundadores de Euskadi.* Madrid: Biblioteca nueva, 2018.

Granja Sainz, José Luis de la. Ángel o demonio, Sabino Arana: el patriarca del nacionalismo vasco: Madrid: Tecnos, D.L. 2015, 2015.

Granja Sainz, José Luis de la. "Ángel o demonio: Sabino Arana como símbolo del nacionalismo vasco." *Memoria y civilización: anuario de historia* n°. 15 (2012): 133–50.

Granja Sainz, José Luis de la. "Cronología de Sabino Arana (1865–1903)." *Sancho el sabio: Revista de cultura e investigación vasca* n°. 31 (2009): 285–98.

Granja Sainz, José Luis de la. "El 'antimaketismo': la visión de Sabino Arana sobre España y los españoles." *Norba. Revista de historia* n°. 19 (2006): 191–203.

Granja Sainz, José Luis de la. "El culto a Sabino Arana: La doble resurrección y el origen histórico del Aberri Eguna en la II República." *Historia y política: Ideas, procesos y movimientos sociales* n°. 15 (2006): 65–116.

Granja Sainz, José Luis de la. *El nacionalismo vasco: claves de su historia.* Madrid: Anaya, 2009, 2009.

Granja Sainz, José Luis de la. *El nacionalismo vasco: un siglo de historia.* Madrid: Tecnos, 2002.

Granja Sainz, José Luis de la. *El siglo de Euskadi: el nacionalismo vasco en la España del siglo XX*: Tecnos, 2003.

Granja Sainz, José Luis de la. "Las alianzas políticas entre los nacionalismos periféricos en la España del siglo XX." *Studia historica. Historia contemporánea* n°. 18 (2000): 149–75.

Granja Sainz, José Luis de la. "Lema Jel." In *Diccionario ilustrado de símbolos del nacionalismo vasco*, edited by Pablo Contreras, Santiago de, Casquete Badallo, Jesús María, MEES, Ludger, and Granja Sainz, José Luis de la, 593–608. Tecnos: Madrid, 2012.

Granja Sainz, José Luis de la. "Nacionalismo vasco." In *Diccionario político y social del siglo XX español*, 866–77: Madrid: Alianza, 2008, 2008.

Izquierdo Ballester, Santiago. *La primera victòria del catalanisme polític: el triomf electoral de la candidatura dels "quatre presidents" (1901)*. Barcelona: Pòrtic, 2001.

La Administración provincial en manos de los nacionalistas. Bilbao: Ed.Vasca, 1919.

Laborda, Juan José. *El Señorío de Bizkaia. Nobles y Fueros (c. 1452–1727)*. Madrid: Marcial Pons, 2012.

Larronde, Jean-Claude. *El nacionalismo vasco: su origen y su ideología en la obra de Sabino Arana-Goiri*. Donostia-San Sebastián: Txertoa, 1977.

Liga De Accion Monarquica. *La administración Provincial en manos de los nacionalistas*. Bilbao: E. López, 1919.

Los nacionalistas en la Diputación de Bizkaya. La actuación de nuestra primera mayoría. Bilbao, 1919.

Macias Picavea, Ricardo. *El problema nacional. (1899)*. Madrid: Fundación Banco Exterior, 1991.

Mallada, Lucas. *Los males de la patria. (1890)*. Madrid: Fundación Banco Exterior, 1990.

Martínez-Cachero Rojo, María. "José María Salaverría (1873–1940) un noventayochista menor." In *Azorín et la Génération de 1898*, 349–62. Pau: Université de Pau et des Pays de l'Adour, Faculté des Lettres, Langues et Sciences Humaines, 1998.

Mateos Lopez, Abdón, ed. *Indalecio Prieto y la política española*. Madrid: Pablo Iglesias, 2008.

Mees, Ludger. "Aguirre, Europa y el Partido Nacionalista Vasco." *Hermes: pentsamendu eta historia aldizkaria = revista de pensamiento e historia* n°. 37 (2011): 58–73.

Mees, Ludger. "El nacionalismo vasco y España: reflexiones en torno a un largo desencuentro." *Espacio, tiempo y forma. Serie V, Historia contemporánea* n°. 9 (1996): 67–84.

Mees, Ludger. "El profeta pragmático: Aguirre, el primer lehendakari (1939–1960)." *Sancho el sabio: Revista de cultura e investigación vasca* n°. 26 (2007): 225–27.

Mees, Ludger. "Modernización, cultura y nacionalismo.: Apróximaciones teóricas y conceptuales en torno al nacionalismo." In *Modernización, desarrollo económico y transformación social en el País Vasco y Navarra : actas del seminario de estudios vascos de la Universidad de Navarra (febrero-mayo de 2002)*, 129–45, 2003.

Mees, Ludger. *Nacionalismo vasco, movimiento obrero y cuestión social (1903–1923)*. Bilbao: Fundación Sabino Arana, 1992.

Mees, Ludger. "Nationalism and Democracy. Manuel Irujo Ollo: The Leadership of a Heterodox Basque Nationalist." *Bulletin of Hispanic Studies (Liverpool. 2002)* 93, no. 10 (2016): 1065–79.

Mees, Ludger. "Nationalist Politics at the Crossroads: The Basque Nationalist Party and the Challenge of Sovereignty (1998–2014)." *Nationalism and Ethnic Politics* 21, n°. 1 (2015): 44–62.

Mees, Ludger. "Tan lejos, tan cerca: el Gobierno Vasco en Barcelona y las complejas relaciones entre el nacionalismo vasco y el catalán." *Historia contemporánea* nº. 37 (2008): 557–91.

Mees, Ludger. "Tras el fracaso de Estella-Lizarra: las pautas y claves del Estatuto de 1936." *Iura vasconiae: revista de derecho histórico y autonómico de Vasconia* nº. 10 (2013): 461–90.

Miralles, Ricardo. *Indalecio Prieto. La nación española y el problema vasco. Textos políticos.* Bilbao: Servicio Editorial Universidad del País Vasco, 2019.

Montero, Manuel. *La Bolsa de Bilbao y los negocios financieros. La formación del mercado de capitales en el despegue industrial de Vizcaya.* Bilbao: Universidad del País Vasco, 1996.

Montero, Manuel. *La burguesía impaciente. Especulaciones e inversiones en el desarrollo empresarial de Vizcaya.* Bilbao: Beitia, 1994.

Morales Moya, Antonio, and Esteban De Vega, Mariano, eds. ¿Alma de España? Castilla en las interpretaciones del pasado español. Madrid: Marcial Pons, 2005.

Morales Moya, Antonio, Fusi Aizpurua, Juan Pablo, and De Blas Guerrero, Andrés de, eds. *Historia de la nación y del nacionalismo español.* Barcelona: Galxia Gutenberg, 2013.

Mosse, George L. "Racism and nationalism." *Nations and Nationalism* 1, nº. 2 (1995): 163–73.

Navarra Ordoño, Andreu. "José María Salaverría escritor y periodista (1904-1940)." Universitat de Barcelona, 2011.

Navarra Ordoño, Andreu. "Un programa político antieuropeísta: 'La afirmación española' de José María Salaverría." *Sancho el Sabio: Revista de cultura e investigación vasca* nº. 24 (2006): 35–56.

Navarra Ordoño, Andreu. "Una geografía imperial: vieja España de José María Salaverría." *Revista de literatura* 67, nº. 134 (2005): 463–82.

Nuñez Seixas, Xosé. "Ecos de Pascua, mitos rebeldes: el nacionalismo vasco e Irlanda (1890–1939)." *Historia Contemporánea* nº. 55 (2017): 447–82.

Nuñez Seixas, Xosé. *Patriotas y demócratas. El discurso nacionalista español después de Franco.* Madrid: Libros de la catarata, 2010.

Nuñez Seixas, Xosé. *Suspiros de España. el nacionalismo español, 1808–2018.* Barcelona: Crítica, 2018.

Olabarri Gortazar, Ignacio. "Un conflicto entre nacionalismos: la 'cuestión regional' en España. 1808–1939." In *La España de las Autonomías.* Madrid: Instituto de Estudios de la Administración Local, 1985.

Olea, Enrique de. *Ntra. Sra. de Begoña. Crónica de los hechos más notables acaecidos con motivo de este nombramiento.* Bilbao: Editorial Vizcaína, 1904.

Orella Martínez, José Luis. *Víctor Pradera: un católico en la vida pública de principios de siglo.* Madrid: Biblioteca de Autores Cristianos, 2000.

Pablo Contreras, Santiago de. "El nacionalismo vasco: más de un siglo en la encrucijada." *Crítica* 59, nº. 961 (2009): 44–49.

Pablo Contreras, Santiago de. *En tierra de nadie : la conformación de una cultura política. II, Los nacionalistas vascos en Araba*: Vitoria-Gasteiz: Ikusager, 2008, 2008.

Pablo Contreras, Santiago de. "¡Grita Libertad! El nacionalismo vasco y la lucha por la independencia de las naciones africanas." *Memoria y civilización: anuario de historia* n°. 15 (2012): 267–84.

Pablo Contreras, Santiago de. "Julio de 1959: El nacimiento de ETA." *Historia Actual Online* n°. 48 (2019): 45–59.

Pablo Contreras, Santiago de. *La patria soñada: historia del nacionalismo vasco desde su origen hasta la actualidad*. Madrid: Biblioteca Nueva, 2015.

Pablo Contreras, Santiago de. *En tierra de nadie. Los nacionalistas vascos en Araba*. Vitoria: Ikusager, 2008.

Pablo Contreras, Santiago de, Casquete Badallo, Jesús María, Mees, Ludger, and Granja Sainz, José Luis de la, eds. *Diccionario ilustrado de símbolos del nacionalismo vasco*: Tecnos, 2012.

Pablo Contreras, Santiago de, y Granja Sainz, José Luis de la. "Nueva documentación sobre el primer nacionalismo vasco: correspondencia inédita de Sabino Arana con Luis de Eleizalde (1900–1902)." *Sancho el sabio: Revista de cultura e investigación vasca* n°. 31 (2009): 255–84.

Pablo Contreras, Santiago de, and Mees, Ludger. *El péndulo patriótico: historia del Partido Nacionalista Vasco*: Barcelona : Crítica, [2005], 2005.

Pando y Valle, Jesús. *Regeneración económica. (1897)*. Madrid: Fundación Banco Exterior, 1990.

Partido Carlista. *Los Fueros Vasco-Navarros (intervienen: Sabino Arana, que defiende la independencia del País Vasco . . . Echave Susaeta . . . Miguel de Unamuno . . . y Jose María de Urquijo)*, Bilbao: S. Amorrotu, 1897.

Perez Nuñez, Javier. "Autonomía y nacionalidad vasca. El debate sobre los Fueros vascos en el Senado de 1864." *Studia Storica. Historia Contemporánea* XII (1994): 109–28.

Real Cuesta, Javier. *Partidos, elecciones y bloques de poder en el País Vasco. 1876–1923*. Bilbao: U. Deusto, 1991.

Riquer I Permanyer, Borja de, and Fontana Lázaro, Josep. *Lliga regionalista: la burguesia catalana i el nacionalisme (1893–1904)*. Barcelona: Edic. 62, 1977.

Rivera Blanco, Antonio. "Prieto, los nacionalistas vascos y la cuestión vasca." In *Indalecio Prieto y la política española*, edited by Mateos López, Abdón, 87–122. Madrid: Fundación Pablo Iglesias, 2008.

Rivera Blanco, Antonio. *Señas de identidad : izquierda obrera y nación en el País Vasco, 1880–1923*. [2a ed.]. ed, Historia. Madrid: Biblioteca Nueva, 2007.

Rubio Pobes, Coro. *Fueros y constitución, la lucha por el control del poder: País Vasco, 1808–1868*. Bilbao: Universidad del País Vasco/Euskal Herriko Unibertsitatea, 1997.

Rueda Laffond, José Carlos. "Antonio Maura: las pautas inversionistas de un miembro de la elite política de la Restauración." *Historia Social* n°. 11 (1991).

Salaverria, José Mª. *La afirmación española*. Barcelona: Gustavo Gili, 1917.

Sanchez De Toca, J. *Centralización y regionalismo ante la política unitaria de Patria mayor*. Madrid: Imp hijos de M.G. Hernández, 1899.

Sánchez De Toca, Joaquín. *Regionalismo, municipalismo y centralizacion*. Madrid: R. Velasco, 1907.

Sanchez, Esther. "Un siglo de vidrio francés: Saint Gobain en España, de 1905 a la actualidad." *Investigaciones de Historia Económica* 7, nº. 3 (2011): 395–407.

Solé Villalonga, Gabriel. "La Reforma de Raimundo Fernández Villaverde." *Hacienda Pública Española* nº. 1999 (1999): 21–31.

Tellechea Idígoras, José Ignacio. *Miguel de Unamuno y José María Salaverría: epistolario (1904–1935)*. Donostia-Donostia-San Sebastián: Fundación Social y Cultural Kutxa, 1996.

Torres Villanueva, Eugenio. *Ramón de la Sota. 1857–1936. Un empresario vasco*. Madrid: LID, 1998.

Tusell Gómez, Javier. *La reforma de la Administración local en España (1900–1936)*. 2 ed. Madrid: Instituto de Estudios Administrativos, 1987.

Tusell Gómez, Javier, and Avilés Farré, Juan. *La derecha española contemporánea: sus orígenes: el maurismo*: Espasa Calpe, 1986.

Unamuno Y Jugo, Miguel de. *En torno al casticismo*. 9ª ed. Madrid: Espasa-Calpe, 1979 [1895].

Urrutia, Ander ed. *Euskara Foru Aldundien zirkularretan: Bizkaia (1917–1919), Gipuzkoa (1918–1923)*. Bilbao: Academia Vasca de Derecho, 2015.

Urrutia León, Manuel María. "Unamuno y el periódico bilbaíno 'El Coitao. Mal llamao.'" *Revista de Hispanismo Filosófico* nº. 11 (2006): 97–110.

Van Der Leeuw, Barbara. "Regionalismo y nacionalismo en el siglo XIX: la batalla de los conceptos (País Vasco, Flandes y Frisia)." *Rubrica contemporanea* 6, nº. 11 (2017): 45–65.

Villacorta, José Luis. *Revista de Vizcaya (1885–1889). Un proyecto de renovación cultural en Bilbao*. Bilbao: Ayuntamiento de Bilbao, 1999.

Wimmer, Andreas, and Glick Schiller, Nina. "Methodological nationalism and beyond: nation-state building, migration and social sciences." *Global Networks* 2, no. 4 (2002): 301–34.

Ybarra Y Berge, Javier. *Política nacional en Vizcaya*. Madrid: Instituto de Estudios Políticos, 1948.

Notes

1. This text is part of the Research Project, "Collective biography and prosopographic analysis beyond the Parliament" (PGC 2018-095712-B-I00), of the Ministry of Science, Innovation and Universities; and in the Basque University System Research Group (IT 1263-19), of the Basque Government/Eusko Jaurlaritza.

2. Originally published in the 1990s, and then translated into Catalan, Michael Billings's analysis has recently been translated into Spanish, vid. Michael Billing,

Nacionalismo banal, Madrid: Capitan Swing, 2014. An example of its application in Ferran Archilés Cardona and Alejandro Quiroga, *Ondear la nación*. *Nacionalismo banal en España*, Granada: Comares, 2018.

3. Vid. Andreas Wimmer and Nina Glick Schiller, "Methodological nationalism and beyond: nation-state building, migration and social sciences," *Global Networks* 2, no. 4 (2002). Its application in the Basque case in, for example, Barbara Van Der Leeuw, "Regionalismo y nacionalismo en el siglo XIX: la batalla de los conceptos (País Vasco, Flandes y Frisia)," *Rubrica contemporanea* 6, nº. 11 (2017).

4. This is, of course, merely an exaggeration, but it is symptomatic of the relatively recent concern with analyzing Spanish nationalism rather than peripheral nationalisms in Spain. Vid. Antonio Morales Moya, Juan Pablo Fusi Aizpurua and Andrés de De Blas Guerrero, eds., *Historia de la nación y del nacionalismo español*, Barcelona: Galxia Gutenberg, 2013. Xosé Nuñez Seixas, *Suspiros de España. el nacionalismo español, 1808–2018*, Barcelona: Crítica, 2018. Xosé Nuñez Seixas, *Patriotas y demócratas. El discurso nacionalista español después de Franco*, Madrid: Libros de la catarata, 2010. José (coord.) Alvarez Junco, *Las historia de España. Visiones del pasado y construcción de identidad*, ed. Fontana, Josep, Villares, Ramón, vol. 12, Historia de España, Madrid: Crítica-Marcial Pons, 2013.

5. Larronde Jean Claude, *El nacionalismo vasco: su origen y su ideología en la obra de Sabino Arana-Goiri*, San Sebastián: Txertoa, 1977. Javier Corcuera Atienza, *Orígenes, ideología y organización del nacionalismo vasco. 1876–1904*, Madrid: Siglo XXI, 1979.

6. This is of course not an exhaustive list: Santiago de Pablo Contreras, "Julio de 1959: El nacimiento de ETA," *Historia Actual Online*, nº. 48 (2019); Santiago de Pablo Contreras, *La patria soñada: historia del nacionalismo vasco desde su origen hasta la actualidad*, Madrid Biblioteca Nueva, (2015); Santiago de Pablo Contreras et al., eds., *Diccionario ilustrado de símbolos del nacionalismo vasco*, Tecnos, 2012; Santiago de Pablo Contreras, "¡Grita Libertad! El nacionalismo vasco y la lucha por la independencia de las naciones africanas," *Memoria y civilización: anuario de historia*, nº. 15 (2012); Santiago de Pablo Contreras y José Luis de la Granja Sainz, "Nueva documentación sobre el primer nacionalismo vasco: correspondencia inédita de Sabino Arana con Luis de Eleizalde (1900–1902)," *Sancho el sabio: Revista de cultura e investigación vasca*, nº. 31 (2009); Santiago de Pablo Contreras, "El nacionalismo vasco: más de un siglo en la encrucijada," *Crítica* 59, nº. 961 (2009); Santiago de Pablo Contreras, *En tierra de nadie: la conformación de una cultura política. II, Los nacionalistas vascos en Álava*: Vitoria-Gasteiz: Ikusager, 2008, 2008; Santiago De Pablo Contreras, *En tierra de nadie. Los nacionalistas vascos en Álava*, Vitoria: Ikusager, 2008, Santiago de Pablo Contreras y Ludger MEES, *El péndulo patriótico: historia del Partido Nacionalista Vasco*: Barcelona : Crítica, [2005], 2005.

7. José Luis de la Granja and Luis Sala Gonzáléz, *Vidas cruzadas. Prieto y Aguirre. Los padres fundadores de Euskadi*, Madrid: Biblioteca nueva, 2018; José Luis de la Granja Sainz, *Ángel o demonio, Sabino Arana: el patriarca del nacionalismo*

vasco: Madrid : Tecnos, D.L. 2015, 2015; José Luis de la Granja Sainz, "Cronología de Sabino Arana (1865-1903)," *Sancho el sabio: Revista de cultura e investigación vasca*, nº. 31 (2009); José Luis de la Granja Sainz, *El nacionalismo vasco: claves de su historia*: Madrid : Anaya, 2009, 2009; José Luis de la Granja Sainz, "Nacionalismo vasco," in *Diccionario político y social del siglo XX español*, Madrid : Alianza, 2008, 2008; José Luis de la Granja Sainz, "El "antimaketismo": la visión de Sabino Arana sobre España y los españoles," *Norba. Revista de historia*, nº. 19 (2006); José Luis de la Granja Sainz, "El culto a Sabino Arana: La doble resurrección y el origen histórico del Aberri Eguna en la II República," *Historia y política: Ideas, procesos y movimientos sociales*, nº. 15 (2006); José Luis de la Granja Sainz, *El siglo de Euskadi: el nacionalismo vasco en la España del siglo XX*: Tecnos, 2003; José Luis de la Granja Sainz, *El nacionalismo vasco: un siglo de historia*, Madrid Tecnos, 2002; José Luis de la Granja Sainz, "Las alianzas políticas entre los nacionalismos periféricos en la España del siglo XX," *Studia historica. Historia contemporánea*, nº. 18 (2000).

8. Mikel Aizpuru Murua, "Las bases sociales del nacionalismo vasco," en Los nacionalistas : historia del nacionalismo vasco, 1876-1960 1995, Mikel Aizpuru Murua, "Vascófilos y bertsolaris, conformadores del nacionalismo vasco en el último tercio del siglo XIX," Gerónimo de Uztariz, nº. 16 (2000), Mikel Xabier Aizpuru Murua, El Partido Nacionalista Vasco en Guipúzcoa (1893-1923): orígenes, organización y actuación política, Bilbao: Universidad del País Vasco/Euskal Herriko Unibertsitatea, Servicio de Publicaciones, 2000, Mikel Aizpuru Murua, "Modelos de movilización y lugares de la memoria en el nacionalismo vasco. Los límites de una cultura política," Historia y política: Ideas, procesos y movimientos sociales, nº. 15 (2006), Mikel Aizpuru Murua, "Nacionalismo vasco, separatismo y regionalismo en el Consejo Nacional del Movimiento," Revista de Estudios Políticos, nº. 164 (2014), Mikel Aizpuru Murua, "Sindicalismo agrarista y nacionalismo vasco (1933-1936)," Historia y política: Ideas, procesos y movimientos sociales, nº. 38 (2017).

9. Ludger Mees, "Nationalism and Democracy. Manuel Irujo Ollo: The Leadership of a Heterodox Basque Nationalist," *Bulletin of Hispanic Studies (Liverpool, 2002)* 93, no. 10 (2016); Ludger Mees, "Nationalist Politics at the Crossroads: The Basque Nationalist Party and the Challenge of Sovereignty (1998-2014)," *Nationalism and Ethnic Politics* 21, no. 1 (2015); Ludger Mees, "Tras el fracaso de Estella: las pautas y claves del Estatuto de 1936," *Iura vasconiae: revista de derecho histórico y autonómico de Vasconia*, nº. 10 (2013); Ludger Mees, "Aguirre, Europa y el Partido Nacionalista Vasco," *Hermes: pentsamendu eta historia aldizkaria = revista de pensamiento e historia*, nº. 37 (2011); Ludger Mees, "Tan lejos, tan cerca: el Gobierno Vasco en Barcelona y las complejas relaciones entre el nacionalismo vasco y el catalán," *Historia contemporánea*, nº. 37 (2008); Ludger Mees, "El profeta pragmático: Aguirre, el primer lehendakari (1939-1960)," *Sancho el sabio: Revista de cultura e investigación vasca*, nº. 26 (2007); Ludger Mees, "Modernización, cultura y nacionalismo: Apróximaciones teóricas y

conceptuales en torno al nacionalismo," in *Modernización, desarrollo económico y transformación social en el País Vasco y Navarra : actas del seminario de estudios vascos de la Universidad de Navarra (febrero-mayo de 2002)* 2003; Ludger Mees, "El nacionalismo vasco y España: reflexiones en torno a un largo desencuentro," *Espacio, tiempo y forma. Serie V, Historia contemporánea,* n°. 9 (1996).

10. https://www.sabinoarana.eus, or also www.sabinetxea.org

11. Agirreazkuenaga J. *The Making of the Basque Question: Experiencing Self-Government, 1793–1877.* Reno: Center for Basque Studies-University of Nevada, 2011. Pp. 311 and ff.

12. The idea that the Basques epitomized "Spanish identity" was an observation made by foreign writers who traveled in the Basque Country in the XIX century, such as Ford. Vid. Richard Ford, *Manual para viajeros por el País Vasco y Navarra y lectores en casa,* Madrid: Turner, 1981. Luis Castells Arteche and Juan Antonio Gracia Cárcamo, "La nación española en la perspectiva vasca," in *Historia de la nación y del nacionalismo español,* ed. Morales Moya, Antonio, Fusi, Juan Pablo, and Blas Guerrero, Andrés de, Barcelona: Galaxia Gutenberg, 2013, p. 974.

13. The two terms form part of the title of a book by José Luis de la Granja, one of the leading experts on Basque nationalism. Vid. Granja Sainz, Ángel o demonio, Sabino Arana: el patriarca del nacionalismo vasco, José Luis de la Granja Sainz, "Ángel o demonio: Sabino Arana como símbolo del nacionalismo vasco," *Memoria y civilización: anuario de historia,* n°. 15 (2012).

14. A detailed chronology of his life can be found in Granja Sainz, "Cronología de Sabino Arana (1865–1903)."

15. Sabino Arana Y Goiri, *Vizcaya por su independencia,* Bilbao: Imp. Amorrortu, 1892.

16. The Euskalerria Society was a group that in a certain way served as a bridge between the liberal *foralism* of the central decades of the nineteenth century and the nationalism of Arana. One of its most prominent leaders, until his death in 1894, was Fidel de Sagarmínaga, one of the main protagonists of the intransigent position facing the *foral* proposal of Cánovas del Castillo, which resulted in the abolition of the *foral* regime (Representative Assemblies and *Foral* Deputations) in 1877.

17. The slogan JEL has continued to be relevant to the present day, given that the name of the Basque Nationalist Party (*Partido Nacionalista Vasco* in Spanish— henceforth PNV) in Euskera is *Eusko Alderdi Jeltzalea.* The suffix *-tzale* indicates an active agent, in this case in relation to the JEL. The fact that it is nowadays a nonreligious party has not resulted in the removal of the term God from its name. As we can see, the weight of Arana's deep religiousness reaches down to the present. Vid. José Luis de la Granja Sainz, "Lema Jel," in *Diccionario ilustrado de símbolos del nacionalismo vasco,* ed. Pablo Contreras, Santiago de, et al. Tecnos: Madrid, 2012.

NationALISM ON THE IBERIAN PENINSULA

18. See, Javier Corcuera Atienza, *Orígenes, ideología y organización del nacionalismo vasco. 1876–1904*. Madrid: Siglo XXI, 1979, 412 and ff.

19. "En Vizcaya late siempre el amor á la santa causa foral, y así como no se puede olvidar á aquellos que nos han causado profundo daño al derogar nuestras libertades, se mira con cariño y simpatía cuanto tienda en favor de ellas. A pesar de esto, nadie tomó en serio el partido llamado nacionalista, fundado por el señor D. Sabino de Arana, ni sus genialidades estampadas en el periódico Bizkaitarra; comentándose, por el contrario, en tono de broma, las condiciones que se exigían para ingresar en la Sociedad Euskeldun Batzokija.

En realidad, no se dio importancia a los sueños de esos euskéricos, ni aun por el mismo gobierno. Buena prueba de ello es que éste ha tenido anteriormente ocasiones para tomar las medidas que acaba de adoptar y no lo ha hecho. Ahora vuela la fantasía de algunos hombres públicos y de varios periódicos presentando al Euskaldun [Batzokija] como un instrumento de los filibusteros para hacer germinar en España la semilla que ha producido la revolución cubana.

El Euskaldun no ha sido eso y puede asegurarse que no ha recibido un céntimo de otras personas que de su presidente señor Arana y de sus socios fanatizados a favor de la errónea idea que intentan." "Los exaltados vizcaínos." *El Noticiero Bilbaíno*, 15 de septiembre de 1895.

Arana was severely criticized, when not ridiculed, for his genealogical obsession with racial purity as shown in the famous eight Basque surnames—which even today continues to provide a motive for humor. In fact, from 1898 onwards, he was aided by people with surnames of "Basque," such as Sota—born in the town of Castro in Cantabria, Chalbaud or Hom. For example, see Javier Ybarra Y Berge, *Política nacional en Vizcaya*, Madrid: Instituto de Estudios Políticos, 1948, pp. 276–277.

20. Granja Sainz, José Luis de la. *Ángel o demonio, Sabino Arana: el patriarca del nacionalismo vasco*. Madrid: Tecnos, 2015, cap. 1.

21. The *Fueros*—from which the adjectives *foral* and *foralist* (i.e., pro-*foral*) are derived—were particular laws of the Basque provinces and Navarre, which had Royal approval. They covered very diverse aspects: public law, penal law, inheritance, taxes . . . They regulated the workings of the Representative Assemblies, which were rudimentary provincial parliaments, and their executive body, the General (or *foral*) Deputation. These laws, which dated back to the late Middle Ages and the Early Modern Age, continued in force until the nineteenth century, with greater or lesser problems; but with the development of liberalism, their scope was increasingly restricted until in 1877 the *foral* institutions were eliminated. All that remained of them were aspects relating to private civil law (above all, inheritance) and some special administrative and tax features contained in the *Concierto Económico* (Economic Agreement). Vid. Alonso Olea, Eduardo J. "Fueros, fiscalidad y la España asimétrica." En *Naciones y Estado. La cuestión española*, editad por Archiles, Ferran and Saz, Ismael, 271–96. Valencia: Publicacions de la Universitat de Valencia, 2014; Laborda, Juan José. *El Señorío*

de Bizkaia. *Nobles y Fueros (c. 1452–1727)*. Madrid: Marcial Pons, 2012; Rubio Pobes, Coro. *Fueros y constitución, la lucha por el control del poder: País Vasco, 1808–1868*. Bilbao: Universidad del País Vasco. Euskal Herriko Unibertsitatea, 1997; Perez Nuñez, Javier, "Autonomía y nacionalidad vasca. El debate sobre los Fueros vascos en el Senado de 1864." *Studia Storica. Historia Contemporánea* XII, (1994): 109–28; Clavero, Bartolomé. "Anatomía de España: Derechos hispanos y derecho español entre Fueros y Códigos." *Per la storia del pensiero giuridico moderno* 2, n°. 34/35 (1989); Clavero, Bartolomé. *Fueros vascos. Historia en tiempo de Constitución*. Barcelona: Ariel, 1985.

22. Vid. Partido Carlista, *Los Fueros Vasco-Navarros (intervienen: Sabino Arana, que defiende la independencia del País Vasco . . . Echave Susaeta . . . Miguel de Unamuno . . . y Jose María de Urquijo)*, Bilbao: S. Amorrotu, 1897.

23. It was during the years of World War I when Ramón de Sota made his very considerable fortune. But in those final years of the nineteenth century and the early years of the twentieth, he already had significant resources. On this individual, vid. Eugenio Torres Villanueva, *Ramón de la Sota. 1857–1936. Un empresario vasco*, Madrid: LID, 1998.

24. By monarchist parties (*dinastismo*), we are referring to the Conservative Party, led by Antonio Cánovas del Castillo, and the Liberal Party, led by Práxedes Mateo Sagasta. Both politicians played a leading role in constructing the regime that emerged with the restoration of the Bourbon dynasty, in the person of King Alfonso XII. The two parties monopolized political representation, with very few exceptions, up until the coming of the Dictatorship of Primo de Ribera in 1923.

25. The Provincial Deputation of Bizkaia was a key institution for the interests of the emergent big industrial bourgeoisie of Bizkaia as it controlled, among other things, the tax policy through its exercise of the powers derived from the Economic Agreement. Vid. Joseba Agirreazkuenaga, Alonso Olea, Eduardo J., ed. *Historia de la Diputación Foral de Bizkaia. 1500–2014*, Bilbao: Diputación Foral de Bizkaia, 2014. For the regulatory capacities afforded by the Economic Agreement, vid. Eduardo J. Alonso Olea, "Concierto Económico y fiscalidad privilegiada: el uso del «paraíso fiscal» vizcaíno. 1878–1937," in *Economía y empresa en el norte de España (Una aproximación histórica)*, ed. Martin Aceña, Pablo, Garate Ojanguren, Montserrat San Sebastián: Diputación Foral de Gipuzkoa- U.P.V., 1994.

26. Arana won in the following districts: in Begoña at the polling station in Casas Consistoriales, in Bilbao at two polling stations in San Nicolás, in the Mercado y Santiago district (at its three polling stations), and in three of the seven polling stations in the Ensanche district; in Deusto at the polling station in Ribera, in Laukiz at the polling station in Campa de Erandio, in Basauri at the polling station in Arizgoiti, in Sopela, in Urduliz, and at the polling station in the Echachu neighborhood in Zamudio. Archivo Foral de Bizkaia (henceforth, AFB). Administrativo. AJo1903/017.

27. This initiative was rejected by the Deputation, which argued that the functions proposed by Arana were already fulfilled by means of the conferences, which the Deputations organized when it was necessary to coordinate some aspect of common interest. On this initiative, vid. Eduardo J. Alonso Olea, "Los proyectos de reinstauración de las asambleas representativas por las Diputaciones provinciales (1876–1937)," in *Contributions to European Parliamentary History: Studies Presented to the International Commission for the History of Representative and Parliamentary Institutions*, ed. J. Agirreazkuenaga, M. Urquijo Bilbao: Juntas Generales de Bizkaia, 1999.

28. The development of Basque nationalism in Gipuzkoa and Álava took place later and encountered difficulties. Vid. De Pablo Contreras, *En tierra de nadie. Los nacionalistas vascos en Álava*, pp. 27 and ff; Mikel Xabier, Aizpuru Murua, *El Partido Nacionalista Vasco en Guipúzcoa (1893–1923): orígenes, organización y actuación política*, Bilbao: Universidad del País Vasco/Euskal Herriko Unibertsitatea, Servicio de Publicaciones, 2000.

29. Arana's complete chronology can be found at www.sabinetxea.org. Likewise, in Granja Sainz, "Cronología de Sabino Arana (1865–1903)."

30. *Regeneracionismo* (regenerationism): A cultural and political movement that at the end of the nineteenth century proposed a broad regeneration and modernization of the Spanish social and political structure. It took the development of the European countries as its model, although this often gave rise to controversy. Vid. De Blas Guerrero, Andrés de. "Regeneracionismo español y cuestión nacional." In *Historia de la nación y del nacionalismo español*, edited by Morales Moya, A., Fusi Aizpurua, J.P., and De Blas Guerrero, A. de. Barcelona: Galaxia Gutemberg, 2013. Chacón Delgado, Pedro José. "El regeneracionismo de 1898: historiografía y nacionalismo español." Dpto. Historia del Pensamiento Político. Universidad del País Vasco/Euskal Herrriko Unibertsitatea, 2003.

31. Vid. Lucas Mallada, *Los males de la patria. (1890)*, Madrid: Fundación Banco Exterior, 1990; Jesús Pando Y Valle, *Regeneración económica. (1897)*, Madrid: Fundación Banco Exterior, 1990; Ricardo Macias Picavea, *El problema nacional. (1899)*, Madrid: Fundación Banco Exterior, 1991.

32. Andrés de De Blas Guerrero, "Regeneracionismo español y cuestión nacional," in *Historia de la nación y del nacionalismo español*, ed. Morales Moya, A., Fusi Aizpurua, J.P., and De Blas Guerrero, A. de Barcelona: Galaxia Gutemberg, 2013. Pp. 565 and ff.

33. "El «peligro catalán» y la «amenaza separatista» están en la raíz de la dinamización de toda suerte de proyectos políticos y administrativos orientados a la reforma de la planta política del Estado; pero ese peligro y esa amenaza resultan también un acicate decisivo para la formulación de unos planteamientos nacionalistas españoles de signo global que tendrán que optar, a partir del 98, por la liquidación o la integración de los nuevos nacionalismos periféricos." De Blas Guerrero, "Regeneracionismo español y cuestión nacional." p. 565.

34. A review of regenerationism, drawing attention to names like Emilia Pardo Bazán, F. Antón de Olmet, T. Giménez Valdivieso, and Vicente Gay, in Morales

Moya, Fusi Aizpurua, and De Blas Guerrero, eds., *Historia de la nación y del nacionalismo español*, pp. 574 and ff.

35. His long parliamentary biography in: Joseba Agirreazkuenaga, et al., *Diccionario biográfico de Parlamentarios de Vasconia (1876–1939)*, Vitoria: Eusko Legebiltzarra-Parlamento Vasco, 2007.

36. J. Sanchez De Toca, *Centralización y regionalismo ante la política unitaria de Patria mayor*, Madrid: Imp hijos de M.G. Hernández, 1899. Years later he published this text, together with his interventions in the debates on decentralization that took place in the Royal Academy of Political Sciences in 1891, in Joaquín Sánchez De Toca, *Regionalismo, municipalismo y centralizacion*, Madrid: R. Velasco, 1907.

37. Vid. Florentino Portero Rodríguez, "El regeneracionismo conservador: el ideario político de Francisco Silvela," en *Las derechas en la España contemporánea*, ed. Tusell Gómez, Javier, Montero García, Feliciano, y Marín Arce, José María Madrid: Antropos, 1997.

38. For example, it was under his government that the fiscal reform of Fernández Villaverde was carried out and the Law of January 30, 1990, on Accidents at Work, was published, which was the basis on which Social Security was developed in Spain. Vid. Gabriel Solé Villalonga, "La Reforma de Raimundo Fernández Villaverde," *Hacienda Pública Española*, nº. 1999 (1999); Eduardo J. Alonso Olea, "De lo privado a lo público. La protección sobre accidentes de trabajo en Vizcaya durante el siglo XX," in *Estado, protesta y movimientos sociales*, ed. Ortiz de Orruño, J. Mª, Castillo, S. Bilbao: UPV-EHU/Asociación de Historia Social, 1998.

39. Real Decreto de 12 de septiembre de 1999. *Gaceta de Madrid*, 13 de septiembre de 1899, nº. 256, pp. 973–974.

40. ". . . Pero recientemente, ya por insano afán de notoriedad, ya por verdaderas neurosis que se producen por causas bien conocidas en colectividades como en individuos aislados, se han determinado manifestaciones en la prensa, en asociaciones y reuniones públicas, que sin alcanzar importancia ni por el número ni por la condición de las personas, ni constituir el menor riesgo para el orden material. atacan con tal audacia el sentimiento de la Patria común, expresan con tan desatinada insistencia propósitos de romper el vínculo nacional, que constituyen una perturbación del orden moral y una mengua para un país que ha alcanzado su unidad a tanta costa y que no puede consentir verla repudiada, ni vilipendiada impunemente." Royal Decree of September 13, 1899.

41. The rights to demonstrate and hold meetings were suspended, as were guarantees concerning the inviolability of the home and the period of detention. Vid. Art. 17 de la Constitución de 1876. 30 de junio de 1876. *Gaceta de Madrid*, nº. 184, de 2 de julio de 1876, pp. 9–12.

42. Vid. Borja de Riquer I Permanyer and Josep Fontana Lázaro, *Lliga regionalista: la burguesia catalana i el nacionalismo (1893- 1904)*, Barcelona: Edic. 62, 1977.

43. Santiago Izquierdo Ballester, *La primera victòria del catalanisme polític: el triomf electoral de la candidatura dels "quatre presidents" (1901)*, Barcelona: Pòrtic, 2001.

44. "La política catalana, por ejemplo, consiste en atraer a sí a los demás españoles; la bizkaina, v. gr., en rechazar de sí a los españoles como extranjeros. (. . .) su patria es muy distinta de la nuestra;(. . .) Cataluña padece por la ingratitud de su propia madre España, mientras que Bizkaya es presa de una nación extraña, que es precisamente la Patria común de los catalanes, baleares, gallegos, valencianos, etc. Ya ve cómo no es razonable la alianza de los catalanes y los bizkainos: pues no son semejantes los sujetos, Bizkaya y Cataluña; ni se parecen por su desgracia; ni tienen un enemigo común; ni son las mismas sus aspiraciones. (. . .) Jamás confundiremos nuestros derechos con los derechos de región extranjera alguna; jamás equipararemos nuestras viejas leyes nacionales, mal llamadas Fueros, con los Fueros de las regiones españolas; jamás haremos causa común con los regionalistas españoles." "Errores catalanistas." *El Bizkaitarra*. 31 de octubre de 1894.

45. "La causa catalanista es causa digna de respeto para todo vasko: Catalunya, dueña legítima del suelo que ocupa, quiere ser libre: tiene derecho a serlo. El opresor de Catalunya es el dominador de Euzkadi: es útil se concierten Catalunya y Euzkadi para el logro de sus respectivos fines: deben concertarse." Granja Sainz, "Las alianzas políticas entre los nacionalismos periféricos en la España del siglo XX." p. 153.

46. That same year, 1901, *Joala* published an article in *La Patria* against "El catalanismo," which he concluded as follows: "Not being a nationalist is a crime; being a Catalanist is another crime." The protest by the editor of the weekly journal, Felipe de Zabala, resulted in his dismissal.

47. Vid. Eduardo J. Alonso Olea, "Primeros Juegos Florales de Bilbao de agosto de 1901. Premios y premiados," *Bidebarrieta. Anuario de Humanidades y Ciencias Sociales de Bilbao*, n°. XI (2002).

48. Another example of Unamuno's interest in *"vascuence"* (Euskera) were his articles published in those years in the *Revista de Vizcaya*. Vid. José Luis Villacorta, *Revista de Vizcaya (1885–1889). Un proyecto de renovación cultural en Bilbao*, Bilbao: Ayuntamiento de Bilbao, 1999. This contains texts by Unamuno such as *El elemento alienígena en el idioma vasco* and ¿Vasco o basco? Texts also coexisted with others with a similar theme by Sabino Arana, such as *Etimologías sueltas* and ¿Basco o vasco?

49. *"Maketos"*—foreigners. The racism underlying this term is far from being specific to Basque nationalism, and was a very common factor in all the nationalisms of the nineteenth and twentieth centuries. Vid. George L. Mosse, "Racism and Nationalism," *Nations and Nationalism* 1, no. 2 (1995).

50. "Nuestra alma es más grande ya que su vestido secular; el vascuence, nos viene ya estrecho; y como su material y tejido no se prestan á ensanche, rompámosle. Hay, además, una ley de economía, y es que nos cuesta menos esfuerzo aprender el castellano que trasformar el vascuence, que es instrumento sobrado complicado y muy lejos de la sencillez y sobriedad de medios de los idiomas analíticos. (. . .) Enterrémosle santamente, con dignos funerales, embalsamado en ciencia; leguemos a los estudios tan interesante reliquia. Y para lograrlo,

estudiémosle con espíritu científico, á la vez que con amor, sin prejuicios, no atentos a cual tesis previa, sino a indagar lo que haya, y estudiémosle con los más rigurosos métodos que la moderna ciencia lingüística prescriba." *El Nervión*, 27 de agosto de 1901.

51. "Muchos de los males que padece hoy España, casi toda su decadencia en el orden espiritual, la vacuidad de su literatura y sus artes, la cobardía mental que a sus hombres caracteriza, provienen de una ola de lujuria que desde las costas de Levante y Mediodía ha inundado Madrid y amenaza invadir la nación toda. (. . .) Peor, mucho peor es lo otro. Y francamente entre esa marranería espiritual de los efebos estéticos y la beocia bizkaitarresca con todo su cortejo de comilona, 'bebilona' y berreo, me quedo con esto." "Marranería espiritual." *El Coitao. Mal llamao*, año I, n°. 2, Bilbao, February 2, 1908, p. 3. Little-known article conserved by Unamuno (CMU: 3-5). Vid. Manuel María Urrutia León, "Unamuno y el periódico bilbaíno 'El Coitao. Mal llamao,'" *Revista de Hispanismo Filosófico*, n°. 11 (2006).

52. Vid. Andrés de Blas Guerrero, *Sobre el nacionalismo español*, Madrid: Centro de Estudios Políticos y Constitucionales, 1989.

53. On the weight of Castile in many interpretations of the essence of Spain, vid. Antonio Morales Moya and Mariano Esteban De Vega, eds., ¿Alma de España? Castilla en las interpretaciones del pasado español, Madrid: Marcial Pons, 2005.

54. Unamuno Y Jugo, *En torno al casticismo*, p. 74.

55. "Ha empezado hace algún tiempo a deshacerse la enormidad de errores que acarrearon las confusiones entre lo fisiológico, lo lingüístico, lo geográfico y lo histórico en los pueblos; es corriente ya que éstos son un producto histórico, independiente de homogeneidad de raza física o de comunidad de origen; poco a poco, va difundiéndose la idea de que la supuesta emigración de los arios a Europa sea acaso en parte emigración de las lenguas arianas con la cultura que llevaban en su seno, siendo sus portadores unos pocos peregrinos que cayeran a perderse en poblaciones que los absorbieron.

De raza española fisiológica nadie habla en serio, y, sin embargo, hay casta española, más o menos en formación, y latina y germánica, porque hay castas y casticismos espirituales por encima de todas las braquicefalias y dolicocefalias habidas y por haber.

Todo el mundo sabe, de sobra con sobrada frecuencia, que un pueblo es el producto de una civilización, flor de un proceso histórico el sentimiento de patria, que se corrobora y vivifica a la par que el de cosmopolitismo. A esto último hemos de volver, que lo merece." Miguel de Unamuno Y Jugo, *En torno al casticismo*, 9ª ed., Madrid: Espasa-Calpe, 1979 [1895]. p. 54.

56. "Pero si Castilla ha hecho la nación española, ésta ha ido españolizándose cada vez más, fundiendo más cada día la riqueza de su variedad de contenido interior, absorbiendo el espíritu castellano en otro superior a él, más complejo: el español. No tienen otro sentido hondo los pruritos de regionalismo, más vivaces cada día, pruritos que siente Castilla misma; son síntomas del proceso de españolización

de España, son pródromos de la honda labor de unificación. Y toda unificación procede al compás de la diferenciación interna y al compás de la sumisión del conjunto todo a una unidad superior a él.

La labor de españolización de España no está concluida, ni mucho menos, ni concluirá, creemos, si no se acaba con casticismos engañosos, en la lengua y en el pensamiento que en ella se manifiesta, en la cultura misma.

Castilla es la verdadera forjadora de la unidad y la monarquía españolas; ella las hizo y ella misma se ha encontrado más de una vez enredada en consecuencias extremas de su obra. Mas cuando España renació a nueva vida, el año 1808, fue por despertar difuso, sin excitación central." Unamuno Y Jugo, *En torno al casticismo*, p. 56.

57. Antonio Rivera Blanco, *Señas de identidad: izquierda obrera y nación en el País Vasco, 1880–1923* [2nd ed.], ed., Historia, Madrid: Biblioteca Nueva, 2007, pp. 54 and ff.

58. "No se debe concebir la cuestión nacional en España como si cada nacionalismo o cada territorio fuese un compartimento estanco, como con frecuencia se ha supuesto implícitamente en la historiografía hispánica. Aunque pueda parecer obvio recordarlo, el desarrollo del nacionalismo español desde fines del siglo XIX condiciona el de los nacionalismos *periféricos*, al igual que acaece el proceso inverso." Nuñez Seixas, *Suspiros de España. el nacionalismo español, 1808–2018*, p. 12.

59. Nuñez Seixas, *Suspiros de España. el nacionalismo español, 1808–2018*, pp. 111 and ff.

60. Although it is extremely interesting, we will not enter the debate over whether there was Basque nationalism prior to Sabino Arana, or whether Sagarmínaga or Juan de Tellitu were nationalists, or pre-nationalists, or something else altogether.

61. On this business venture by José Martínez de la Rivas. Vid. Ignacio Arana Perez, "Aproximación al fracaso de un ambicioso proyecto empresarial. Astilleros del Nervión," in *Symbolae Ludovico Mitxelena Septuagenario Oblatae*, Vitoria: Fac. Filología, Historia y Geografía, 1985. We are referring to the three armored cruisers *Infanta María Teresa*, *Vizcaya*, and *Almirante Oquendo*, launched at this shipyard on the Nervión Estuary and sunk at the battle of Santiago de Cuba on July 3, 1898.

62. Prior to the Cuban War, distinguished writers had already declared the need for Spain to be regenerated. For example, Macias Picavea, *El problema nacional. (1899)*, Pando Y Valle, *Regeneración económica. (1897)*, and Mallada, *Los males de la patria. (1890)*.

63. Vid. Javier Bello Portu, "Pío Baroja, artífice, colaborador e impulsor de la generación del 98," *Bidebarrieta*, nº. 4 (1999).

64. In 1917 he wrote that: "Yo no sólo soy enemigo del nacionalismo, sino de la misma idea de la patria. 'El mundo para todos los hombres,' ese sería mi lema, y si éste pareciese demasiado amplio, me contentaría con este otro: 'Europa para los europeos.'" Pío Baroja, *Las horas solitarias. (Notas de un aprendiz de psicólogo)*, Madrid: Ediciones 98, 1917, p. 97.

65. Baroja, *Las horas solitarias. (Notas de un aprendiz de psicólogo).*

66. Miguel Ángel García De Juan, "Pío Baroja y su germanofilia en la conflictiva segunda década del siglo XX," *Revista de Literatura* LXXVII, n°. 154 (2015). To see that agreement in some matters does not imply agreement in others; Unamuno was openly pro-Allied and even showed contempt for Germanophilia. Vid. José María Salaverría. "El catedrático hablador." *ABC*, 31 de enero de 1917.

67. Baroja, Pío. "Los carlistas y el tormento," *Vida Nueva*, 18 de diciembre de 1898.

68. "La sensualidad pervertida" in Pío Baroja, *Obras Completas*, ed. Mainer, José Carlos 25 vols., Barcelona: Opera Mundi, 1998. The quotation is in vol. III, p. 1,135.

69. Baroja, *Obras Completas*, Vol. III, p. 1020.

70. On example, among many others, is the nationalist mayor of Bilbao, Gregorio Ibarreche. Vid. Joseba Agirreazkuenaga, (dir.), *Bilbao desde sus alcaldes: Diccionario biográfico de los alcaldes de Bilbao y gestión municipal, en tiempos de revolución democrática y social. 1902-1937*, Bilbao: Ayuntamiento de Bilbao, 2003.

71. Vid. Manuel Montero, *La burguesía impaciente. Especulaciones e inversiones en el desarrollo empresarial de Vizcaya*, Bilbao: Beitia, 1994; Manuel Montero, *La Bolsa de Bilbao y los negocios financieros. La formación del mercado de capitales en el despegue industrial de Vizcaya*, Bilbao: Universidad del País Vasco, 1996.

72. "Roosevelt, President United States. Washington. The Basque Nationalist Party congratulates you on Cuba's independence by the most the noble Federation you preside over, which was able to end slavery. Your powerful states provide an example of magnanimity and culture, justice and freedom, unknown to history, inimitable for European powers, particularly Latin powers. If Europe—including the Basque nation, its oldest people, which enjoyed freedom for many years, ruled by a Constitution that was praised by the United States—were to imitate you, it would be free. Arana Gori."

73. Españolismo /Españolista: In general these terms refer to Spanish nationalism, but they usually have a pejorative connotation insofar as they are related to a centralist and exclusive view of "Spanish identity."

74. Vid. Granja Sainz, "El 'antimaketismo': la visión de Sabino Arana sobre España y los españoles."

75. *La Patria*, 29 de junio de 1902.

76. Vid. Corcuera Atienza, *Orígenes, ideología y organización del nacionalismo vasco. 1876-1904.*

77. *La Piña*: A political group linked to the political ambitions of the Bizkaian magnate Víctor Chávarri Salazar (1856-1900). In order to protect his economic interests, essentially in the mining, industrial, and railway sectors, he organized a political group, officially called the *Unión Liberal*, which during the 1890s almost completely monopolized the Bizkaian political representation. Vid. Eduardo J. Alonso Olea, *Víctor Chávarri (1854-1900). Una biografía.* San Sebastián: Eusko Ikaskuntza-Ayuntamiento de Portugalete, 2005.

78. On José Mª Urquijo and José Acillona Garay, Marquis of Acillona, vid. Agirreazkuenaga, *Diccionario biográfico de Parlamentarios de Vasconia (1876-1939).*

79. A brief biography can be found in Iñigo Camino, *Nacionalistas (1903–1930)*, Bilbao: Alderdi, 1985.
80. "El calificativo más adecuado al movimiento [nacionalista vasco] no es tanto el de separatismo como el de antimaquetismo. Es ante todo y sobre todo una explosión de enemiga hacia el español no vascongado, el maqueto, establecido en Bilbao y que allí trabaja. Las raíces del movimiento son de carácter económico, radicando en el desarrollo industrial de la región minera. Es un hecho análogo a tantos otros fenómenos sociales semejantes (. . .).

Culpan a la llamada invasión [maqueta] de males que lleva consigo el proceso mismo económico. Es la cantinela de siempre, basada en profunda ignorancia del dinamismo social, ignorancia que es la base principal del movimiento antimaquetista, cuyo actual cabecilla [Sabino Arana], aunque no de talento, carece en absoluto de sentido histórico, a pesar de las historias de que tiene atiborrada la mollera, y se muestra en sus escritos ayuno por completo de cultura científica en cuestiones sociales." Miguel de Unamuno, "El antimaquetismo," *El Heraldo de Madrid*, 18 de septiembre de 1898.
81. Vid. Enrique de Olea, *Ntra. Sra. de Begoña. Crónica de los hechos más notables acaecidos con motivo de este nombramiento.*, Bilbao: Editorial Vizcaína, 1904.
82. Vid. Esteban Antxustegi Igartua, *El debate nacionalista. Sabino Arana y sus herederos*, Murcia: Universidad de Murcia, 2007. Especially chapter II.
83. We will not enter into the debate on whether prior to Arana there were pre-nationalisms, in figures like Fidel de Sagarmínaga, for example, or even earlier writers. Vid. Corcuera Atienza, *Orígenes, ideología y organización del nacionalismo vasco. 1876–1904*. Javier Fernández Sebastián, "Antecedentes: fuerismo, carlismo y nacionalismo," in *Los nacionalistas : historia del nacionalismo vasco, 1876–1960*, Vitoria: Fundación Sancho el Sabio, 1995.
84. On the processes of negotiating the Economic Agreement, vid. Eduardo J. Alonso Olea, *El Concierto Económico (1878–1937). Orígenes y formación de un Derecho histórico*, Oñate: Instituto Vasco de Administración Pública, 1995. On the diverse aspects of the Economic Agreement, vid. Eduardo J. Alonso Olea, "Para repensar el Concierto Económico: de 'migaja' a Derecho Histórico," *Historia Contemporánea*, nº. 13 (1996).
85. "Anduvieron allá de la Ceca a la Meca, postrándose cual viles siervos a los pies de los Ministros y de la reina española, como infelices penados que van a pedir indulgencia, y dejándose tratar de potencia a potencia por los empleados de Hacienda. Y toda esta rastrera bajeza con pretensiones de diplomacia ¿para qué? Para ceder y retirarse cuando chocaron con alguna resistencia y confiar la solución del asunto a un senador [Víctor Chávarri], si tan falto como ellos de patriotismo, más exento de vergüenza." "Traidores." *Bizkaitarra*. 29 de enero de 1894.
86. The main cause of this resurgence was the reform of the tax on alcoholic drinks, covered by the Economic Agreement. On the technical aspect of the conflict of 1904, vid. Alonso Olea, *El Concierto Económico (1878–1937). Orígenes y formación de un Derecho histórico*; Eduardo J. Alonso Olea, "Los conflictos fiscales

entre las Diputaciones vascongadas y el Ministerio de Hacienda. (1876–1937),"
Forum Fiscal de Bizkaia, nº. Marzo-1997 (1997). One of the consequences was the
formation of the Autonomist *Foral* League of Gipuzkoa, in Luis Castells Arteche,
Los Conciertos Económicos. La Liga Foral Autonomista.1904–1906, San Sebastián:
Haranburu, 1980.

87. Article 83 of the 1876 Constitution recovered the formula employed in the 1845
Constitution: "the Municipal Councils will be appointed by the residents to
whom the law confers this right" (Constitución de la Monarquía española de 30
de junio de 1876. *Gaceta de Madrid.* 2 de julio de 1876). The second provision
of the Municipal Law established that: "The King can appoint from amongst
the Councillors of the provincial capitals . . ." (Ley de 16 de diciembre de 1876,
reformando las Leyes municipal y provincial de 20 de agosto de 1870 con arreglo
a las bases que se consignan). This regulation was ratified in article 49 of the
Municipal Law (Real Decreto de 2 de octubre de 1877). It was in 1917—except in
the case of Madrid, where the mayor continued to be appointed by the government—when mayors began to be elected by the councillors.

88. On the mayoralty of Ibarreche, vid. Agirreazkuenaga, *Bilbao desde sus alcaldes:
Diccionario biográfico de los alcaldes de Bilbao y gestión municipal, en tiempos de
revolución democrática y social.1902–1937.*

89. An extensive biography in Javier Cangas De Icaza, *Gregorio de Balparda. (Forja y
destino de un liberal)*, Bilbao: Laida, 1990.

90. Gregorio de Balparda Y De Las Herrerias, "El bizcaitarrísmo," *Nuestro Tiempo*,
nº. 123 (1909).

91. Gregorio de Balparda Y De Las Herrerias, *Errores del nacionalismo vasco*,
Madrid: Juan Pueyo, 1918; Gregorio de Balparda Y De Las Herrerias, *Historia
crítica de Vizcaya y de sus fueros*, 3 vols., Madrid: Artes de la Ilustración, 1924.

92. Gregorio Balparda Y De Las Herrerias, *La Tradición de Vizcaya y el bizcaitarrismo*, Bilbao: Casa de Misericordia, 1908.

93. "Tocado de raquitismo mental incurable, el partido bizcaitarra ni en las cuestiones políticas propiamente dichas, ni en la administración de la provincia y de los
municipios, ni en la negociación del concierto económico, ni en la reforma tributaria, ha tenido ni tendrá jamás una política propia; su sino es el que antes he
dicho, ser utilizado por otros." Balparda Y De Las Herrerias, "El bizcaitarrísmo,"
p. 297.

94. "Sus extravagantes doctrinas, aderezadas con todo un vocabulario de motes
más ó menos afortunados, para ridiculizar las cosas de España y con todo el
aparato de neologismos que constituyen el rito en *Jel*, comenzaron tomándose
á risa como obra de un desequilibrado; harto conseguir fue, sin embargo, que
no causasen indignación y que, aun cuando en broma, comenzasen algunos á
enredarse en discusiones. Apenas se comprende hoy la libertad con que en su
campaña anti-española se expresa; sus dicterios contra España, y los españoles
y la bandera española y todo lo español, y los denigrantes retratos de *maketos
y maketófilos*, su lenguaje punzante y sarcástico, herían más hondamente á los

buenos españoles en los días de los contratiempos de Melilla y de las desdichadas campañas de Cuba y de Filipinas." Balparda Y De Las Herrerias, "El bizcaitar-rísmo," pp. 307-308.

95. "Pero entre el catalanismo y el bizcaitarrismo hay dos diferencias que saltan á la vista; una por su fundamento, puesto que las aspiraciones nacionalistas, injustificadas respecto de Cataluña, son simplemente ridículas aplicadas á una agrupación social como Vizcaya, que sin la agregación de otros elementos de origen análogo no llega siquiera á constituir una región, y que, desde que á principios del siglo XI empieza á tenerse alguna idea de ella (lo que se diga de tiempos anteriores es el mentir de las estrellas), no ha vivido jamás otra vida política, internacional, jurídica, artística, social, científica, ni religiosa que la de Castilla aun en épocas muy anteriores á la constitución de la unidad nacional. Y á parte de ésta, hay entre el catalanismo y el bizcaitarrismo otra diferencia, por razón de su origen, que se conservará indeleble hasta la desaparición de ambos, y es la siguiente: que la confección del nacionalismo catalán, con todo lo que tiene de artificioso y de decadente, es obra de inteligencias escogidas, de una cultura eminente: ¿qué tiene de extraño que haya atraído el interés primero y la adhesión después de hombres de positivo valer, (. . .) y de las esperanzas de algunos de los actuales representantes en Cortes solidarios y que el movimiento haya repercutido, no solo en la política general, sino en los estudios, en las bellas artes y en la prosperidad económica de Barcelona?

En cambio, el bizcaitarrismo es la obra indocumentada ó incoherente de un hombre que se lanzó á su predicación sin preparación científica ni experiencia suficientes, ni conocimiento del sentido y fondo de las instituciones jurídicas y políticas de Vizcaya, y no digamos de las de España y del resto del mundo, y en el que la probidad y el desinterés con que realizó su propaganda á costa de su fortuna y de su salud, serán parte á justificar su figura moral pero no á elevar su talla intelectual ni su personalidad política. La propaganda de Sabino Arana no se hizo, naturalmente, entre un público de eruditos, y como la base de su doctrina consistía en problemas intrincadísimos de crítica histórica acerca de los orígenes del Señorío, de la significación de ciertas batallas del siglo XIV, de si la incorpo-ración á Castilla en la misma época fué *real ó personal* etc., etc., el bizcaitarrismo lleva desde su nacimiento el sello de una pedantería inenarrable, provista de una erudición de cuarta clase que repele á todas las personas de algún gusto intelec-tual." Balparda Y De Las Herrerias, "El bizcaitarrísmo," pp. 296-297.

96. Antxustegi Igartua, *El debate nacionalista. Sabino Arana y sus herederos.*

97. "Mauristas y republicanos." *El Noticiero Bilbaíno,* 30 de noviembre de 1913.

98. José Carlos Rueda Laffond, "Antonio Maura: las pautas inversionistas de un miembro de la elite política de la Restauración," *Historia Social,* n°. 11 (1991).

99. On Maurism in general, vid. Maria Jesús González Hernández, *Ciudadanía y acción. El conservadurismo maurista, 1907-1923,* Madrid: Siglo XX, 1990; Javier Tusell Gómez and Juan Avilés Farré, *La derecha española contemporánea: sus orígenes: el maurismo*: Espasa Calpe, 1986.

100. "Se nos dice que nuestro partido está falto del sentimentalismo que poseen los catalanistas, los vascos y los carlistas, pero ¿no es sentimentalismo hacer política españolista?

  Nuestro sentimentalismo es velar por el vigor de la Patria; hay que ser español antes de todo y por encima de todo; hay que tener sentido de España, llevar nuestra savia a los países que nos quieren, hacer labor económica, dar impulso a nuestra cultura, procurar que España sea lo que fue, lo que debe ser, en los momentos actuales." "La asamblea conservadora." *El Noticiero Bilbaíno*, 1 de diciembre de 1913, p. 3.

101. For the more general aspects of this question, vid. Alejandro Acosta López, "Aliadófilos y germanófilos en el pensamiento español durante la Primera Guerra Mundial. Balance historiográfico de una Guerra Civil de palabras," *Studia historica. Historia contemporánea*, n°. 35 (2017).

102. In the district of Bilbao, the candidacy was headed by Mariano de la Torre, Luis Urrutia, and José Ramón Bilbao. In Durango, the candidacy was headed by the nationalists Rotaeche, Elguezabal, Manuel Eguileor, all put forward by nationalists, and Enrique Ornilla and Hilario Bilbao, by the *Jaimistas*. In Markina, the candidacy was headed by the nationalists Urrengoechea, Landaburu, and Zubicaray, together with the *Jaimista* José María Garay Lesúnaga.

103. An example of the peculiar way in which municipal economic control was understood is that the accounts of the Town Councils were approved by the Government Ministry, not by the Treasury. In the Basque Country, that control was exercised by the Deputations, which is why the Deputation of Bizkaia altered the budget headings, which were obligatory in the whole state, using its own budgetary criteria.

104. Here we find diverse reactions, ranging from the reply of the Town Council of Bermeo, which expressed its delight that the Deputation was finally utilizing Euskera as a language for administrative relations, to that of Balmaseda, which sarcastically noted that it seemed they had received an official document from the Deputation because of the coat of arms on the letterhead, but that they were unable to understand or identify *Sota eta Aburto 'tar Ramon*, who appeared as the signatory. Vid. Ander Urrutia, ed. *Euskara Foru Aldundien zirkularretan: Bizkaia (1917–1919), Gipuzkoa (1918–1923)*, Bilbao: Academia Vasca de Derecho, 2015.

105. The debate on the successes and failures of the nationalist management of the Deputation was also expressed in pamphlets in which some praised the former while others emphasized the latter. Vid. *Los nacionalistas en la Diputación de Bizkaya. La actuación de nuestra primera mayoría*, Bilbao 1919; *La Administración provincial en manos de los nacionalistas*, Bilbao: Ed. Vasca, 1919; Liga De Accion Monarquica, *La administración Provincial en manos de los nacionalistas*, Bilbao: E. López, 1919.

106. Enrique Fuentes Quintana, *Las reformas tributarias en España. Teoría, historia y propuestas*, Barcelona: Crítica, 1990, p. xxi.

107. Raymond Carr, *España: 1808–1975*, 4nd., Barcelona: Ariel, 1988, pp. 486–487.

108. Cambó's visit, the *"traída de catalanes"* ("invitation to the Catalans"), was provoked by the policy of the Treasury Ministry to tax the extraordinary incomes proceeding from the war. We believe it is interesting to point out that the Deputations did not take any measures in relation to this new tax, at least officially. Vid. Idoia Estornes Zubizarreta, *La construcción de una nacionalidad vasca: el autonomismo de Eusko Ikaskuntza (1918–1931)*, San Sebastián: Eusko Ikaskuntza-Sociedad de Estudios Vascos, 1990., pp. 94–95. Alba's reform—an unsuccessful reform—had enemies that were more direct and powerful than the Basque Deputations. Vid. José Luis (Dir.) Garcia Delgado, Cabrera Calvo-Sotelo, Mercedes, Comin Comin, Francisco, *Santiago Alba. Un programa de reforma económica en la España del primer tercio del siglo XX*, Madrid: Instituto de Estudios Fiscales, 1989.

109. Acta de la sesión secreta de la Diputación de Guipúzcoa. 9 de julio de 1917. AFB. Administrativo 2654/103.

110. The complete text can be found in: Acta de la Asamblea de las Diputaciones vascongadas celebrada en la ciudad de Vitoria el día 16 de julio de 1917. AFB. Administrativo 2654/103, Estornes Zubizarreta, *La construcción de una nacionalidad vasca: el autonomismo de Eusko Ikaskuntza (1918–1931)*, pp. 103–104, and Joseba Agirreazkuenaga, ed. *La articulación político-institucional de Vasconia: Actas de las "Conferencias" firmadas por los representantes de Alava, Bizkaia, Gipuzkoa y eventualmente de Navarra (1775–1936)*, 2 vols., Bilbao: Diputaciones Forales de Bizkaia, Gipuzkoa y Alava, 1995. T. II.

111. Agirreazkuenaga, Joseba, ed. *La articulación político-institucional de Vasconia: Actas de las "Conferencias" firmadas por los representantes de Alava, Bizkaia, Gipuzkoa y eventualmente de Navarra (1775–1936)*. Bilbao: Diputaciones Forales de Bizkaia, Gipuzkoa y Alava, 1995, vol. 2, p. 1.239.

112. Acta de la Asamblea de las Diputaciones vascongadas celebrada en la ciudad de Vitoria el día 16 de julio de 1917. AFB. Administrativo 2654/103.

113. Acta de la Asamblea de las Diputaciones vascongadas celebrada en la ciudad de Vitoria el día 16 de julio de 1917. AFB. Administrativo 2654/103.

114. Acta de la Asamblea de las Diputaciones vascongadas celebrada en la ciudad de Vitoria el día 16 de julio de 1917. AFB. Administrativo 2654/103.

115. The Deputation of Bizkaia received telegrams of support from the Juventud de Tolosa (*Jaimistas* of Gipuzkoa and Álava), the Laurak-Bat Society, and the Deputation of Lérida, together with all the Municipal Councils of the province. AFB. Administrativo 2654/104.

116. Acuerdo del Ayuntamiento de Bilbao. 20 de julio de 1917. AFB. Administrativo 2654/104. The Bizkaia Deputation approved the convening of an Assembly of Municipal Councils without any problem. Acta de la sesión secreta de la Diputación de Vizcaya. 28 de julio de 1917. AFB. Administrativo 2654/104.

117. Carta de la Asamblea de Senadores y Diputados españoles a la Diputación de Vizcaya. 19 de julio de 1917. AFB. Administrativo 2654/104.

118. Acuerdo del pleno del Ayuntamiento de Bilbao. 3 de agosto de 1917.
119. Acta de la Asamblea de las Diputaciones vascongadas celebrada en la ciudad de Vitoria el día 16 de julio de 1917. AFB. Administrativo 2654/103. Hilario Bilbao was the brother and heir of Esteban Bilbao. We will encounter him again in the Deputation years later, in a very different context.
120. Circular de la Diputación de Bizkaya a los Ayuntamientos de la provincia. 1 de agosto de 1917. AFB. Administrativo 2654/103.
121. Circular del presidente de la Diputación de Vizcaya a los exdiputados provinciales. 2 de agosto de 1917. AFB. Administrativo 2654/103.
122. Acta de la reunión de comisionados de la Diputación de Vizcaya con exdiputados provinciales. 7 de agosto de 1917. AFB. Administrativo 2654/103.
123. "It is unquestionable that this Message neither satisfies nor fulfils the aspirations of many who are meeting together here. There are things that it was very hard for us to approve, but we made a great sacrifice in our political convictions, conceding in all of them to reach a unanimous agreement and, we signed the Message believing we were doing a great service to the country." Acta de la reunión de comisionados de la Diputación de Vizcaya con exdiputados provinciales. 7 de agosto de 1917. AFB. Administrativo 2654/103.
124. Acta de la reunión de comisionados de la Diputación de Vizcaya con exdiputados provinciales. 7 de agosto de 1917. AFB. Administrativo 2654/103.
125. Acta de la reunión de comisionados de la Diputación de Vizcaya con exdiputados provinciales. 7 de agosto de 1917. AFB. Administrativo 2654/103.
126. Acta de la reunión de comisionados de la Diputación de Vizcaya con exdiputados provinciales. 7 de agosto de 1917. AFB. Administrativo 2654/103.
127. Acta de la reunión de comisionados de la Diputación de Vizcaya con exdiputados provinciales. 7 de agosto de 1917. AFB. Administrativo 2654/103.
128. Acta de la reunión de comisionados de la Diputación de Vizcaya con exdiputados provinciales. 7 de agosto de 1917. AFB. Administrativo 2654/103.
129. Acta de la reunión de comisionados de la Diputación de Vizcaya con exdiputados provinciales. 7 de agosto de 1917. AFB. Administrativo 2654/103.
130. Acta de la reunión de comisionados de la Diputación de Vizcaya con exdiputados provinciales. 7 de agosto de 1917. AFB. Administrativo 2654/103. With respect to this point he recalled his proposal of 1914, which we referred to above and that was not approved.
131. Acta de la reunión de comisionados de la Diputación de Vizcaya con exdiputados provinciales. 7 de agosto de 1917. AFB. Administrativo 2654/103.
132. The Assembly was attended by representatives from 107 Bizkaian Municipal Councils, and the Deputation was represented by Ramón de la Sota, Luis de Urrutia, Luis de Urrengoechea, Vicente Fatrás, José Ramón de Bilbao, Alejandro Pisón, Hilario Bilbao, José Mª de Garay, Vicente Ibarra, Fernando de Zubicaray, Félix de Landáburu, and Manuel Eguileor. The representatives for Lanestosa and de Mallabia excused themselves, but agreed to the minutes.
    The agreements reached were as follows:

1st. Bizkaia solemnly protests against the promulgated laws that damage its *foral* regime.

2nd. The Deputation of Bizkaia, in carrying out the procedures with which it is commissioned today, has the complete trust of all the Bizkaian Municipalities that promise it their committed and unconditional support. Acta de la Asamblea de Ayuntamientos de Vizcaya. 9 de agosto de 1917. AFB. Administrativo 2654/103.

133. In addition to Martínez de Aragón, it seems that Gandarias, Chávarri, Zubiría, Ampuero, and Ajuria were also opposed to the Deputation's initiative. Vid. Estornes Zubizarreta, *La construcción de una nacionalidad vasca: el autonomismo de Eusko Ikaskuntza (1918–1931)*, p. 112. We say "it seems" because in December Ampuero placed himself at the disposal of the president of the Bizkaian Deputation to lobby on its behalf in the Ministry of Education and the Treasury, and most importantly, to deliver the message. Carta de José Joaquín Ampuero (diputado por Durango) al presidente de la Diputación de Vizcaya. 12 de diciembre de 1917. AFB. Administrativo 2654/103.

134. Estornes Zubizarreta, *La construcción de una nacionalidad vasca: el autonomismo de Eusko Ikaskuntza (1918–1931)*, p. 112.

135. Carta del presidente de la Diputación de Guipúzcoa al presidente de la Diputación de Vizcaya. 23 de octubre de 1917. AFB. Administrativo 2654/103.

136. Although this did not stop them from making other petitions shortly after García Prieto took office. Vid. Nota entregada al presidente del Gobierno. 10 de noviembre de 1917. AFB. Administrativo 2651/52. This included a request not to apply the General Regulations concerning the secretaries of Municipal Councils.

137. Estornes Zubizarreta, *La construcción de una nacionalidad vasca: el autonomismo de Eusko Ikaskuntza (1918–1931)*, p. 113.

138. González Hernández, *Ciudadanía y acción. El conservadurismo maurista, 1907–1923*, p. 81.

139. González Hernández, *Ciudadanía y acción. El conservadurismo maurista, 1907–1923*, pp. 82–83. Ybarra Y Berge, *Política nacional en Vizcaya*, pp. 442–443.

140. "España parece que quiere ir a una liquidación espiritual. En ella, con todos los errores y desvaríos que se quieran señalar, quedan de un lado los parlamentarios catalanes, las Juntas Militares, las *diputaciones vascongadas*, los productores de Córdoba, los municipios de Coruña y Salamanca, todos los que ansían la renovación; y de otro el rey, los partidos turnantes, el trust, la oligarquía, el quietismo, la podredumbre." Letter from Ossorio to Maura. 1 August 1917, in González Hernández, *Ciudadanía y acción. El conservadurismo maurista, 1907–1923*, p. 75. (Our italics.)

141. Vid. Alonso Olea, "Los conflictos fiscales entre las Diputaciones vascongadas y el Ministerio de Hacienda. (1876–1937)."

142. Vid. Juan Pablo Fusi, "Los nacionalismos y el Estado español," *Cuadernos de historia contemporánea*, n°. 22 (2000). Sobre la postura vasca, vid. Agirreazkuenaga, ed. *La articulación político-institucional de Vasconia: Actas de las "Conferencias" firmadas por los representantes de Alava, Bizkaia, Gipuzkoa y eventualmente de*

Navarra (1775–1936). The contrast with the situation permitted by the Economic Agreement, in Eduardo J. Alonso Olea, *Continuidades y discontinuidades de la administración provincial en el País Vasco. 1839–1978. Una «esencia» de los Derechos Históricos*, Oñati: IVAP, 1999.

143. Vid. Royal Decree, which declared that for exclusively administrative purposes which were the competence of the provinces, the latter could form communities following publication of the proceedings. *Gaceta de Madrid*, nº 353, de 19 de diciembre de 1913, pp. 815–817.

144. Xosé Nuñez Seixas, "Ecos de Pascua, mitos rebeldes: el nacionalismo vasco e Irlanda (1890–1939)," *Historia Contemporánea*, nº. 55 (2017), p. 456.

145. For example, in 1916, after leaving the leadership of Basque Naitonalist Communion, Luis Arana led a breakaway group (*Euskeldun Batzokija*). In 1921, the Basque Nationalist Party (*Aberri*) was founded by Eli Gallastegi. Vid. Granja Sainz, *El nacionalismo vasco: un siglo de historia*.

146. On the question of fiscal pressure in the provinces, where the Economic Agreement was in effect, vid. Eduardo J. Alonso Olea, "La fiscalidad empresarial en Vizcaya 1914–1935. Un beneficio del Concierto Económico," *Hacienda Pública Española*, oº. 2-3/1997 (1997); Eduardo J. Alonso Olea, "La recaudación de Impuestos Especiales. Vizcaya (1876–1937)," *Zergak. Gaceta Tributaria del País Vasco*, nº. 1-1998 (1998).

147. On this turbulent election, Ybarra Y Berge, *Política nacional en Vizcaya*, pp. 444 and ff; Carmelo de Echegaray, *Cartas a D. Serapio de Múgica. (1899–1925)*, San Sebastián: Grupo Doctor Camino de Historia Donostiarra, 1987, p. 507; Javier Real Cuesta, *Partidos, elecciones y bloques de poder en el País Vasco. 1876–1923*, Bilbao: U. Deusto, 1991, p. 143; Ludger Mees, *Nacionalismo vasco, movimiento obrero y cuestión social (1903–1923)*, Bilbao: Fundación Sabino Arana, 1992, pp. 290 and ff; Ignacio Arana Perez, *El monarquismo en Vizcaya durante la crisis del reinado de Alfonso XIII (1917–1931)*, Pamplona: EUNSA, 1982, p. 35.

148. Five deputies were elected but the election in the district of Baracaldo was annulled, which left them with four (Rotaeche, Orueta, Ramón de la Sota y Llano, and Arroyo). Vid. Ybarra Y Berge, *Política nacional en Vizcaya*, pp. 455–456. Domingo (*Txomin*) Epalza was elected when the elections were repeated in the summer, p. 478. Their biographical profiles can be found in Agirreazkuenaga, *Diccionario biográfico de Parlamentarios de Vasconia (1876–1939)*.

149. Ybarra Y Berge, *Política nacional en Vizcaya*, pp. 457–472; Arana Perez, *El monarquismo en Vizcaya durante la crisis del reinado de Alfonso XIII (1917–1931)*, pp. 37–38.

150. "Se autoriza al gobierno de S.M para que de acuerdo con las diputaciones vascongadas presente en el plazo más breve posible un proyecto de ley que satisfaga las aspiraciones contenidas en el mensaje aprobado por aquellas Corporaciones y entregado al Sr. Presidente del Consejo de Ministros el día diez y siete de Diciembre último." Acta de la Conferencia de las Diputaciones vascongadas. 20 de marzo de 1918. A.A.D.V. R.E.A.- C.E. 2654/103.

151. Vid. DSC. Apéndice 35 al n° 7, de 2 de abril de 1918.

152. "Yo tengo que decirlo de alguna manera, sin que ello agravie personalmente al Sr. Sota; pero tengo que manifestaros, Sres. Diputados, que cualquier extranjero tiene mayor capacidad para sentarse en este Congreso que el Sr. Sota. Porque el Sr. Sota, que tuvo la fortuna, la dicha, el honor, de ser español, ha abjurado públicamente de su Patria. Y esta abjuración de su Patria no es una abjuración implícita, deducida de los principios que profesa; es una abjuración positiva, práctica. Es decir, que no es que, a consecuencia de unos principios erróneos, sea el Sr. Sota antiespañol, sino que, a consecuencia de extravíos afectivos, el Sr. Sota no ama a España; el Sr. Sota odia a España. (Rumores)." DSC. 5 de abril de 1918, p. 159.

153. The ideas of Vázquez de Mella, in the context of extreme right-wing thought in the first third of the twentieth century, in Pedro Carlos González Cuevas, "Tradicionalismo, catolicismo y nacionalismo: la extrema derecha durante el régimen de la Restauración (1898–1930)," *Ayer* n°. 71 (2008).

154. Vid. José Luis Orella Martínez, *Víctor Pradera: un católico en la vida pública de principios de siglo*, Madrid: Biblioteca de Autores Cristianos, 2000; Pedro Carlos González Cuevas, *Acción Española: teología política y nacionalismo autoritario en España (1913–1936)*, Madrid: Tecnos, 1998, pp. 50–57.

155. "Fué la Diputación, no fué el presidente de la Diputación, ni el vicepresidente, ni la plana mayor del partido bizcaitarra, fue la Diputación; y por eso al volver los comisionados, dió un voto de gracias a los que en Barcelona les habían recibido y agasajado. Desde entonces se suceden en Vizcaya una serie de asambleas, parodia de las que se celebraron por los parlamentarios. Y consecuencia de todo ello fué el mensaje que entregaron al Gobierno en 17 de Diciembre, en el cual se con-tienen las aspiraciones de este partido, mensaje en el cual se pide que se organice el Estado de tal manera que queden a los organismos forales o regionales todas las facultades más esenciales del Estado, porque se reserva solamente al Estado lo relativo a las relaciones internacionales, a la defensa del territorio, a las aduanas y a la moneda, y, en cambio, se pide que se deje a los organismos regionales la declaración y regulación de los derechos individuales, la declaración de los derechos de los Municipios, la Administración de Justicia, la enseñanza; en una palabra, se pide la destrucción del Estado." Gregorio Balparda's speech. DSC. 5 de abril de 1918, pp. 161–162.

156. That same year Balparda published a collection of texts, articles, and talks—some already familiar since the year 1908, others from subsequent years—in which he once again focused on attacking Basque nationalism, underscoring its false interpretation of *foral* history and stressing the liberal content of the *Fuero*. Vid. Balparda Y De Las Herrerias, *Errores del nacionalismo vasco*.

157. Antonio Arroyo´s speech. DSC. 5 de abril de 1918, p. 163.

158. Estornes Zubizarreta, I. *La construcción* . . . p. 120; Echegaray, C. de. *Cartas* . . . p. 509.

159. Not all Basque socialists were as opposed to certain *foral* or autonomist demands

as Prieto; the former included his coreligionists from Eibar, for example, or a republican like Gascue, one of the greatest defenders of the liberal view of the *Fuero*. Vid. Rivera Blanco, *Señas de identidad : izquierda obrera y nación en el País Vasco, 1880–1923*, pp. 136 and ff. On Gascue and his view of the *Fueros*, Francisco Gascue, *El Fuerismo histórico y el Fuerismo progresivo en Guipúzcoa*, San Sebastian: Tip. La Voz de Guipúzcoa, 1909.

160. "In short, Indalecio understood better than anyone else that only by absorbing the idea of the *Fueros* into the highest law, the Constitution, would it be possible for the demand to be modernized, while at the same time this would remove it from the romantic and/or traditionalist dreams that had recklessly accompanied Carlism, integralism and clericalism in earlier epochs, and that now accompanied nationalism." Ricardo Miralles, *Indalecio Prieto. La nación española y el problema vasco. Textos políticos*, Bilbao: Servicio Editorial Universidad del País Vasco, 2019, p. 78.

161. DSC. 17 de abril de 1918, pp. 453 y ss. It can also be found in Miralles, *Indalecio Prieto. La nación española y el problema vasco. Textos políticos*, pp. 265–273. Also included in: Rivera Blanco, *Señas de identidad : izquierda obrera y nación en el País Vasco, 1880–1923*, pp. 225–230.

162. Rivera Blanco, *Señas de identidad : izquierda obrera y nación en el País Vasco, 1880–1923*, p. 147.

163. Vid. Daniel Guerra Sesma, "Socialismo y cuestión nacional en la España de la Restauración (1875–1931)," *Revista de Estudios Políticos*, n°. 137 (2007).

164. A general view of the figure of Indalecio Prieto in the context of Spanish politics, which also includes his relation with the Basque Nationalists, in Abdón Mateos Lopez, ed. *Indalecio Prieto y la política española*, Madrid: Pablo Iglesias, 2008.

165. *Euzkadi*, 18 de mayo de 1919.

166. Vid. Antonio Rivera Blanco, "Prieto, los nacionalistas vascos y la cuestión vasca," in *Indalecio Prieto y la política española*, ed. Mateos López, Abdón Madrid: Fundación Pablo Iglesias, 2008, pp. 94–95.

167. Vid. Estornes Zubizarreta, I. *La construcción* . . ., pp. 121–135.

168. *Primer Congreso de Estudios Vascos. Recopilación de los trabajos de dicha asamblea, celebrada en la Universidad de Oñate del 1 al 8 de septiembre de 1918, bajo el patrocinio de las Diputaciones Vascas*. Bilbaína de Artes Gráficas. Bilbao, 1919–1920, pp. 311–314

169. The Manifesto of the Nationalist Assembly of Lugo, in 1918, and the appearance of the *Irmandades da Fala* (in 1916), were therefore not chance occurrences.

170. Estornes Zubizarreta, I. *La construcción* . . ., p. 139. Nuñez Seixas, "Ecos de Pascua, mitos rebeldes: el nacionalismo vasco e Irlanda (1890–1939)."

171. This bill not only called for the repeal of the Law of 1839 "and as many regulations dictated for its execution and for its fulfilment and development," in an implicit reference to the Law of 21 July 1876. The bill's second article also indicated that the Basque provincial Deputations should determine the transitional regime that was to be formed by virtue of the previous article, while the third article authorized

"the government, at the appropriate time, to deal and agree with the legitimate representatives of Álava, Gipuzkoa, Navarre and Bizkaia on the foundations on which the mutual and cordial coexistence of those territories with the Spanish state shall rest." That is, the bill went far beyond the simple derogation of a law dating back nearly 80 years. Bill tabled by Mr. Epalza and others derogating the Law of 25 October 1839. Signed by Domingo de Epalza, Ramón de la Sota, and Anacleto de Ortueta November 4, 1918. DSC. 6 de noviembre de 1918, apéndice 7° al n° 90.

172. DSC. 13 de diciembre de 1918, pp. 3.558 y ss.

173. Romanones was Minister of State under García Prieto. A sign of the reigning political instability was the fact that, between March 1918 and July 1919, a period of sixteen months, there were five governments.

174. Acta de la Conferencia de las Diputaciones vascongadas. 19 de noviembre de 1918. AFB. Administrativo. 2654/109.

175. For a detailed account of these events, vid. Ybarra Y Berge, J. de. *Política nacional* . . ., pp. 504–525. The text of the rowdy Assembly of Municipal Councils of Bizkaia, in Certificado del Secretario del Ayuntamiento de Bilbao. 24 de enero de 1918. AFB. Administrativo. 2654/109. Also see, Mees, *Nacionalismo vasco, movimiento obrero y cuestión social (1903–1923)*, pp. 289 y ss.

176. Vid. oficio del Gobernador Civil de Vizcaya al Presidente de la Diputación de Vizcaya. 21 de diciembre de 1918. AFB. Administrativo. 2654/109.

177. Romanones, García Prieto, Alba, Alcalá Zamora, Maura, Dato, Sánchez de Toca, De la Cierva, and several other personages. Several Basques were also appointed to it: Senante, Orueta, Chalbaud, and Pradera. Estornes Zubizarreta, I. *La construcción* . . ., p. 146.

178. Estornes Zubizarreta, I. *La construcción* . . ., pp. 146–47.

179. Arana Perez, Ignacio. "Las Iniciativas autonómicas en el siglo XX (I)," in *Muga*, n°. 58. 1987, pp. 46–47.

180. Carta de J. de Orueta al Presidente de la Diputación de Vizcaya. 31 de diciembre de 1918. AFB. Administrativo. 2654/109.

181. Arana Perez, I. "Las Iniciativas autonómicas . . .," p. 46.

182. Sub-ponencia para Alava, Guipúzcoa y Vizcaya. 9 de enero de 1919. AFB. Administrativo. 2654/109. Artículo 1°.

183. At present the quota functions in this way, but based on the budget of outlays not assumed by the Basque Autonomous Community.

184. Estornes Zubizarreta, I. *La construcción* . . ., p. 147.

185. Vid. "La propuesta del Sr. Alba." *El Pueblo Vasco*. 20 de enero de 1919.

186. "Queda confiado a la iniciativa de los Ayuntamientos de cada una de las provincias Vascongadas y la de Navarra, con el asesoramiento que estimen oportuno, el proyecto de restauración y adaptación a las actuales circunstancias de sus antiguos organismos forales. estos proyectos habrán de redactarse y de aprobarse conforme a los artículos 2° y 3° de esta ley." Disposición adicional transitoria Tercera del Proyecto de ley de Bases de organización y régimen municipal. D.S.C. apéndice 11 al n° 110. 21 de enero de 1919, p. 19.

187. Ignacio Arana Perez, "Las iniciativas autonómicas en el siglo XX (II)," *Muga*, n°. 59 (1987), p. 47.

188. González Hernández, *Ciudadanía y acción. El conservadurismo maurista, 1907–1923*, p. 99.

189. Ignacio Olabarri Gortazar, "Un conflicto entre nacionalismos: la 'cuestión regional' en España. 1808–1939," in *La España de las Autonomías*, Madrid: Instituto de Estudios de la Administración Local, 1985, p. 123.

190. Vid. De Blas Guerrero, "Regeneracionismo español y cuestión nacional," pp. 586, 587.

191. Antonio Maura Foundation. Archive. Box 265.

192. Vid. Javier Tusell Gomez, *La reforma de la Administración local en España (1900–1936)*, 2 ed., Madrid: Instituto de Estudios Administrativos, 1987.

193. Joseba Agirreazkuenaga, "El tránsito del discurso foral al autonomista: El 'vasco-catalanismo' de 1917," en *Conciliar la diversidad pasado y presente de la vertebración de España : VII y VIII Seminarios Ernest LLuch*, ed. J. Astigarraga and C. Arrieta J. Bilbao: UPV-EHU, 2009.

194. Joseba Agirreazkuenaga Zigorraga, "La transición por la "Constitución Vascongada" (1852): De la "Constitución Foral" (1808) al "Estatuto de la autonomía de las regiones de Álava, Guipuzcoa y Vizcaya" (1919), in *I Seminari Catalunya-Euskadi. La Institucionalització política: de les Constitutions històriques als Estatus d'Autonomia (1808–2005)*, Barcelona: Generalitat de Catalunya-Museu d'Historia de Catalunya, 2007.

195. It is well known that Sota supported the Allied cause with his shipping company, which earned him a knighthood from King George V. Vid. Torres Villanueva, *Ramón de la Sota. 1857–1936. Un empresario vasco*.

196. His grandfather, José Salvador de Lequerica, had been one of the founders of the first modern industries of Bilbao, Santa Ana de Bolueta. Vid. Eduardo J. Alonso Olea, *Casilda de Iturrizar Urquijo. Viuda de Epalza (1818–19009. Una biografía*, Bilbao: Fundación Bilbao 700- III Millennium Fundazioa, 2019.

197. José Félix de Lequerica, together with his brother Enrique, and José Luis Costa Arana, participated in the formation of the Compagnie General des Verreries Espagnoles S.A., a company that manufactured glass, with its head office in Bilbao and factories in Lamiako (Biscay) and Jerez de la Frontera (Cádiz). They were the Spanish associates of the French glass multinational Saint Gobain. Vid. Esther Sanchez, "Un siglo de vidrio francés: Saint Gobain en España, de 1905 a la actualidad," *Investigaciones de Historia Económica* 7, n°. 3 (2011).

198. *Txomin* Epalza, heir to some of the shares that Tomás José de Epalza held in Santa Ana de Bolueta, founded by J. F. de Lequerica's grandfather, was a member of this company's council, together with Sánchez Mazas, grandson of another of the company's founders. Vid. Eduardo J. Alonso Olea, Erro Gasca, Carmen, Arana Pérez, Ignacio, *Santa Ana de Bolueta, 1841–2016. Renovación y supervivencia en la siderurgia vizcaína*, 2 ed., Bilbao: Santa Ana de Bolueta, 2016.

199. *Cunero*: a candidate who stands in an electoral district with which he has no ties of birth or of any other kind, but where his election is guaranteed.

200. José Mª Salaverria, *La afirmación española*, Barcelona: Gustavo Gili, 1917.

201. Andreu Navarra Ordoño, "Un programa político antieuropeísta: 'La afirmación española' de José María Salaverría," *Sancho el Sabio: Revista de cultura e investigación vasca*, n°. 24 (2006), p. 44.

202. Salaverria, José Mª. "El país más liberal y retrogrado." *ABC*, 30 de agosto de 1923.

203. On this writer, vid. Andreu Navarra Ordoño, "José María Salaverría escritor y periodista (1904–1940)" (Universitat de Barcelona, 2011), Iker González-Allende, "From the self to the nation: willpower in José María Salaverría," *Romance notes* 49, n°. 1 (2009); Navarra Ordoño, "Un programa político antieuropeísta: 'La afirmación española' de José María Salaverría"; Andreu Navarra Ordoño, "Una geografía imperial: vieja España de José María Salaverría," *Revista de literatura* 67, n°. 134 (2005); Miren Bilbao Notario, "Jose María Salaverría: España en su pensamiento político, 1873–1940" (Universidad de Deusto, 2001); María Martínez-Cachero Rojo, "José María Salaverría (1873–1940) un noventayochista menor," in *Azorín et la Génération de 1898*, Pau :Université de Pau et des Pays de l'Adour, Faculté des Lettres, Langues et Sciences Humaines, 1998; José Ignacio Tellechea Idígoras, *Miguel de Unamuno y José María Salaverría: epistolario (1904–1935)*, Donostia-San Sebastián: Fundación Social y Cultural Kutxa, 1996.

204. Vid. Arana Perez, *El monarquismo en Vizcaya durante la crisis del reinado de Alfonso XIII (1917–1931)*.

205. The district of Bilbao-Centre was made up of the municipalities of Barrika, Begoña, Berango, Deusto, Etxebarri, Erandio, Getxo, Laukiniz, Leioa, Loiu, Plentzia, Sopela, Urduliz, Zamudio, and part of Bilbao (the districts of Casas Consistoriales, Santiago, and Atxuri). These were basically the municipalities and districts situated on the right bank of the Nervión tidal river.

    The district of Bilbao-Ensanche (the expansion district) was made up of the municipalities of Arrigorriaga, Basauri, and Bilbao (the districts of Bilba la Vieja, San Francisco, Cortes, Station, Gran Via, and San Vicente). That is, the municipalities and districts situated on the left bank of the Nervión tidal river.

206. Vid. Arana Perez, *El monarquismo en Vizcaya durante la crisis del reinado de Alfonso XIII (1917–1931)*.

207. On the divisions in Basque nationalism, besides the one mentioned, vid. Gaizka Fernandez Soldevilla, "De Aberri a ETA, pasando por Venezuela. Rupturas y continuidades en el nacionalismo vasco radical (1921–1977)," *Bulletin d 'Histoire Contemporaine de l 'Espagne* n°. 51 (2015).

208. Their biographies in Agirreazkuenaga, *Diccionario biográfico de Parlamentarios de Vasconia (1876–1939)*.

209. This was the case not only in politics but also in the business field; he was a member of a company dedicated to the distribution and screening of films clearly aligned with the catholic doctrine, Seleccine S.A.

210. Ybarra Y Berge, *Política nacional en Vizcaya*. In his prologue Rafael Sánchez Mazas, the first person to speak about fascism in Spain, pointed to one of the effects the "family policy" carried out in those years: "The third effect was to

create in the struggle against separatists and reds a valiant school of patriotism—later to be fatally, bloodily and nationally united. The two decisive legions were created in two struggles: the military one in Africa, and the civil one in Vizcaya. Vizcaya was like a spiritual and political Africa for the spiritual and political cadets of a reconquered Spain," p. vii.

211. Vid. Jose Luis de la Granja Sainz, *Nacionalismo y II República en el País Vasco. estatutos de autonomía, partidos y elecciones. Historia de Acción Nacionalista Vasca: 1930–1936*, Madrid: C.I.S.- Siglo XXI, 1986, José Luis de la Granja *República y Guerra civil en Euskadi. Del Pacto de San Sebastián al de Santoña*, Oñati: IVAP, 1990. José María Tapiz, *El PNV durante la II República (organización, interna, implantación territorial y bases sociales)*, Bilbao: Fundación Sabino Arana, 2001. and Ludger Mees, "Tras el fracaso de Estella: las pautas y claves del Estatuto de 1936," *Iura vasconiae: revista de derecho histórico y autonómico de Vasconia*, nº. 10 (2013).

212. Mees, "Tras el fracaso de Estella: las pautas y claves del Estatuto de 1936.", p. 468.

213. A decree conferring on the Management Commissions of the Deputations of Álava, Vizcaya, Guipúzcoa and Navarra, the task of directing the work of drawing up the project or projects for a statute or statutes that would establish and regulate the autonomous faculties that, as a widening of the existing faculties in these provinces, could be granted to them in keeping with the Constitution. *Gaceta de Madrid*, no. 343, December 9, 1931, pp. 1.550–1.551. It was no accident that on that same day a special issue of the *Gaceta de Madrid* was published containing the constitutional text of the Republic, which was also published in a normal issue the following day, December 10.

214. Vid. Javier Ugarte Telleria, *La nueva Covadonga insurgente. Orígenes sociales y culturales de la sublevación de 1936 en Navarra y el País Vasco*, Madrid: Biblioteca nueva, 1998. Jordi Canal I Morell, *El carlismo. Dos siglos de contrarrevolución en España*, Madrid: Alianza Editorial, 2000.

215. On the *Galeuzca* phenomenon, vid. Xosé Estévez Rodríguez, "Nacionalismos y estatutos en la II República Española." In *Cultura vasca*, edited by Barandiarán, José Miguel de, San Sebastián: Erein, 1977, Xosé Estévez Rodríguez. "Apuntes para una historia de las relaciones políticas entre Galicia, Euskadi y Catalunya (1900–1950)." *Letras de Deusto* 13, nº. 27 (1983): 5–28, Xosé Estévez Rodríguez, *De la Triple Alianza al Pacto de San Sebastián (1923–1930): antecedentes del Galeuzca*. Bilbao: Universidad de Deusto, Servicio de Publicaciones, 1991, Xosé Estévez Rodríguez, "Galeuzka: Euzkadi, Catalunya e o nacionalismo galego na II República." *Murguía: revista galega de historia* nº. 7 (2005): 105–13, Xosé Estévez Rodríguez," Galeuzca en el surco ondulante de la memoria." In *España en la encrucijada de 1939: Exilios, cultura e identidades*, 175–94: Bilbao: Universidad de Deusto, 2007. Xosé Estévez Rodríguez," El Galeuzca histórico: la búsqueda trinacional de la soberanía (1923–1959)." *Hermes*, nº 28 (2009): 72–83. On the relations between Catalan and Basque nationalists, not only at this moment, but before and after, vid. Alexander Ugalde and Enric Ucelay-Da Cal, "Una alianza

en potencia en un contexto más amplio: la mirada distante de los movimientos nacionalistas vasco y catalán (1910–1936)." In *Patrias diversas, ¿misma lucha? alianzas transnacionalistas en el mundo de entreguerras (1912–1939)*, edited by Ucelay-Da Cal, Enric, Nuñez Seixas, Xosé and González I Villalta, Arnau. Barcelona: Bellaterra, 2020. Vid. *Infra.*

216. Vid. Agirreazkuenaga, *Diccionario biográfico de Parlamentarios de Vasconia (1876–1939)*.

217. *El Liberal*, 21 November 1933.

218. DSC, nº. 273, December 5, 1935, pp. 11.116 and ff.

219. DSC, no. 273, December 5, 1935, p. 11.116.

220. His biography can be found in Agirreazkuenaga, *Diccionario biográfico de Parlamentarios de Vasconia (1876–1939)*.

221. DSC, no. 273, December 5, 1935, p. 11.118.

222. DSC, no. 273, December 5, 1935, p. 11.119.

223. Basque and Catalan nationalism were kept well-informed about events in Latin America by their respective diasporas. Vid. Xosé Manoel Nuñez Seixas, "¿Negar o reescribir la Hispanidad? Los nacionalismos subestatales ibéricos y América Latina, 1898–1936." *Historia Mexicana* LXVII, nº. 1 (2017): 401–58.

224. DSC, no.273, December 5, 1935, p. 11.120.

225. DSC, no. 273, December 5, 1935, p. 11.121.

226. DSC, no. 273, 5 December 1935, pp. 11.124–11.126. Vid. note 62.

227. DSC, no. 273, 5 December 1935, p. 11.126.

228. DSC, no. 273, December 5, 1935, p. 11.128.

229. We will not go into the recent questioning of whether that victory was so clear-cut. Vid. Manuel Alvarez Tardio and Roberto Villa García, *1936: Fraude y Violencia*, Madrid: Espasa, 2017. Eduardo González Calleja and Francisco Sánchez Pérez, "Revisando el revisionismo. A propósito del libro *1936. Fraude y violencia en las elecciones del Frente Popular*," *Historia Contemporánea*, nº. 58 (2018).

230. *El Liberal*, February 29, 1936.

231. Analyzed in José Luis de la Granja and Luis Sala González, *Vidas cruzadas. Prieto y Aguirre. Los padres fundadores de Euskadi*, Madrid: Biblioteca nueva, 2018, José Luis de la Granja Sainz, "Los padres fundadores de Euskadi en la Guerra Civil: José Antonio Aguirre e Indalecio Prieto," *Sancho el sabio: Revista de cultura e investigación vasca*, nº. 1 (2018).

232. On the nationalisms during the war, vid. Xosé Manoel Nuñez Seixas. "Las patrias de la República: La experiencia de los nacionalistas periféricos durante la Guerra Civil española (1936–1939)." *Historia Contemporánea* nº. 38 (2009): 13–47.

233. Granja Sainz, "Los padres fundadores de Euskadi en la Guerra Civil: José Antonio Aguirre e Indalecio Prieto.", p. 19.

234. A broad study of this organization, in Granja Sainz, *Nacionalismo y II República en el País Vasco. estatutos de autonomía, partidos y elecciones. Historia de Acción Nacionalista Vasca: 1930–1936*.

235. Vid. Tapiz, *El PNV durante la II República (organización, interna, implantación*

territorial y bases sociales). The Assembly of Tolosa (1932–33), besides the appearance of a new batch of leaders (Aguirre, Irujo, Monzón and Landáburu) also saw a clear affirmation by the party in favor of Independence.

236. Here we can find a wide range of elements that served as motives for confrontation: ranging from the application of Income Tax in the Basque Country (a tax that was not agreed upon until Francoism), the activities of the Mixed Committees on Profits [*Jurados Mixtos de Utilidades*] , to the better-known problem of the tax on wine; and also the bitter debates on the Law of the Local Regime in 1935, in which the right attempted to ignore the special situation of the Basque municipalities; all of the which formed part of a general tendency. Vid. for example, Eduardo J. Alonso Olea, "Los conflictos fiscales entre las Diputaciones vascongadas y el Ministerio de Hacienda. (1876–1937)," *Forum Fiscal de Bizkaia*, n°. Marzo-1997 (1997).

237. Concerning his "conversion" to autonomism, vid. Antonio Rivera, "Indalecio Prieto y la 'conversión' autonomista del socialismo vasco," in *Nacidos para mandar. Liderazgo, política y poder. Perspectivas comparadas*, ed. Mees, Ludger and Núñez Seixas, Xosé Manoel Madrid: Tecnos, 2012.

238. An organization that emerged precisely in reaction to the autonomist campaign of 1918–1919, vid. Moreno Luzón, Javier, "De agravios, pactos y símbolos: el nacionalismo español ante la autonomía de Cataluña." *Ayer* n°. 63 (2006): 119–51.

239. Núñez Seixas, "De gaitas y liras: Sobre discursos y prácticas de la pluralidad territorial en el fascismo español (1930–1950)." In *Falange, las culturas políticas del fascismo en la España de Franco (1936-1975)*, edited by Ruiz Carnicer, Miguel Angel. Zaragoza: Institución "Fernando el Católico", 2013, p. 298.

240. Decreto-Ley de 23 de junio de 1937. *B.O.E.* 24 de junio de 1937. n° 247, p. 204. Vid. Eduardo J. Alonso Olea, "El otro exilio interior: la abolición del Concierto Económico en junio de 1937. Un exilio institucional," *Murguía: revista galega de historia* 37, n°. Xaneiro-Xuño 2018 (2018).

241. *Levelling* in this context refers to the extension of the administrative regime of the rest of Spain to the Basque Country. It was a term frequently used in the XIX century as a synonym for the abolition of the *Fueros*. A clear and recent case is what happened with UPyD, which only obtained one representative for Álava in the Basque Country. This was due to special electoral conditions: the parity of representation among the Historical Territories, in 2009 and 2012. In the general election of 2019 in the Basque Country, *Ciudadanos* (Citizens)—the heir to UPyD's discourse on *leveling*—only won 3.14% (40,000 votes) and VOX won 2.21% (28,000) of the vote. In the *foral* elections—for the provincial parliaments—that same year, *Ciudadanos* won 1.3% (14,440 votes) and VOX won 0.7% (7,807 votes) in the entire Basque Country.

242. While in general VOX obtained good results in the general election and the local election of 2019, this was far from the case in the Basque Country. Was this another chance occurrence? In the light of this text this was not something unusual: the main leader of Vox was born in Bilbao, but brought up in Álava.

Catalan Nationalism, International Politics, and Relations with the Basque Country and Galicia (1901–1936)

Giovanni C. Cattini

Introduction

The persistent presence of stateless Iberian nationalisms has very clearly been a matter of interest for international historiography since the latter half of the twentieth century. In this respect, the launch of a process of self-determination in Catalonia in 2012 has doubtless been a source of puzzlement for international public opinion, which has looked for the roots of the problem of Catalonia's fit within the Spanish state over longer timeframes. The present essay sets out to analyze the first third of the twentieth century, when a political movement that was openly Catalan nationalist rose to become a leading player in Catalonia's public life, gaining control of local institutions (town halls and provincial governments), devising an early formula for home rule under the *Mancomunita de Catalunya* (1914–1923) and achieving political autonomy during the years of the Second Spanish Republic under the *Generalitat de Catalunya* (1931–1939). The present study aims to trace the stages and political cultures of Catalan nationalism, the international models from which the movement drew inspiration in the early decades of the twentieth century and, lastly, its relationships with other stateless counterparts on the Iberian Peninsula, namely Basque and Galician nationalisms, which strove to create a stable alliance with Catalan nationalism.

Society, Economics, and Culture:
The Material Foundations of Catalan Nationalism

Since the latter half of the twentieth century, the historiography[1] that has analyzed the emergence of a political Catalan nationalism has emphasized a number of elements that help to understand the origins of the movement. First, Catalonia's strong industrialization led to the development of a social and economic structure that differed sharply from the remainder of agrarian Spain in the nineteenth century, which, with the exception of the Basque Country, did not experience similar processes of economic modernization. Against this backdrop, the Catalan oligarchy voiced demands and called for policies that were only partially listened to, and this gave rise over the long run to a rejection of the policies developed by the leading Spanish political parties. Second, the formation of the Spanish nation-state was pursued through the adoption of centralist models bent on uniformity that threatened the continued existence of case law and customs that were deeply rooted in various Spanish regions. In response, the regions put forward counterproposals for political decentralization to enable different identities to coexist within the Spanish nation. In addition, the influence of Romanticism and its upholding of autochthonous cultures and languages contributed to the rediscovery and potentialities of the Catalan, Basque, and Galician languages by a bourgeoisie that paradoxically had adopted the Spanish language as the language of culture and social advancement. Indeed, diglossia, as the reality of an urban oligarchy, made a show of knowing how to use the Spanish language in order to distance itself from the lower classes, which were overwhelmingly Catalan speakers.

These developments, together with the Catalan elite's inability to exert influence on the higher echelons of power in the Spanish capital, slowly led the oligarchy itself to gravitate away from the Spanish state's majority political parties and toward the notion of doing politics from and for Catalonia through a genuinely "Catalan nationalist" political party. This shift can also be explained by the appearance of an intellectual sector that grew proportionally larger and more diverse from one century to the next: while the great opinion makers continued to exist as they had since the eighteenth century, there also appeared an increasingly plentiful group dedicated to generating ideas suited to the specific moment, adapting big ideas to specific arenas and turning them into strategies. This group, which was made up of thinkers, literary figures, artists, and members of the liberal professions more broadly, used its cultural standing to claim a role in proposing "remedies" to the nation's "ills."[2] This was especially possible in regional spaces where the development of an industrial society was an established fact and it translated into the emergence of new professional sectors, the spread of administrative jobs in the private sector and the state's new structures, and an accelerating process of urbanization, which would bring Barcelona in thirty years to over a million inhabitants by 1931.

These middle classes were made up not only of small business owners, but also of a broad swath of liberal professions, such as lawyers, judges, and other posts in the legal system, physicians, pharmacists, veterinarians, architects, master builders or masons, and engineers. These liberal professions, which had risen by roughly 4.5% throughout the middle years of the nineteenth century, grew to an exponential level by the turn of the century: while there had been 6,800 liberal professionals in 1877, the figure climbed to 7,200 in 1887; 8,000 in 1900; 9,000 in 1910; and 9,500 in 1920. The trend for instructors in upper secondary-school (batxillerat) and university studies also increased, albeit more slowly, climbing from roughly 4,000 in 1887 to 4,600 in 1900 and over 6,000 in 1920. Regular clergy (also known as clerics regular), some of whom worked in education, also saw a sharp rise over the period under analysis.

In addition to the middle classes described above, it is important to note the growth and consolidation of office clerks, counter staff, and shop assistants connected to the spheres of commerce, banking, and the public administration. While the sector had 40,000 people in 1877, the figure rose to roughly 47,000 in 1887, 62,000 in 1900, and ultimately 128,000 in 1920. Lastly, within this broad and heterogeneous middle-class world, many individuals worked in the arts industries and entertainment world, giving shape to a new urban cultural milieu of major importance at the turn of the century.[3]

In this context, the city of Barcelona capitalized on a sweeping process of urbanization: from roughly 400,000 inhabitants in 1887, the city's population ballooned to 530,000 in 1900 after the incorporation of six adjoining municipalities, and it was nearly 590,000 in 1910 as a result of a growth process that would reach its high point in subsequent years, when the first major waves of migrants would push the city to over a million inhabitants by 1930. Significant growth rates were also the keynote feature of municipalities in the greater Barcelona metropolitan area, which benefited from a surge of industrial development in the Catalan capital: Sabadell went from 19,000 inhabitants in 1887 to 28,000 in 1910 and 46,000 in 1930; Terrassa grew from 13,000 in 1887 to 22,000 in 1910 and 40,000 in 1930; and Badalona underwent a nearly identical process, expanding from 13,000 to 21,000 to 44,400 inhabitants at the time of the proclamation of the Second Spanish Republic.

The distinctive growth of Barcelona's greater metropolitan area is a feature that cannot be extrapolated to the rest of Catalonia's municipalities, despite the obvious top-heaviness of the Catalan capital, because most of the main centers at provincial or district levels were characterized by demographic stability. For example, Girona grew from 15,000 to 16,000, Lleida from 22,000 to 24,000, Tortosa from 25,000 to 28,000, and Mataró from 18,000 to 19,000, while Reus actually declined from 29,000 to 25,000, Tarragona fell from 27,000 to 23,000, and other places like Manresa (approx. 22,000 inhabitants) and Igualada (approx. 10,000 inhabitants) remained stable in population terms.

Nonetheless, it is safe to say that the process of urbanization was a reality that affected a growing number of Catalonia's populace and prompted the growth of cities with over 10,000 inhabitants, especially in the greater Barcelona metropolitan area: whereas urban residents accounted for only 29% of Catalonia's total population in 1860, the figure rose to 42% in 1900 and 54% in 1930.[4]

The Politicization of Catalan Nationalism
at the End of the Nineteenth Century

Against this backdrop of economic and demographic growth, the historiography has stressed that the decade of the 1880s holds the key to the politicization of the Catalan nationalist movement. This politicization was made possible thanks, above all, to the tenacity of the republican thinker and activist Valentí Almirall (1841–1904),[5] who had stood out for his uncompromising federalist ideals since the six-year period known as the *Sexenio Democrático*, which came after the Glorious Revolution of 1868. Almirall pursued a wide-ranging program of Catalan nationalist political and civic organizing: he founded the Catalan language newspaper *Diari Català*[6] (1879–1881), in an effort to articulate a political discourse that would serve as a broad tent for the various sensibilities within the Catalan nationalist world, ranging from the literati at the publication *La Renaixensa* to the Vic-based Catholics at *La Veu del Montserrat* (1878). To this end, Almirall tempered his thinking, adapting it to a regionalist incrementalism that would per-mit the transformation of Spain into a composite state and thereby bring about its modernization and the acceptance of possible home rule for Catalonia.[7] This explains why he softened the democratic and republican aspects of his convictions, defending accidentalism in the forms of government, so that he could rally all the sectors of the het-erogeneous Catalan nationalist world to line up behind his discourse and then, together with them, pursue a policy of negotiating with the central authorities to secure an acknowledgement and strengthening of regional life within the state as a whole. In this context, Almirall convened the first Catalan nationalist congress [*Primer Congrés Catalanista*] to open in Barcelona on October 9, 1880.[8] Although the congress attendees had their differences, the event concluded a few weeks later with agreements to launch an academy of the Catalan lan-guage, to appoint a committee to preserve Catalan law and, above all, to found the Catalan Centre [*Centre Català*, 1882], the first association to have a clearly defined responsibility to engage in politics, although its original plan did not include standing in elections. The Catalan Centre organized the second Catalan nationalist congress [*Segon Congrés Catalanista*] in June 1883. This time, the event was scheduled to conclude its sessions in autumn of that year, but it was unable to do so because of the uprising of republicans in support of Manuel Ruiz Zorrilla: the state of siege and the strained political climate at the time advised against carrying on. Nor should be it forgotten that many of the participants in the congress were close to the insurgents or that the Federal Republican Party had prepared a draft constitution for the

Catalan state in May of that same 1883. It was a time that coincided with a revival of Federal Republican forces throughout Spain, but it also made clear the importance of the Catalan question in beginning to assume on the agenda of the non-dynastic parties.

Nonetheless, the Catalan Centre was gradually expanding its capacity to interact with the most important associations in Catalonia. For example, the Catalan Centre took charge of the meeting of business and cultural associations at the *Llotja*, Barcelona's ancient exchange building, in January 1885, and led the Catalan committee that delivered the *Memorial de Greuges*, a declaration of grievances, directly to Alfonso XII in March of that year. The speaker for the committee that submitted the text to the king was Valentí Almirall, the leader of the Catalan Centre. The declaration denounced the negative effects of centralism and standardization on the entirety of Spanish society, which had consequently been unable to escape secular decline. Catalan discontent was further aggravated by free-trade agreements, which proved detrimental to industrial interests, and by maneuverings against Catalonia's homegrown legal code. The *Memorial de Greuges* proposed that Alfonso XII intervene in defense of Catalan interests, halting the government's measures in accordance with the Constitution of 1876, which attributed a shared sovereignty between Crown and Parliament [*Cortes*]. In the long run, the *Memorial de Greuges* also defended a hypothetical decentralization of the Spanish state, at the top of which the king would rule according to the example set by the Aragonese Confederation. The proposal had no chance of success, but the uproar in the state's official media was such that the ultimate winner proved to be the cause to politicize Catalan nationalism: the *Memorial de Greuges* would go down in history as the first victory in Catalonia's struggle to advance its claims.[9]

At that point, Valentí Almirall took on a leading role within the new politics of Catalan nationalism, publishing short treatises, articles, and books, most notably *Lo Catalanisme*,[10] in order to lay the scientific groundwork for Catalonia's demands. Almirall's book *Lo Catalanisme* set forth the arguments that would serve as the basis for Catalan nationalism, emphasising what the author called the "scientific foundations of particularism" ["*fonaments científics del particularisme*"] as well as practical solutions to address Catalonia's fit within the Spanish state. Along these lines, Almirall reviewed the various forms of composite states then in existence and threw his support behind the federal system, which was possible both in a republic and in a monarchy.

Notably, only a few weeks before the publication of *Lo Catalanisme*, Almirall had experienced abject failure when the first-ever Catalan nationalist candidacy for the Spanish Parliament went down to defeat.[11] What the failure of Almirall's political project demonstrated to Catalan nationalists was the consolidation of the political order of the moment and, consequently, of the dynastic parties in Catalonia, in the second decade of the Bourbon Restoration. What was also clear, however, was the difficulty of the Catalan nationalists to achieve their own political space as well as the depressed state of their "vital forces" within Catalonia. One of the most striking consequences of the Catalan Centre's election defeat was a growing opposition to Almirall from the contributors to *La Renaixensa* and from university students gathered around the *Centre Escolar Catalanista*, a Catalan nationalist student group. After a number of reciprocal accusations, the dissidents (who numbered roughly 40% of the Catalan Centre's membership) left to found the League of Catalonia [*Lliga de Catalunya*], a name chosen in clear allusion to the Irish cause.[12]

In any event, Catalan political debate at the close of the 1880s revolved around interpretations of the Spanish civil code. This was because the framework law of May 11, 1888, which was limited in scope to Castile and Andalusia, nevertheless posed a serious threat to those regions that possessed their own legal systems based on ancient *fueros*, or privileges. Specifically, Articles 12 and 15 of the proposed legislation would be made applicable in any case not provided for in the *fuero*-based legal codes. The Spanish state's attempted standardization set off alarms in Catalan society. A host of organizations prepared reports to submit to the government and a groundswell of demonstrations in defense of Catalan law swept through the villages and district capitals of all Catalonia (as well as Aragon, the Balearic Islands, Galicia, Navarre, and the Basque Country), resulting in the significant spreading of Catalan nationalist ideas throughout Catalonia. The demonstrations and protests prompted José Canalejas, the new minister for

Grace and Justice, to amend the controversial articles, resulting in what the young politician Narcís Verdaguer defined in a famous tract as "the first victory of Catalan nationalism" [*"la primera victòria del catalanisme"*].[13]

In the autumn of 1890, the world of Catalan nationalism saw an important passing of the torch when, for the first time, the young law student Enric Prat de la Riba (1870–1917) gave a speech that would serve as one of the most important theoretical planks of contemporary Catalan nationalism. Speaking as president of the university student association *Centre Escolar Catalanista*, Prat drew a sharp distinction between nation and patria or homeland and state. In other words, he made it clear for the first time, and in a compelling manner, that "Catalonia was the only homeland of the Catalans" [*"Catalunya era l'única pàtria dels Catalans"*], while Spain was "but an indicative name of a geographical division, like Europe" [*"sols un nom indicatiu d'una divisió geogràfica, com ho és Europa"*], and that it was not "a nation, but a state" [*"una nació, sinó un Estat"*]. From then to the end of his life, Prat de la Riba kept the substance of his message on the key concept of the Catalans' homeland practically unchanged, despite any adjustments made in response to circumstances. Indeed, he would reiterate it in his seminal work *La nacionalitat catalana* (1906) [in English, *The Catalan Nationality*]. Ultimately, Prat's first address transcended its moment by laying the groundwork for modern Catalan nationalism.[14]

In his 1890 speech, Prat de la Riba also defended the essence of Catalonia as a subject nation, comparing it to Poland, Ireland, and other European nations without a state (including the Basque Country and Galicia). He decried the falsely proclaimed equality of Spanish law, because that law discriminated against Catalonia's language, its own legal system, and the output of its firms, which did not benefit from the protection of customs tariffs that, by contrast, safeguarded Spain's grain producers.

A year and a half later, in March 1892, the first meeting of the Catalan Nationalist Union [*Unió Catalanista*, 1890][15] was held in the city of Manresa. The purpose of the gathering was to draft the now-famous foundational principles for a Catalan regional constitution [known, in Catalan, as the *Bases per a la Constitució Regional*

Catalana], which was the first proposal put forward from Catalonia to enact an asymmetric reform of the state in order to ensure Catalonia's autonomy within the unity of Spain. As a political program, the manifesto, which went down in history as the *Bases de Manresa*, was a milestone in nineteenth-century Catalan nationalism.[16] However, it is also important to drive home that the *Bases de Manresa*, in reality, were still very much an embryonic project with a set of programmatic principles that would have to be fleshed out in greater detail in the years to come. Whatever their shortcomings, the Manresa principles clearly registered, on the Spanish political agenda, that a portion of Catalonia was mobilizing, making its voice distinctive from mobilizations in the 1880s. The *Bases de Manresa* proposed wide-ranging home rule for Catalonia with a local parliament elected by organic suffrage, the protection of its legal and linguistic features, and the introduction of a new territorial division based on districts (known as *comarques*) and municipalities in contrast to the provincial division of 1833. In short, the Manresa manifesto straddled a declaration of principles to carry out proselytism for the cause of Catalan nationalism and a fuzzy notion of Catalan constitutionalism.

In subsequent years, the Catalan Nationalist Union convened assemblies all across Catalonia in order to give concrete form to its program, spread the formation of new associations throughout the territory, and foster the creation of a Catalan language press in the various districts. After Manresa, notable meetings took place in Reus (1893), Balaguer (1894), Olot (1895), and Girona (1897). Because of this activism, more than a hundred Catalan nationalist organizations sprang into existence between 1890 and 1910, and some of the leading institutions in Catalan civil society became "Catalanized." In this respect, the "Catalan nationalist assault" was punctuated by two landmark events that occurred in 1895: first, the Catalan nationalist poet and dramatist Àngel Guimerà ascended to the presidency of the Barcelona Athenaeum [*Ateneu Barcelonès*], accompanied by the writer and poet Joan Maragall in the role of secretary; and second, the jurist Joan Josep Permanyer became president of the Academy of Jurisprudence and Legislation [*Acadèmia de Jurisprudència i Legislació*] in the Catalan capital.[17] Notably, Guimerà's inaugural speech raised a great uproar because it marked the first time that the Catalan language had been used in a presidential address to open the year. Never before had the country's own language been employed at the Barcelona Athenaeum and Guimerà's action sparked outrage from a large number of members who understood that the institution's official language was Spanish, just as it was in all other representative bodies of the state, and that consequently all events should be held in Spanish. The outcry led some to cancel their membership in protest, but it also prompted the institution's new board, led by Valentí Almirall with Enric Prat de la Riba as secretary, to overhaul the statutes to ensure the full equality of Catalan and Spanish languages within the Barcelona Athenaeum. Ultimately, the change was approved by a vast majority of the members. Beyond this, the first minutes of a governing body to be written in Catalan came out of a meeting at the Academy of Jurisprudence and Legislation on September 21, 1896, under the presidency of the Catalan nationalist jurist Joan Josep Permanyer, one of the chief authors of the *Bases de Manresa*.[18] Nevertheless, the road toward normalization of the use of Catalan was not a straightforward one. This is apparent from the address of Permanyer himself when, as president of the institution in 1896, he spoke out in favor of the Catalinization of all legal life in Catalonia. And the reply from the authorities of the Spanish state was an unwavering *no*.

International Examples and Alliances for the Creation of a Decentralized Spain

The legacy of the Catalan nationalist movement's politicization lay in the creation of a political culture that blended a Catalan nationalist rhetoric with the adoption of an asymmetric federalism. It was focused on achieving an autonomous government with a parliament legislating all areas of public life, except for international security and the printing of currency and minting of coinage, which would remain as powers of the central state. At the time, the highest aspiration shared by Catalan nationalist leaders, as well as many leaders of other stateless nationalities, was to be like the Hungarians per the dual monarchy of the Austro-Hungarian Empire that had emerged after Austrian defeat at the hands of the Prussians in 1866. The Hungarians held up an enormously suggestive mirror because the dual monarchy had risen from the ashes of an empire notorious for its centralism and despotism: the compromise of 1867 had made the dual monarchy possible, with the Austrians and Hungarians sharing only an emperor-king, foreign affairs, defense, and certain joint costs. As an example, this exerted a hugely seductive power over Catalans who aspired to be Hungary within the Kingdom of Spain. Indeed, they interpreted the modern Austro-Hungarian Empire as a reincarnation of the Spanish Habsburg monarchy, when the Crowns of Castile and Aragon had retained their own distinctive features while acting in a spirit of cooperation under the same monarch.[19] During the Universal Exposition of 1888 in Barcelona, the League of Catalonia prepared a summary of the points in the *Memorial de Greuges* of 1885, and presented it to Maria Cristina of Austria, a Habsburg and the widow of Alfonso XII, who had died in 1886. This document would become known as the "Message to the Queen Regent" [*Missatge a la Reina Regent*], and what it called for was precisely the introduction of a dual system in which Catalonia could become the Hungary of Spain. No less important were the examples of the Irish parliamentary struggle to achieve home rule, illustrated by the impact of the activities of the Irish leader Charles Parnell between 1880 and 1890, and the broad grassroots associations of the Czech model, especially the groups in the Sokol movement: the Sokol blending of political activism and physical exercise would be followed in Catalonia with the founding in 1928 of the Palestra Association by Josep M. Batista i Roca (1895–1978).

As for Catalan nationalism's relations with the Galician and Basque nationalist movements, they can be divided into cultural and political types, though these distinctions are sometimes quite evanescent as in the case of Manuel Murguía, whose activism ranged from literature to history and politics. Cultural relations appeared to firm up around the spread and occasional translation of authors writing in the Galician and Basque traditions, such as the aforementioned Manuel Murguía and his fellow Galicians Eduardo Pondal, Rosalía de Castro, and Manuel Curros Enríquez, or their Basque counterparts José María de Iparraguirre and Claudio de Otaegui, to name but a few. The budding political relations were fueled by nationalists connected to the

League of Catalonia and by the distinguished figures who published a journal called *La España Regional*, which set out to rethink the structure of the state according to the historical nationalities that were identified with Catalonia, Castile, the Basque Country, and Galicia. The jurist Josep Pella i Forgas (1852–1918), who was a trailblazer in the comparative study of regionalist movements seeking redress, focused on the European level, including Spain, and examined their particular linguistic cultural characteristics, because, as he wrote, "the language is a dearer treasure than the freedoms and constitutions of peoples, according to the Hungarians, because constitutions can be restored, but not a language, which is the very essence of nationality." ["*el idioma es un tesoro más precioso que las libertades y constituciones de los pueblos, dicen los húngaros, porque las constituciones pueden restablecerse, y no el idioma, que es la misma nacionalidad.*"][20]

In this context, the end of the century witnessed further repeated efforts from the Galicians mentioned above, Manuel Murguía, Aureliano J. Pereira, Aurelio Ribalta, and Alfred Brañas, plus from the Basques Fidel de Sagarminaga, Eduardo de Velasco, and Aristides Artiñano Juan Iturralde, and the Navarrese Basque Arturo Campión.[21] Among all the non-Catalan writers, it was doubtless the Galician jurist Alfred Brañas who had the deepest influence on Catalan circles and stayed most closely in contact. Brañas's popularity was such that he was invited to the *Jocs Florals* literary contest in 1893. To express his gratitude, Brañas gave an address on the fellowship of Galicia and Catalonia, united against the oppression of the centralist state. His speech, as the editor of the *La España Regional* wrote, enraged General Martínez Campos, "who made a show of his displeasure" ["*quien hizo ostentación de su disgusto*"].[22] On his visit to Barcelona, Brañas was also invited to the Catalan employers association *Foment del Treball Nacional* to give a talk on regionalist movements in Northern Europe from Ireland to Scotland and Norway, without neglecting to remark on the commonality of their demands with the demands of Galicia, Catalonia, the Basque Country, and Navarre.[23] Alfred Brañas would have a lasting impact on figures like Enric Prat de la Riba and Francesc Cambó, two of the foremost conservative Catalan nationalist politicians of the first third of the twentieth century.[24]

Local Politics and Catalan Nationalism (1898–1914)

The disaster of 1898, which saw Spain lose the last of its colonies, led
to a severe crisis in the public coffers, but also prompted a return of
Catalan capital that had hitherto been invested in the Spanish West
Indies and now provided an important injection of capital into Catalan
industry. The events of 1898 radicalized the world of Catalan nationalism. A new message was sent to the queen regent and two manifestos
appeared: *Als Catalans* ["To the Catalans"] and *Al Poble de Catalunya* ["To the People of Catalonia"]. In September 1899, the Catalan
National Centre [*Centre Nacional Català*, or CNC] was founded by
a group linked to the charismatic lawyer Prat de la Riba, one of the
leading lights in Catalan nationalism of the period. Amid the crisis,
two major events had a crucial effect on the definition of the Catalan
political context: the first was a call for a new economic arrangement
known as the *Concert Econòmic*, which General Polavieja's eventual
rise to power in Madrid seemed to make possible, while the second
was a tax protest movement known as the *Tancament de Caixes*, which
occurred when the proposed economic arrangement fell through and,
even worse, the Villaverde budget increased the tax burden (1899).
In response to the tax hikes, Catalan merchants refused to pay. They
locked their cash boxes, tensions escalated sharply, and the matter
ended in the imprisonment of a number of merchants and the resignation of Barcelona's mayor Dr. Bartomeu Robert, who stepped down
in solidarity with the tax strikers. Prat de la Riba grasped the changing
times and the need to distance himself from the more dogmatic positions of the apolitical members of the Catalan Nationalist Union who
opposed participation in elections. A meeting of minds between the
CNC and businesspeople in the Regionalist Union [*Unió Regionalista*],
which had been created out of the remnants of the movement that supported General Polavieja in Catalonia, led to the proposal of a joint
slate for the elections of May 1901. Known as the candidacy of the
"four presidents," the list was headed by Albert Rusiñol, former president of the *Foment del Treball Nacional* (the employers association
that brought together most of the Catalan businesses of the period),
and also included the former Barcelona mayor Dr. Bartomeu Robert,

who now served as president of the Economic Society of Friends of the Country [*Societat Econòmica d'Amics del País*]; the architect Lluís Domènech Muntaner, former president of the Barcelona Athenaeum; and Sebastià Torres, president of the protectionist business association *Lliga de Defensa Industrial i Comercial Catalana*. The joint slate was an unqualified success, securing the election of all four presidents and prompting the birth of a new political party, the Regionalist League [*Lliga Regionalista*], which would play a crucial role in all of Catalan public life until 1931.[25]

The new Regionalist League, with its cadre of modern political figures, shifted Catalan politics away from the political order of the Bourbon Restoration, in which the dynastic parties held power. Within a few years, the leading actors in Catalonia were a right-wing Catalan nationalist party (the Regionalist League), left-wing republican Catalan nationalist parties (the *Centre Nacionalista Republicà* and the *Unió Federal Nacionalista Republicana*), and a Spanish nationalist republican party (the *Partido Republicano Radical*, or PRR). The final grouping became known as the Lerrouxists (after their leader Alejandro Lerroux), and the greater part of the historiography[26] takes the view that one of the PRR's functions was to undercut the impact of Catalan nationalism among the working classes. At this point, Catalan nationalist demands were no longer confined to intellectual coteries, but stood at the very heart of social and political life.

The politicization of the Catalan nationalist movement and the attainment of ever greater shares of political power at the local level, both in town halls and in provincial governments, and at the state level, with representation in the Spanish Parliament in Madrid, led the Regionalist League to articulate its discourse differently from the approach followed by Catalan nationalists in the closing decades of the nineteenth century.[27] The demands of peoples for a state were not shunted into the background, but they did not carry the same weight as they had in earlier periods, precisely because politics and management of the public administration became the central focus. The Regionalist League, which was the prime Catalan nationalist political force until the dictatorship of Primo de Rivera (1923–1930), was shaped into a modern mass party with a hierarchical organization, at the top of which stood a political action committee, a small circle that most notably included Enric Prat de la Riba, Lluís Duran i Ventosa (1870–1954), and Francesc Cambó (1876–1947). Prat was the master weaver of the political relationships that would be needed to guide the restoration of Catalan home rule, while Duran was the mastermind of regionalist theory, and Cambó was the master political organizer and member of parliament in Madrid for the conservative wing of Catalan nationalism. The political rhetoric of the Regionalist League focused on a critique of the centralism of the Spanish state, the petty tyranny of local bosses known as *caciques*, the exclusion of the Catalan oligarchy from the center of power, and the need for the party's presence to carry through a reform and regeneration of the state. The Regionalist League campaigned for the decentralization of the state in order to secure Catalonia's autonomy in such a way that it would not compromise Spain's national unity. Indeed, the Regionalist League sought to have an influence on the central authorities and was never a pro-independence party. From the viewpoint of party propaganda, the daily newspaper *La Veu de Catalunya* was the mouthpiece used by Prat and Cambó to circulate their ideas and political pragmatism, and it offered an outlet where Catalan intellectuals could publish articles on widely varied aspects of the culture of their times.[28]

With joint action orchestrated from Catalonia by Prat and from Madrid by Cambó, the Regionalist League succeeded in pushing through a law to enable Spain's provinces to reorganize into larger *mancomunitats* [in Spanish, *mancomunidades*], permitting the concentration of the powers of provincial governments into a regional government. The legislation restored a modicum of home rule under the government of the *Mancomunitat de Catalunya* in 1914 at a time when the passage of home rule for Ireland appeared imminent, until World War I halted the process. At the cultural level, the political elite of Catalan regionalism was able to connect with a new generation of intellectuals who forged a far-reaching cultural politics in the name of a budding *Noucentisme* movement. *Noucentisme* propounded elite activity by intellectuals and gave support to the political activity of Prat de la Riba, first in the provincial government of Barcelona and later in the *Mancomunitat de Catalunya*. The focal point of their nationalism lay in their support for the language and its renewal, and they believed that the main driver of cultural nationalization and the renewal of institutions should be the activity of intellectuals. Eugeni d'Ors (1881–1954) symbolized the commitment of the new generation of intellectuals in the *Noucentisme* movement, who took part in the regionalist modernizing program and defined its space, calling for new ways to understand the nation based on civility and an ethos of responsibility, culture, Mediterreanean-ness, continuity, youth, the spirit of the twentieth century, and so on. All working together, young intellectuals and professionals (e.g., educators, physicians, economists, urban planners, architects, and more) strove for the regeneration of Spain starting in Catalonia.[29]

The Cultural Politics of the Catalan Nationalist Movement and Its Relations with Basques and Galicians

During the opening decade of the twentieth century, the main histori-cal, cultural, and symbolic reference points became well established in a cross-class Catalan nationalist movement that solidified its historicist discourse, citing the birth of the Catalan nation in its medieval glories and justifying its struggle on the basis of the freedoms lost after Catalan defeat in the War of the Spanish Succession in 1714. In these years, the Catalan nationalist movement adopted the *Senyera*, with its four red bars on a yellow field as the flag of Catalonia, selected *Els Segadors* [the song of "The Reapers"] as the national anthem, and made September 11 into Catalonia's national day.[30]

The four-bar *Senyera* won out over the flags of St. George and St. Eulalia at the end of the nineteenth century when it started being flown at all Catalan nationalist events and events held in defense of Catalonia's economic and/or legal interests. In 1896, the *Cant de la Senyera* was first sung by the *Orfeó Català* choral group in a ceremony to bless the flag. The song, featuring lyrics penned by the poet Joan Maragall (1860–1911) and music composed by Lluís Millet (1867–1941), would confirm the *Senyera* as the quintessential national flag of the Catalans. In the first decade of the twentieth century, every political demonstration was characterized by the presence of the *Senyera* in that role.[31] The anthem *Els Segadors*, whose origins dated back to a popular song at the time of the Catalan revolt against the troops of

Felipe IV in 1640, won out over other patriotic compositions, such as the abovementioned *Cant de la Senyera* by the poet Joan Maragall. The popularization of the song had begun in 1893 when the *Orfeó Català* added it to the group's repertory, though it would take some years before it became firmly established as the Catalan national anthem. From 1897, a whole host of Catalan nationalist organizations began to use *Els Segadors* systematically, and the *Orfeó Català* itself decided to conclude its concerts with the song. Particularly effective was an abbreviated version crafted by Emili Guanyavents (1899), which made it easier for people to learn the lyrics. From the closing years of the nineteenth century, Catalan nationalist organizations also began to use the song in the traditional laying of floral wreaths at the monument to Rafael Casanova each September 11 to commemorate the date in 1714 when Barcelona fell to the Bourbon troops of Felipe V and the secular institutions of Catalan home rule were abolished. Even so, the song did not have an easy life because the Spanish authorities regarded its combative lyrics as a provocation to Spain. As a result, the authorities took repeated action to ban its performance.[32]

In the same period, the date of September 11 became firmly set as a unifying holiday focused on Catalan demands and one of the most telling examples of contemporary Catalan nationalism.[33] This occurred in spite of the fact that the War of the Spanish Succession had not been one of the major subjects in the works of the writers, historians, and intellectuals behind the Catalan Renaissance, which had focused more on the splendors of the medieval saga of the Crown of Aragon. The first attempts to celebrate September 11 took place around 1886, but the turning point came in 1901, when thirty young members of the *Associació Catalunya i Avant* were arrested for laying floral wreaths at the statue of Rafael Casanova on the appointed day. The event acted as a catalyst to mobilize the public and the Regionalist League's members of parliament, and their mobilization was to prove crucial in persuading the authorities to release the detainees on September 13. On September 15, a large civic demonstration marched through the streets of Barcelona to the statue of Casanova to lay a new floral wreath in tribute. The event proved a success, drawing on the participation of over ten thousand people, and the commemoration of the date of

September 11 became fixed in the collective imagination as the most important anniversary in Catalonia's history.

In terms of the relations between Catalan, Basque, and Galician nationalisms, another landmark event took place in Barcelona in November 1905. Some three-hundred officers in the Barcelona garrison attacked and destroyed the newsrooms and printing facilities of the satirical magazine ¡Cu-Cut! and *La Veu de Catalunya*. The officers claimed to be acting in response to the effrontery of a cartoon that had ridiculed them. The events triggered an enormous outcry, and the Catalan nationalist members of parliament in Madrid spoke out in protest. However, the Spanish Parliament responded by condemning the Catalan nationalists and passing a new law known as the *Ley de Jurisdicciones*, which put crimes against the homeland and its symbols under military jurisdiction. Catalan members of parliament and a few others (such as the old Spanish republican Nicolás Salmerón) walked out of the chamber in protest. In Catalonia, a decision was taken to form an electoral coalition bringing together every Catalan political party except the republican Lerrouxists. Adopting the name of Catalan Solidarity [*Solidaritat Catalana*], the coalition achieved their first triumph in the provincial elections of March 1906. At that point, the coalition agreed on a common platform in support of the regeneration of Spain, and decentralization and repeal of the *Ley de Jurisdicciones*. (This became known as the Tivoli program, after the Barcelona theater where the members met.) In the general election of April 1907, Catalan Solidarity enjoyed enormous success, winning forty-one of the forty-four seats in play across Catalonia with a turnout of 70% of the electorate (an unprecedented level that would not be repeated until the Second Republic).

In these years, contacts with the Galician and Basque nationalists continued. The Galicians, who did not have a movement similar to the Regionalist League, were nevertheless absorbing the Catalans' rhetoric and went on to found the Galician Solidarity party [*Solidaridad Gallega*] in 1907. While Galician Solidarity gained significant wins at the provincial level in A Coruña and Lugo, it did not achieve a modernization of Galician political life similar to its Catalan counterpart and consequently failed to consolidate its political program. That said, the experience proved very important as a precursor to later Galician nationalism.[34] As is often recalled, however, the Basque case did feature a coalition known as the *Liga Foral Autonomista*. Founded in 1904 and based in the province of Gipuzkoa, the coalition was a pioneer in forming a unified platform in defense of a mutual economic arrangement, although it does not appear to have had an influence on the Catalan regionalists. In any event, upon the death of Sabino Arana, father of the Basque Nationalist Party (PNV), Arana's successor, Ángel Zabala, rejected an alliance with the *Liga Foral Autonomista* because he regarded it as "Spanish nationalist" and kept the PNV out of the coalition in spite of its successes in 1905. With the resounding victory of Catalan Solidarity two years later, the problems of Basque solidarity returned to the center of the debate. Sectors of the clergy, however, prevailed in ensuring that no alliance was formed between "the followers of Christ and those of Satan," making it impossible to bring about solidarity in the Basque Country along the same lines as in Catalonia.[35] The Galician and Basque cases served an internal function in consolidating the idea that the regeneration of Spain remained possible through the action of its historical nations, whose reawakening was crucial to the achievement of the task.

The Workers' Movement and Catalan Nationalism

Catalan Solidarity ran aground in the summer of 1909, when the uprising against the war in Africa culminated in what is known as the "Tragic Week" ["*Setmana tràgica*"],[36] and it became clear that the regionalist political program still had to come to terms with the social question. In this context, it must be remembered that the first decade of the twentieth century had been characterized by various attempts to reorganize the workers' movement, which had been dismantled in the previous decade when the government cracked down on anarchist terrorism. The first attempt at reviving the labor unions had come about with the first general strike of the twentieth century, which lasted for a full week in Barcelona in February 1902. Workers had demanded a reduction in the working day from ten hours to nine hours, but the strike failed because of the intransigence of the employers association, which refused to give ground and instead called on law enforcement to crush the strike.[37] As a consequence of the strike's failure, the socialist General Union of Workers [*Unión General de Trabajadores*, or UGT], which had not backed the strike, lost nearly all of its support in Catalonia. Also, the credibility of the cross-class Regionalist League was seriously undermined in the eyes of workers because of its support for the employers. In those initial years of the twentieth century, the propaganda of Alejandro Lerroux, an Andalusian journalist living in Barcelona since 1901, attracted many followers from the lower classes of Barcelona because of his revolutionary radicalism and the accusations he hurled at employers, whom he branded as Catalan nationalists and exploiters of the working class. In addition, Lerroux knew how to create a broad base of popular support that was built on preexisting circles of sociability, such as Catalonia's athenaeums and republican centers, which he skillfully reorganized to keep himself at the center of Catalan politics for nearly a decade. Lerroux's success can be explained by the inability of those in the Catalan nationalist left to organize a political force that was viewed as credible by Catalonia's lower classes.[38]

In the end, it was precisely the organizing of the workers' movement that wrested support from Lerroux. The first step in union organizing occurred under the same circumstances as the rise of Catalan Solidarity, when Barcelona workers' associations issued a call for workers' solidarity in the summer of 1907 in order to demand the right to strike and to implement a reduction in the working day to eight hours. The socialists, anarchists, and republicans in Barcelona's working classes were the driving force behind the first congress of Workers' Solidarity [*Solidaritat Obrera*], which took place in 1908 and grew to include every Catalan workers' association. The gathering spurred the creation of a regional resistance confederation known as the *Confederació Regional de Caixes de Resistència—Solidaritat Obrera*. The new body's mouthpiece was the daily newspaper *Workers' Solidarity* [*Solidaridad Obrera*], whose life was characterized by suspensions and bans, making it a prime example of the precariousness and repression suffered by the Catalan workers' movement in the first third of the twentieth century.[39] This organizing of the workers' movement ground to a halt in the wake of the Tragic Week, the above-mentioned antimilitarist revolt with its revolutionary and anti-clerical overtones, which had broken out in Barcelona and other urban centers of Catalonia and been put down in a brutal crackdown. Dozens of rationalist and freethinking schools were shut, hundreds of people were thrown in prison, and five men were sentenced to death, prominent among them being the distinguished anarchist thinker and educator Francesc Ferrer i Guàrdia.[40] In the following year, however, the original instigators of Workers' Solidarity succeeded in holding their second congress, at which the attendees decided to found a new statewide trade union under the name of the National Confederation of Labour [Confederació Nacional del Treball, or CNT] with a clear revolutionary syndicalist orientation. The first congress of the new CNT took place in Barcelona in September 1911, but it ran into trouble from the outset because the Spanish government immediately outlawed it.[41] The CNT was not created with the intention of supplanting the socialist UGT labor union, but rather to move toward a unified working class, a complex goal and one that was achieved only for brief periods in the subsequent twenty years.

The *Mancomunitat de Catalunya* and the Campaign for Catalan Autonomy in 1918

The abovementioned effects of the Tragic Week (1909) led to the disbanding of Catalan Solidarity and a deepening of the divisions among the political forces that had formed the party. The republican Catalan nationalists, who had split off from the Regionalist League in 1904 and set up the Republican Nationalist Centre [Centre Nacionalista Republicà] in 1905, seized on the moment to launch a new political party, the Republican Nationalist Federal Union [Unió Federal Nacionalista Republicana], which enjoyed fleeting success in the elections of 1910. However, it was unable to grab a foothold and remained marginal in relation to the Regionalist League[42] which, by contrast, maintained its centrality and, in 1912 and 1913, capitalized on the struggle in the Spanish Parliament to spearhead a decentralization of the state, which it achieved in December 1913 when a decree on territorial reorganization into *mancomunidades* was signed into law by the conservative Eduardo Dato. As noted earlier, the new decree allowed the provincial governments of a region to work together, and the provincial governments of Catalonia quickly took advantage of the option. In April 1914, they created the *Mancomunitat de Catalunya* presided over by Enric Prat de la Riba. In the following years, the *Mancomunitat* spent its paltry budgets on setting up cultural and educational institutions, building infrastructure, and creating services, all with the aim of giving Catalonia a national structure, transforming the territory into a kind of first "region-state." The program of the *Mancomunitat* can be summarized in a remark made by Enric Prat de la Riba himself, when he proposed furnishing every municipality in Catalonia with a highway or access road, telephone lines, a public school, and a public library in every district.[43]

Indeed, Prat had started to give concrete shape to his program when he won the presidency of the government of the Barcelona province [*Diputació de Barcelona*] in 1906. His first step had been to create, in 1907, the Institute for Catalan Studies [*Institut d'Estudis Catalans*], which was at the forefront of his cultural project and became the most prestigious public institution in Catalonia after the establishment of the *Mancomunitat*. In this vein, the Institute for Catalan Studies was intended to address three major challenges for the normalization of Catalan culture. First, it was the best tool to defend Catalan culture from those more developed in the immediate vicinity, such as the Spanish and French cultures (which counted on the resources of their respective states). Second, it was the indisputable tool to achieve the internal cohesion of the Catalan scientific community. And third, it was needed by them to obtain visibility and recognition internationally.[44]

The years that followed were marked by a relentless process of state-building. The first element was the acculturation and preparation of Catalan society through the founding of specialized schools like the *Escola Elemental del Treball*, which was led by socialist Rafael Campalans as headmaster and helped to train hundreds and hundreds of young workers, and the *Escola Superior d'Agricultura*, which had a library, technical agricultural services and livestock, as well as a committee for reforestation. In the same vein, schools were set up for business studies, the trades, civil service in local government, nursing, and the performing arts. (These were called *Escolas d'Estudis Comercials*, the *Escola Superior de Bells Oficis*, the *Escola de Funcionaris d'Administració Local,* the *Escola d'Infermeres Auxiliars de Medicina,* and the *Escola Catalana d'Art Dramàtic.*) To provide support for the spread of culture, the *Mancomunitat de Catalunya* also founded public libraries, which were the first of their kind in the Spanish state, and it appointed civil servants trained in library sciences at the *Escola de Bibliotecàries.* Prat de la Riba, Eugeni d'Ors, and Jordi Rubió i Balaguer designed a network of libraries that worked in a coordinated manner to transmit the core values of Catalan culture.[45] The National Library of Catalonia opened its doors in 1914 with the intention of being the driving force for the entire future Catalan library system. The same goal of acculturation also explains the creation, in 1914, of the Institute for General Education [*Institut d'Educació General*], which was conceived as an autonomous body for the moral, civic, and hygienic training of adults.[46]

While these efforts went ahead, Prat de la Riba also promoted training for the specialized services and offices needed to provide support for the governmental activity, first of the provincial government [*Diputació de Barcelona*] and then of the larger *Mancomunitat.* They included services for the conservation of monuments, for excavations, and for geographical and geological maps of Catalonia (all undertaken in conjunction with the history and archaeology section and the science section of the Institute for Catalan Studies), as well as a health-care service, an office of legal affairs, a social policy service, and a social museum. These undertakings were enough to give rise, in the words of Jaume Bofill i Mates, to the myth of Prat as master [*"Prat-Mestre"*], or Prat as the hub of a wheel [*"Prat-Radial"*]. In other words, Prat took on the image of a politician who had successfully united a majority of the intellectual and professional sectors of Catalonia around a common project. It is especially important to emphasize Prat's "national culturism," which put Catalonia's culture at the core of his idea of state-building regenerationism and thereby sought to integrate the bourgeoisie and the working classes through "economic and social nationalisation" [*"nacionalització econòmica i social"*].[47]

The *Mancomunitat de Catalunya* was created only months before Europe descended into a spiral that would lead to World War I and that would, despite Spain's neutrality, open deep divisions throughout the state between sectors who backed the Allies and sectors who were pro-German. In any event, Catalan industrial production and its economy in general benefited from the new state of affairs. Toward the end of the war, however, international politics was to have a profound impact on Catalonia. The Easter Rising in Ireland in 1916 and the Russian Revolution in 1917 showed clearly that nothing in world politics would ever be the same, now that it was grasped for the first time, and that taking up arms could achieve goals that had hitherto been regarded as impossible.

Catalan nationalist intellectuals and writers who had been students of international politics in other decades, such as the prominent Antoni Rovira i Virgili (1882–1949), were pushed aside when the Easter Rising broke out in Dublin in 1916. From that moment onwards, new Catalan nationalist intellectual sectors rose up to capitalize on the mirror of Ireland, but without success. World War I sent an earthquake through the world of Catalan nationalism, breaking the mirror of the Austro-Hungarian Empire and its dual monarchy once and for all. Then, with US President Woodrow Wilson's announcement of his fourteen points, a new era opened under a banner calling for the recognition of self-determination.

On the political terrain, the Regionalist League worked throughout the years of World War I to secure benefits for the Catalan economy. For example, they assisted exports through the granting of a tariff-free port for Barcelona. However, their efforts fell short because of the intransigence of the great landowners elsewhere in the state. The reactionary turn of Spanish politics, with the repeated closure of parliament throughout the period under analysis, prompted the Regionalist League to try leading an alternative parliamentary assembly. They came up with the idea of calling all of Catalonia's members of parliament to a meeting in Barcelona on July 5, 1917. Nearly every member of parliament elected in Catalonia took part, despite their political differences, and they agreed that, to achieve political regeneration, it would be necessary to restructure the state to grant autonomy to Catalonia and any other region that wanted it and to convene a constituent assembly at the parliament in Madrid or, if not possible, to call all of Spain's members of parliament and senators to another assembly elsewhere. Prime Minister Dato did not wish to make any concessions, and he disbanded the second assembly of parliamentarians, which took place in Barcelona on the following July 19 with the additional presence of Spanish republican and socialist members of parliament. The revolutionary general strike of August 1917, however, also brought a sharp turnabout in the movement led by the Regionalist League, which threw its support behind the oligarchy out of a fear of social revolution: in November, a national unity government was formed under the premiership of the liberal Manuel García Prieto, with the presence of two ministers from the Regionalist League in his cabinet: Joan Ventosa i Calvell at the Ministry of Finance and Felip Rodés at the Ministry of Public Instruction. This was the first time that the Regionalist League had held statewide power, but the move drew sharp criticism from republicans, nationalists, and anyone else in attendance at the assembly in July who accused the Regionalist League of betrayal.

The general elections of February 1918 gave an ample victory to the Regionalist League at the Catalan level, leading to the formation of a national unity government in Madrid led now by Antonio Maura, with Francesc Cambó at the Ministry of Development and Joan Ventosa i Calvell at the Ministry of Supplies. When the new coalition did not last longer than nine months, a sense of failure spread far and wide among Catalan nationalists, and even more so if one looks ahead to the fruitless campaign for Catalan autonomy in late 1918 and early 1919. Indeed, the *Mancomunitat de Catalunya*'s school for local civil servants had originally launched the idea in the summer of 1918 to mobilize the municipal governments of Catalonia in favor of Catalan autonomy.[48]

A few months later, the process led to the drafting of foundational principles for a statute of autonomy that was delivered by Josep Puig i Cadafalch, president of the *Mancomunitat* and Prat's successor after the latter had died on August 1, 1917, to Spanish Prime Minister García Prieto on November 28, 1918. García Prieto, however, remained unmoved, and Spanish public opinion reacted by launching an anti-Catalan nationalist campaign that translated into a boycott of Catalan products and a formidable demonstration in Madrid on December 9, 1918, which attracted between 40,000 and 100,000 participants.[49] On December 10 and 11, the parliamentary sessions at which the Catalan proposal was debated unfolded in a climate of deep hostility toward autonomy. As a result, Francesc Cambó led a walkout by the Catalan minority on December 12. Four days later in Barcelona, Cambó delivered a well-known speech in which he stressed that Catalonia's struggle could not be linked to one form of government or another, and he boiled down his views as follows: "Republic? Monarchy? Catalonia!"

In subsequent months, two drafts of Catalonia's statute of autonomy were written: one by an extra-parliamentary committee appointed by the central government and the other by the *Mancomunitat de Catalunya* and Catalan members of parliament who were not satisfied with the Madrid initiative. In January 1919, the proposal for Catalonia's autonomy was finalized, and it won the backing of 1,046 Catalan municipalities out of a total of 1,072. However, the focus was once again diverted, this time by an outbreak of clashes between the Spanish nationalists of the Spanish Patriotic League [*Liga Patriótica Española*] and radical Catalan nationalists, and also by growing social strife in Barcelona, which led to the suspension of constitutional protections in the Catalan capital on January 16, 1919, at the behest of the Romanones government. On February 5, a strike began at Barcelona's main electricity generating plant, known popularly as *La Canadenca* [or "The Canadian," because of the plant's majority Canadian shareholder], and by February 21 it had spread into a general strike under the aegis of the anarchist union, the CNT. In response, the Spanish Prime Minister Romanones took the decision to dismiss Parliament on February 27, the very day of the scheduled voting on the Catalan members' proposal and its eventual transformation into a referendum. Just as had happened in August 1917, social unrest once again crushed the momentum for autonomy and the Regionalist League aligned itself behind the need to keep public order.[50]

Over the same period, the Regionalist League sought to forge relationships with Galician and Basque nationalists. In the Galician case, the Catalan regionalists closely followed the Brotherhood of the Language movement [in Galician, *Irmandades da Fala*], which took its first steps in the spring of 1916.[51] In September 1917, Cambó paid a visit to Galicia to strengthen relationships with the Galician nationalist movement. A few months later, in November 1917, a Galician delegation arrived in Barcelona to take part in the Galician Week being held there. By mid-December, a Catalan Week was being put on Galicia. On one hand, this connection gave an impetus to the Galician nationalist movement. On the other hand, however, it prompted a campaign of mudslinging to discredit the movement, with mainstream publications linked to the Galician branches of the Spanish political parties claiming that it was being paid for by the Catalans. The climate of mutual under-standing between Cambó's regionalists and the Galician nationalists was then plunged into crisis during the Catalan politician's term as minister, when the construction of a railway between Ferrol and Gijón was rejected and the proposed creation of the National Institute for Agriculture [*Instituto Nacional Agrario*] was blocked.[52]

Even more important were the influences of Catalan nationalism on the Basque nationalist movement. Cambó and his men paid visits to the Basque provinces to forge an alliance with Basque nationalists in order to bolster a pro-autonomy campaign at the statewide level. The first step in the strategy was to win approval among the Basque nationalists for the Catalans' incrementalist strategy. In this context, the Basque nationalists took charge of the Biscay provincial govern-ment in the elections of 1917, and the new president Ramon de Sota spoke a few words in support of the creation of a Basque *mancomu-nidad* along Catalan lines. In the autumn of 1918, the Basque national-ists, like their Catalan counterparts, were affected by the end of World War I and launched a campaign to obtain a statute of autonomy that, like the Catalan one, ended in failure.[53]

Years of *Pistolerismo* and the
Birth of New Catalan Nationalist Parties on the Left

The failure of Catalonia's campaign for autonomy played out amid the social unrest of the postwar period, which was marked by industrial restructuring and clashes between the employers association and the anarchist CNT. The CNT had sprung up in 1910 and become hege-monic among the Catalan working classes in 1916 and 1917. From 15,000 members in 1915, the CNT grew to 74,000 members in 1918 and then skyrocketed to 427,000 members in 1919, only a year later. The CNT's spectacular growth in the early postwar period was driven by winds of change from Russia and an expectation of the imminence of revolution, as well as by the CNT's effectiveness in bringing about the end of trade-based unions, replacing them with unified, industry-wide unions. As a result, all the workers in a factory belonged to the same union even if they were sometimes engaged in different trades, and they joined all of their forces together into a single struggle against the employers association. Very quickly, escalating violence came to typify the postwar years. As Albert Balcells recalls, the CNT and the employers association had both settled on seeking to monopolize their representation of the classes in conflict, dispensing with government arbitration or bargaining in order to force the other side into unconditional surrender.[54] These approaches led to violent exchanges between the *pistoleros*, or hired gunmen, of the employer-backed Free Trade Union [*Sindicat Lliure*] and those of the Catalan labor movement. From 1919 to 1923, hundreds of people were murdered, most of them in the CNT, thanks to the cover given to the hired gunmen of the Free Trade Union by Martínez Anido, the civil governor of Barcelona. Included among the many victims were two prominent figures: the republican lawyer Francesc Layret (murdered in November 1920) and the CNT leader Salvador Seguí (murdered in March 1923). This social violence also brought with it a crisis in political representativeness that can be explained by the inability of the political order coming out of the Bourbon Restoration to democratize itself and enable the participation of the masses in the new era.[55]

Tensions erupted in the world of Catalan nationalism with the entry of Cambó into the national unity government of Antonio Maura in August 1921 and with the concerns Cambó's actions raised among his own adherents. His decision shook the Catalan nationalist political space, prompting the youth section of the Regionalist League [*Joventut Nacionalista de la Lliga*] to split off under the leadership of writers and intellectuals like Jaume Bofill i Mates, Nicolau d'Olwer, and Ramon d'Abadal. The splinter group called a meeting to unify all the sectors dissatisfied with the Regionalist League. Held in early June 1922, the meeting also brought together all the nationalist republican sectors of Antoni Rovira i Virgili and went down in history as the Catalan National Conference [*Conferència Nacional Catalana*], from which emerged the political organization Catalan Action [*Acció Catalana*]. Also taking part in the meeting was Francesc Macià (1859–1933), a former army officer and former member of parliament for the Regionalist League who had entered politics in the wake of the Spanish military's attack on the satirical magazine ¡Cu-Cut! and *La Veu de Catalunya* and who had evolved from a pro-monarchy regionalism to an openly pro-independence stance, founding the first radical nationalist organization, the Nationalist Democratic Federation [*Federació Democràtica Nacionalista*].[56] At the Catalan National Conference, Macià presented a starker breakaway program that did not win support from a majority of those present. As a result, he founded a new party a few weeks later that would become the touchstone for pro-independence efforts: Catalan State [*Estat Català*]. In this period, political Catalan nationalism was a seedbed of republican and left-wing organizations, such as the previously mentioned Catalan Action and Catalan State, as well as the Socialist Union of Catalonia [*Unió Socialista de Catalunya*], which was founded in 1923 as the first socialist political party that was also Catalan nationalist in outlook and a proponent of the self-determination of peoples. In subsequent years, these organizations would have a profound influence on Catalan politics and succeed in elbowing aside conservative Catalan nationalism in order to establish the hegemony of the left.[57]

The international models changed as well: with the collapse of the Austro-Hungarian Empire, new nationalist proposals emerged, with the Irish example becoming the touchstone not only for Catalan nationalists, but also for their Basque and Galician counterparts.[58] Right from the start, some Catalan intellectuals criticized the Irish uprising, viewing it as a provocation that would help Germany and rebound against the legitimate demands of moderate Irish nationalists for home rule. On the other hand, the example set by members of Sinn Féin also sparked enthusiasm among some. One of the critics was Antoni Rovira i Virgili, who interpreted the events in line with the daily newspaper of the republicans, taking the view that federalism and dialogue were the way to solve national conflicts, but also rejecting the executions meted out by the British authorities. On the other hand, exponents of the new radical nationalism, such as Daniel Cardona

(1890–1943) and Manuel Serra i Moret (1884–1963), adopted the proposals of Patrick Pearse and James Connolly as their own.[59] This influence can also be seen in the case of Francesc Macià, who wrote in the publication *Estat Català* on November 15, 1922, that "England [is] fighting against the mightiest nations in the world and yet, conversely, must yield before the Irish people, because they fight for an ideal of liberty" ["*Anglaterra, lluitant contra les nacions més poderoses del món i, en canvi, ha de cedir davant del poble irlandès, perquè lluita per un ideal de llibertat*"]. On another occasion, Macià stated: "And what is Catalonia before Spain? What would we do before four or five hundred thousand men? I say to them this. But what of Ireland? With only four and a half million inhabitants, it has defeated England which, with its colonies, has some five hundred million inhabitants, the most powerful navy in the world and an army that can rally more than four million fighters, with all the materiel necessary. What does this tell us Catalans? That at every point of a bayonet and at every bullet, there is some part of those invisible forces that carries them unfailingly, above all else, to victory" ["*I què és Catalunya davant d'Espanya? Què faríem nosaltres davant de quatre-cents mil o bé cinc-cents mil homes? Jo els hi dic: I Irlanda? Amb quatre milions i mig d'habitants, davant d'Anglaterra que, amb les seves colònies, en té uns cinc-cents milions, amb la marina més poderosa del món, amb un exèrcit que pot organitzar de més de quatre milions de combatents, amb tot el material necessari, ha vençut. Què ens diu això catalans? Doncs que a cada punta de baioneta i a cada bala hi ha part d'aqueixes forces invisibles que són les porten, indefectiblement, per damunt de tot, a la victòria*"].[60] These words clearly showed the influence of the Irish revolutionary model and a commitment toward armed struggle to achieve national liberation, marking a profound shift in the imagination of Catalan nationalism. Indeed, a new climate of insurrection was pervasive in postwar European society. Abelard Tona, a future volunteer in the insurrection led by Macià at Prats de Molló (France), summed it up in his memoirs as follows: "Catalan nationalism was entering a phase that had never before even been whispered about: organized violence. Everyone talked incessantly in hushed voices. And yet, while it seemed so extraordinary to me at the time, it was a path logically determined by the historical process of our people. From a push for regionalist autonomy, theoretically tinged with nationalism and always tied to the idea of shaking up the Spanish state, we entered a new phase of nationalism as principle and as practice, which had only one overriding aim—independence—and one means to achieve it—violence. To this end, groups of varying success sprang up to organize into paramilitary forces. The first, of course, had been formed by Francesc Macià" ["*[. . .] entrava en una fase del catalanisme encara mai no fressada, la violència organitzada. Tot jo era un fremiment. I tot i això, que en aquell moment se'm feia tant extraordinari, era un camí lògicament determinat del procés històric del nostre poble. D'un autonomisme regionalista, teòricament acolorit de nacionalisme, sempre amarrat a la idea d'una revolució de l'Estat espanyol, entràvem a la nova fase del nacionalisme com a principi i com a pràctica, el qual només tenia un veral: la independència, i un mitjà per conquistar-la: la violència. Per on sorgien, amb més o menys encert, agrupacions que pretenien organitzar-se en una forma paramilitar. La primacia, és clar, havia estat de Francesc Macià.*"].[61]

The Catalan leader made no bones about his views. Even the lower house of the Spanish Parliament had to listen to his words on June 22, 1923. That day, Macià rose to protest against the public-order measures enacted in Catalonia and the disdain with which Catalonia's requests for greater autonomy had been met. In the course of his speech, he accused the moderate regionalists of having sold out for a few public appointments, and went on to say: "Either we remain under the rule of the oppressor state, the centralist state, in moral slavery, a hundred times worse than material slavery, or we turn to violence. No other solution is left" ["*O nosotros continuamos bajo el dominio del Estado opresor, del Estado centralista, en una esclavitud moral, peor cien veces que la material, o vamos a la violencia. No queda otra solución*"]. When an outcry went up from a section of the chamber, Macià further remarked that an armed resistance was being organized in Catalonia to achieve independence: "It is painful to think that a force is organising in Catalonia today and preparing to face the oppressor state tomorrow" ["*Es doloroso pensar que en Cataluña hoy se organiza, se prepara una fuerza para mañana hacer frente al Estado opresor*"]. Then he went on to add: "We know that war is a most harrowing crisis that peoples go through at some moment in their History, but never is it so justified as when it concerns the liberty and full sovereignty of a people" ["*Nosotros sabemos que una guerra es una crisis dolorosísima que pasan los pueblos en un momento de su Historia, pero nunca es tan justificada como cuando se trata de la libertad y de la plena soberanía de un pueblo*"]. Macià also stressed that he sought to secure a hegemony in favor of Catalan independence, and said clearly that this political sector was to represent the great moral strength of his country: "We seek to give this great moral strength to the Catalan state, so that every element of Catalonia contributes with all of its prestige, excluding none, that none shall ever be spurned however little they may be. This is why we want the Catalan state: this is why we have formed the Catalan state" ["*Nosotros queremos dar esa gran fuerza moral al Estado catalán, para que todos los elementos de Cataluña acudan a darle todo su prestigio, sin excluir a ninguno, que jamás es despreciado por pequeño que sea. Por eso nosotros queremos el Estado catalán; por eso nosotros hemos formado el Estado catalán*"].[62] In conclusion, he addressed himself to the Catalan left and made an appeal for the cooperation of the federalists and all other elements that accepted the sovereignty of the Catalan nation-state. Macià's words, which were met with shouts of protest from various members of the Spanish Parliament, were to have great significance because it would prove to be his last appearance in the chamber before the military coup of Primo de Rivera.

The Triple Alliance and Primo de Rivera's Coup d'Etat

In early July 1923, a few days after Francesc Macià's speech in the Spanish Parliament, Galician, Catalan, and Basque nationalists engaged in a number of contacts intended to lead to the formulation of a triple alliance. This marked a new phase in the alliance between the three nationalisms—Basque, Catalan, and Galician—because Cambó's Regionalist League had fallen into disrepute as a consequence of the Catalan conservative politician's failure in his role as minister in developing support of Galician and Basque interests. Indeed, his administration had been detrimental to both groups. As a result, they sought new interlocutors among the emerging Catalan political organizations.[63] The leadership on the Catalan side fell to

Catalan Action, which laid out the need for a peninsula-wide strategy in the editorial pages of *La Publicitat*, where Antoni Rovira i Virgili staunchly defended the need for such an alliance, declaring that the Regionalist League's strategy to expand regionalism had failed, and that the time had now come to forge alliances among the nationalist sectors of Galicia, the Basque Country, and Catalonia. The aim, according to Rovira i Virgili, was to create "a common front of the three peninsular nationalisms against the decadent Spanish state [because it] would increase the strength of each one of the subjugated nationalities and bring nearer the hour of their redemption. Until now, it has happened that the state has been able to combat separately each one of the opposing nationalisms that have challenged it. If they coordinated their campaigns with one another, it would make the enemy's task that much harder" ["*El front comú dels tres nacionalismes peninsulars contra l'Estat espanyol decadent [ja que es] multiplicaria la força de cada una de les nacionalitats sotmeses i acostaria l'hora de llur redempció. Fins ara ha succeït que l'Estat ha pogut combatre separadament cada un dels nacionalismes adversari que li han plantat cara. Si entre aquests s'establís una coordinació en llurs campanyes, la feina de l'enemic es complicaria molt*"].[64]

In Catalonia, the Catalan State party and the Catalan Nationalist Union [*Unió Catalanista*] also joined the initiative, while support in the Basque Country came from the moderate Basque Nationalist Communion [*Comunión Nacionalista Vasca*] and the more radical Basque Nationalist Party [*Partido Nacionalista Vasco*], while support in Galicia came from the Brotherhood of the Language [*Irmandades de Fala*] and the Galician Nationalist Brotherhood [*Irmandade Nazonalista Galega*]. There was even a proposal, appearing primarily in *Aberri*, the Basque Nationalist Party house organ, to include the Berber nationalists in colonial Morocco, who were then at war with Spain, though that proposal never came to fruition. Nor should it be forgotten that the Battle of Annual in Spanish Morocco, precisely in July 1921, had represented a resounding defeat of the Spanish army by the troops of Abd el-Krim. Consequently, the proposals of the Basque Nationalists in *Aberri* deeply wounded the sensibility of Spanish nationalists and, of course, the military.[65]

These nationalist organizations gathered in Barcelona on September 11, 1923, Catalonia's national day, and they reached an agreement on the foundation of the Triple Alliance, which was to pursue self-determination and not conceal any suggestion of the Irish insurrectional strategy. That September 11, during the traditional laying of wreaths at the statue of Rafael Casanova, the police took brutal action when, according to Abelard Tona's memoirs, the members of the delegation of the Triple Alliance arrived "with the flags of the Basque Country, Galicia and Catalonia on full display and [they were] ceremoniously dressed in black" [*"amb les banderes d'Euskadi. Galícia i Catalunya desplegades i cerimoniosament vestits de negre"*].[66] This was viewed by the authorities as the straw that broke the camel's back. Two days after the event, on September 13, 1923, General Miguel Primo de Rivera declared a military inspectorate to maintain public order. On September 15, the king named Primo de Rivera as prime minister, but the general proceeded to transform the government into a military directorate whose first act was to declare a state of war throughout Spain and to suspend constitutional protections. The coup curtailed any attempt by the Triple Alliance to take action. Primo de Rivera's success can be explained by a conjunction of factors that stemmed, first, from the structural crisis of the state that had emerged from the Bourbon Restoration, in which the presence of the military in public life had become practically chronic, and, second, from social upheaval and the mobilization of nationalist movements, which contributed to growing misgivings in the military, especially after the disastrous Battle of Annual in 1921. Moreover, Primo de Rivera's coup encountered no opposition and soon quashed the demands of the workers' movement and political Catalan nationalism.[67]

The military directorate acted indiscriminately against all Catalan nationalists, even the more moderate elements. In this context, the dictator launched a specific decree against separatism on September 18, 1923, with the explicit aim of persecuting Catalan nationalism and expanding the category of crimes against the unity of the homeland that had been prosecuted since the *Ley de Jurisdicciones* of 1906. Bans were put in place against the display of the Catalan flag and the official use of the Catalan language, and draconian new punishments were instituted for anyone who took up arms against the state. Within a few weeks, the dictatorship disbanded town halls, provincial governments, and workers' associations, institutions, and athenaeums (educational institutions), starting with the most iconic example: the People's Encyclopaedic Athenaeum [*Ateneu Enciclopèdic Popular,* or AEP]. Founded in 1902, the AEP was one of the civic institutions with the greatest reach among the public. It had no specific party or union affiliation, but sought instead to contribute to the cultural betterment and education of workers and the lower classes of Barcelona more generally.[68] The dictatorship also shuttered the *Centre Autonomista de Dependents del Comerç i de la Indústria* (CADCI), which had been founded in 1903 to defend the interests of office workers and shop assistants and to espouse nationalist ideas. The CADCI had grown into a key leading cultural and social institution in the Catalan context. The radicalization of CADCI's members in the early 1920s had transformed the institution into one of the main proving grounds of radical Catalan nationalism. Indeed, the campaign for home rule based on the principle of self-determination had been instigated at the CADCI in the summer of 1922.[69] The closure of so many centers went hand in hand with the persecution of a whole host of nationalist party members, including a large number of priests. Even the football stadium of F.C. Barcelona was closed in June 1925 on the pretext that fans had whistled during the playing of the Spanish national anthem. In short, the dictatorship shut down over 150 associations in three months (including the peaceful youth group known as *Pomells de Joventuts,* which had been created at the initiative of Josep Maria Folch i Torres to bring together young Catalans for patriotic and religious purposes), while many other associations disbanded of their own accord in response to the threat of fines and administrative obstacles, and roughly twenty local newspapers in the districts of Catalonia suspended publication.[70]

On October 27, 1923, a royal order was issued by the directorate-general of primary education [*Dirección General de Educación Primaria*] dictating that Spanish would be the only language of instruction. On February 15, 1924, another royal order provided for the mandatory inspection of all schools to verify the application of these measures under penalty of closing any schools that failed to meet the new requirements. The moves of the military directorate went on to ban workers' demonstrations on May 1 and the demonstrations of nationalists on September 11. The repressive policies continued with a purge of staff in all town halls and provincial governments and the implementation of a new municipal statute (April 1924) designed to clamp down on the possibilities of home rule, and a new provincial law (March 1925) that legally abolished the *Mancomunitat de Catalunya*.

In addition, the CNT was declared illegal in May 1924, and its mouthpiece, *Workers' Solidarity [Solidaridad Obrera]*, was banned. Anarchist, communist, and radical nationalist organizations were all forced into exile to escape from the crackdowns of the dictatorship, while the more moderate socialist organizations adjusted to the new reality and found a way to work with the dictatorship.

One highlight among the various initiatives against the dictatorship came in early September 1924,[71] when Francesc Macià proposed the creation of the League of Oppressed Nations *[Lliga de les Nacions Oprimides]* to bring together the national struggles of Catalonia, the Basque Country, Galicia, Ireland, Egypt, India, the Philippines, and the Republic of the Rif in Spanish Morocco in order to achieve independence. This was a strategic move to unite the nationalities of the Spanish state with the most important protest movements of the time: the Irish rebellion, led by Edmond Valera, and the cause of the Rif warriors, who at the time represented a thorn in the side of the Spanish army, which did, ultimately, succeed in subduing them. Macià's project was very much a child of its times, given that the Italian poet Gabriele d'Annunzio had sought a similar alliance during the occupation of the city of Fiume/Rijeka, and the Russian revolutionary Vladimir Lenin had likewise tried to play the card of an alliance of oppressed nations in an antiimperialist vein. However, the impossibility of bringing about a practical synthesis of these proposals for internationalist solidarity led Macià to abandon the project. So much so that a few months later, in January 1925, the Catalan pro-independence leader launched the Action Committee of the Free Alliance *[Comitè d'Acció de la Lliure Aliança]*, which united Basque Nationalists and elements of the CNT under his presidency. Macià's coalition would later be joined as well by liberals hostile to the dictatorship, such as Sánchez Guerra, and by republican military personnel, Galician nationalists and communists. However, his initiative was short-lived and did not translate into specific support. In fact, the most important armed action organized by radical Catalan nationalism, the failed invasion of the guerrilla army through the French border at Prats de Molló (October 1926), was carried out solely by Catalan nationalist militants with the backing of anarchists and international antifascists. The attempted Catalan insurrection represented a hybrid synthesis between the armed volunteers characterizing the Irish struggle for independence and the struggle of Italian antifascists who, from their French exile, had sought to marshal a Garibaldi legion to overthrow fascism in Italy.[72]

The trial of the Catalans, which was held in Paris in January 1927, cast Francesc Macià as the champion of Catalonia's freedoms and the indisputable leader of the dictatorship's foes in the eyes of the Catalan and Spanish communities in exile. In a statement published in the *Petit Journal* of Paris, the Catalan leader made it clear that the "Catalan separatist spirit is not the spirit of hate that has always been attributed to us by Spanish governments. Catalonia wishes to be free and to form an independent Catalan Republic and it also seeks the freedom of all the peoples of the Iberian Peninsula. [. . .] Once the peninsular peoples are free, we will accept every fraternal bond of free accord. *What we do not seek, nor can we accept, are the self-same bonds imposed by force!* Proof of what we say are the alliances that we have made, before and despite the dictatorship, with the Basque Country and Galicia, places where separatism is also felt, and our broader alliance with all the workers of Spain" [the *"esperit separatista català no és l'esperit d'odi que sempre ens han atribuït els governs espanyols. Catalunya vol ser lliure i constituir-se en República catalana independent, i vol també la llibertat de tots els pobles de la Península. [. . .] Un cop els pobles peninsulars fossin lliures, acceptaríem tot lligam fraternal per lliure acord. El que no volem ni podem acceptar són aquests mateixos lligams imposats per la força! Prova del que diem són les aliances que tenim, d'abans i tot de la dictadura, amb el País Basc i Galícia, llocs on el separatisme també és sentit, com també la nostra més ampli aliança amb tots els obrers d'Espanya"*].[73]

The prestige of the Paris trial also helped Macià to gain the support of the Catalan communities living in South America, which he visited throughout 1928, culminating with the island of Cuba on September 30 and October 1 and 2, when the Constituent Assembly of Catalan Separatism [*Assemblea Constituent del Separatisme Català*] was held. This is the gathering that produced the Catalan Revolutionary Separatist Party [*Partit Separatista Revolucionari Català*] and approved a draft constitution for the Catalan Republic.

After a brief stopover in New York in mid-October, Macià returned to Europe. Unable to obtain a residence permit for France or Switzerland, he reestablished his domicile in Brussels and lent his support to the insurrection attempted by José Sánchez Guerra, who led a failed military conspiracy against the dictatorship in Valencia in January 1929. Throughout 1929, Macià pulled the strings of political action from Belgium, despite serious friction with Catalan State party members who had remained in Spain under the leadership of Jaume Aiguader and were not satisfied with the decisions taken at the Cuban assembly in October 1928. Meanwhile, Macià himself kept up contacts and relationships with all the Catalan political forces battling against the dictatorship, even those that did so with the Spanish state in mind and not in the pursuit of Catalonia's independence.

A few years after Sánchez Guerra's attempted coup, the dictatorship of Primo de Rivera collapsed in January 1930 and was replaced by the "soft" dictatorship, or *dictablanda*, of Dámaso Berenguer. In the event, the nationalists of Galicia, the Basque Country, and Catalonia did not succeed in meeting together to agree on a joint strategy for the proclamation of a federal republic. Indeed, among the nationalist forces, it was the Catalan nationalism of the left taking part in the well-known meeting in August 1930 that produced the Pact of San Sebastián. This pact, which was spearheaded by the Spanish republican movement, was supposed to produce a roadmap for the establishment of a republic in Spain and to permit Catalan autonomy. As Xosé Estévez has argued, however, the proponents of the Triple Alliance squandered the opportunity to do politics with statewide forces and to put forward a federal reform of the state.[74]

Jaume Aiguader was the representative of the Catalan State party at San Sebastián. The agreement reached among the anti-dynastic forces did establish the right of the Catalan people to vote on a statute

of autonomy, but it would then require passage by the Spanish constituent assembly. Thus, home rule for Catalonia was clearly a subordi-
nate matter: historians have engaged in a good deal of debate over the
reasons for Macià's acceptance of these proposals, with the majority
taking the view that the Catalan leader perceived that there was marginal support for the separatist option and so he felt compelled to pursue a incrementalist approach to reach his goals.[75] It should be noted
that Macià amended his proposals because of misunderstandings with
Jaume Aiguader, the leader of the Catalan State party in Catalonia,
and because an entire wing of the separatist rank and file, including
Abelard Tona, Martí Vilanova, Jaume Miravitlles, and a whole host of
others, had broken away to launch the Catalan Communist Party in
late 1928.[76] Another key factor to bear in mind is that the most ardent
nationalist sectors, led by Daniel Cardona, set up the nationalist group
Nosaltres Sols! [in English, roughly "Us Alone!"] in November 1930.[77]

In September 1930, Macià journeyed back to Catalonia to take part
in events, even though he was not covered by the amnesty. Arrested
by the police on September 26, he became a symbol of the struggle for
amnesty, winning the support of all the opposition political forces in
Catalonia, including the anarcho-syndicalists. Expelled from the state,
the Catalan leader was only able to return in late February 1931, when
he set up home in Barcelona and worked to secure a broad national
front of left-wing forces able to solve the problem of the Catalan people
in the context of a confederation of Iberian peoples.

The Second Spanish Republic,
Social Change, and Catalan Politics

In 1930 and 1931, a major shift occurred in the balance of power within
the world of Catalan nationalism. The left achieved political hegemony
through strategic alliances with political parties of other traditions that
were nevertheless willing to work together. In this context, left-wing
Catalan nationalism in the 1930s could be characterized as a synthesis
of heterogeneous contributions that spanned from federal republicanism to radical nationalism by way of social democratic ideals.[78]

These forces converged to govern Catalan society in a period of
deep social and economic complexity. It should be recalled that many

European cities at the end of World War I had made the decisive shift into a mass society. Barcelona became a modest but clear example of the process. The mass media sprang forward, marked by the notable presence of cinema and the first steps of radio (1924). The period also saw large-scale projects, such as the construction of the metro and the International Exposition of 1929, which attracted a great deal of manual labor. The Catalan population grew from 2,084,000 in 1910 to 2,344,000 in 1920 and as high as 2,791,000 by 1930, resulting in a population growth of some 40% in twenty years, which had a major impact. In addition, the population increase was concentrated in Barcelona and other nearby cities, which formed a peri-urban belt for the first time, though it was very limited, spanning only L'Hospitalet, Santa Coloma, Sant Adrià, and Badalona.[79] Though the scale of the phenomenon was smaller than in other European cities, the truth is that the population figures contained a crucial new feature. For the first time, Barcelona's newcomers were arriving not from the poor districts of Catalonia, but from other regions of Spain. As a result, they were not Catalan speakers. The immigrants came essentially from Murcia and Almeria, and they represented a revolutionary new political force that would increase the instability of an industrial society like Catalonia's, which was to suffer the consequences of the severe global economic crisis that began in 1929.

The backdrop of political parties in the period was character-ized by the hegemony of the Republican Left of Catalonia [*Esquerra Republicana de Catalunya*, or ERC]. ERC was a product of the confer-ence of left-wing forces that took place in Barcelona in March 1931 in preparation for the elections of April 12.

ERC brought together Francesc Macià's Catalan State party; the republicans of Lluís Companys (1882–1940) and Marcel·lí Domingo (1884–1939); a group connected to the weekly publication *L'Opinió* involving the lawyers Joan Lluhí Vallescà, Antoni Xirau, Pere Comes, and Joan Casanelles; separatist groups, such as the nationalist youth wings of the *La Falç* [in English, "The Sickle"] under the business rep-resentative Josep Tarradellas, and *Els Néts dels Almogàvers* [in English, "The Grandsons of the Almogavars"], both of which had existed before the dictatorship and were now reorganized; Barcelona republicans, such as Republican Democratic Advance of Sant Andreu de Palomar [*Avenç Democràtic Republicà*] under the leadership of Dr. Josep Dencàs; and powerful organizations out in the districts of Catalonia, such as Republican Youth of Lleida [*Joventut Republicana de Lleida*] under Humbert Torres, Republican Nationalist Development of Reus [*Foment Nacionalista Republicà de Reus*] under Josep Andreu Abelló, and Federal Centre of Girona [*Centre Federal de Girona*] under Miquel Santaló, as well as other republican centers and athenaeums throughout the territory. With an advanced social program that was also deeply nationalist in outlook, ERC knew how to connect with diverse sectors of the Catalan populace, and thus held on until the Spanish Civil War in 1936–1939.[80] Specifically, ERC was able to appeal both to the petite bourgeoisie and middle classes and to sectors of the workers' movement and tenant farmers. In addition, ERC benefited in its early years from the charismatic leadership of Francesc Macià, who was the party's mainstay in its infancy, and then of Lluís Companys, who succeeded Macià and carried on until the end of the civil war. Another advantage of the party was that it was regarded as a guiding light by a broad swath of the country's workers, and because its membership included leading figures like Pere Foix, Martí Barrera, and Sebastià Clarà, who had a past as labor activists in the CNT. Similarly, tenant farmers felt represented by a leader like Lluís Companys because of his commitment to their Union of Rabassaires [*Unió de Rabassaires*] in its struggles against the landowners association *Insititut Agrícola Català de Sant Isidre*, which was close to Cambó's Regionalist League. That said, the most significant tensions within ERC were between the nationalist sector, led by Josep Dencàs and Miguel Badia, which was engaged in a fierce battle with the CNT, and the more intellectual and republican sectors, which were linked to the group at *L'Opinió* or to the circle around Lluís Companys.[81]

To the ERC's left, a variety of communist organizations sprang up. The previously mentioned Catalan Communist Party merged with the Catalan-Balear Communist Federation [*Federació Comunista Catalano-Balear*] under Joaquim Maurin to create the Workers and Peasants Bloc [*Bloc Obrer i Camperol*]. These organizations used the myth of the Soviet Union to argue that the solution to national problems lay in adopting the same structure as the USSR. In his 1935 book *Els moviments d'emancipació nacional* [in English, *National Emancipation Movements*], Andreu Nin was critical of Stalin's political evolution, but he expressed his belief that the establishment of the USSR was an admirable first step toward the creation of a union of European socialist republics, the seed for a future universal union of socialist republics that would unite the world's population. Throughout the 1930s, the communist sectors in Catalonia championed the need to form a union of Iberian socialist republics. However, disagreements between the two chief organizations, the Workers' Party of Marxist Unification [*Partido Obrero de Unificación*, or POUM], founded in 1935, and the Unified Socialist Party of Catalonia [*Partit Socialista Unificat de Catalunya*, or PSUC], founded in July 1936 upon the outbreak of the civil war, resulted in the suppression of POUM after the violent street clashes in Barcelona known as the May Days of 1937.[82]

Among reformist sectors, the Socialist Union of Catalonia [*Unió Socialista de Catalunya*, or USC], which had been founded in Barcelona in July 1923 by republican Catalan nationalists like Gabriel Alomar, Manuel Serra i Moret, and Rafael Campalans, argued for an incremental policy of social change and took part in the ERC's candidacies. This alliance, which overstated its real strength, did secure some seats first in the lower house of the Spanish Parliament and later in the Catalan Parliament. More moderate, centrist, liberal, and republican was the Republican Catalan Nationalist Party [*Partit Catalanista Republicà*, or PCR], which was the result of a merger between Catalan Action, founded in 1922 under the leadership of Lluís Nicolau d'Olwer and Jaume Bofill, and the splinter group of Catalan Republican Action under Antoni Rovira i Virgili.

The mainstay of the Catalan political right continued to be the Regionalist League. However, the Regionalist League stood accused by the republicans of having enabled the dictatorship of Primo de Rivera, and the party could no longer count on its leader, Francesc Cambó, who underwent surgery for throat cancer in London and did not regain the political centrality that he had once enjoyed in the years prior to the dictatorship. In the lead-up to the municipal elections of April 12, the Regionalist League backed the Constitutional Centre party [*Centro Constitucional*] that the Spanish liberals had founded to prop up the Alfonsist monarchy, but the Constitutional Centre proved the clear loser at the ballot box. From 1933 onwards, the Regionalist League reinvented itself as a moderate republican party called the Catalan League [*Lliga Catalana*].[83]

Lastly, the other major party that had dominated Catalan politics in the first third of the century was Alejandro Lerroux's Radical Republican Party [*Partido Republicano Radical*, or PRR]. The reorganization of republicanism in the struggle against the dictatorship ended up dislodging the Lerrouxists, who had enjoyed broad popular support thanks to propaganda tying Catalan nationalism to the conservative regionalism of the Regionalist League. In the new circumstances, however, ERC wrested voters from the PRR, pushing the party to the margin of Catalan politics. The PRR was unable to adapt its rhetoric to the fact that a broad swath of republicanism had "Catalanised" under the dictatorship, while a segment of moderate Catalan nationalism had "republicanized." By contrast, Lerroux took on a governmentalist aspect that instead made him more relevant in Spanish politics, where he soon turned the party into a center-right republican alternative to the left.

Among the labor unions, the CNT remained at the forefront. At first, it maintained good relationships with the authorities of the Second Republic in anticipation of wide-ranging sociopolitical changes. Very soon, however, the relationships turned deeply adversarial. In the words of Josep Peirats, the anarchist militant from Valencia, the "honeymoon period" [*"lluna de mel"*] shifted into a "phase of guerrilla warfare" [*"fase de guerrilla"*], typified by strikes and labor disputes, and then culminated in a "season of insurrection" [*"cicle insurreccional"*], linked with the uprising in the Alt Llobregat in Catalonia in January 1932 and the events at Casas Viejas in Andalusia in January 1933.[84] The radical wing of the CNT, made up of members of the Iberian Anarchist Federation [*Federación Anarquista Ibérica*, or FAI] (founded in Valencia in 1927), argued for the radicalization of the conflict with the institutions of the Republic in order to bring about a social revolution. By contrast, the moderate wing of the CNT, represented by individuals like Joan Peiró and Àngel Pestaña, was critical of the FAI proposals and came out with the "Manifesto of the Thirty" [*Manifiesto de los Treinta*] in August 1931. The rifts between the radical and moderate wings of the CNT led to the expulsion of various signatories to the above manifesto throughout 1932 and, in 1933, a number of the CNT's member unions ultimately broke away.[85]

The Government of Catalonia and the Resumption of Contacts among Catalans, Basques, and Galicians (1931–1933)

The Republican Left of Catalonia (ERC) held on as the leading political force in Catalonia after the municipal elections of April 12, 1931. On April 14, Macià proclaimed the Catalan Republic within the Iberian Federal Republic, but the Catalan Republic lasted only until April 17, when the ministers sent by the Republic reached an agreement with Macià to create the Government of Catalonia [*Generalitat de Catalunya*], including a promise of wide-ranging home rule to be regulated by a statute approved by the Catalan people through referendum and then by the Spanish constituent assembly. Initially, Madrid and Barcelona stayed on good terms, and the result was the enactment of such important decrees as the abolition of the *Ley de Jurisdicciones* (the controversial law of 1906 that had allowed military courts to sit in judgment of offenses against the Spanish homeland and been used to persecute Catalan nationalism), as well as the dissolution of the provincial governments in Catalonia and the compulsory use of Catalan in the schools.

However, the legislative passage of Catalan autonomy proved complicated. The constitutional charter pushed by the Catalans (the Statute of Núria, August 1931) proposed the right of the Catalan people to self-determination, the creation of a Catalan state within the Spanish Federal Republic, the official recognition and use of the Catalan language, the possibility of a federation of all Catalan-speaking territories (from the region of Valencia to the Balearic Islands), and a wide-ranging transfer of powers to the *Generalitat de Catalunya*. The statute was quite ambitious, but it was not maximalist in that it left important powers to the Spanish Republic. Indeed, the vast majority of the Catalan parties voted for it, including the Regionalist League.[86]

Yet the new Spanish constitution, which was ratified on December 9, 1931, established a democratic republic that was secular and unitary, while also recognizing the autonomy of the regions. In this respect, it established that any statutes of autonomy had to be approved by the Spanish Parliament, it blocked the federation of regions, it imposed the official recognition and use of the Spanish language, it limited powers over education, and it established that Spanish law was to prevail over regional laws. In short, the Spanish constitution had been written with a view to limiting the powers that the Catalan Statute had demanded for the *Generalitat de Catalunya*.

Meanwhile, the passage of Catalonia's statute of autonomy had run into opposition from a broad swath of the Spanish Parliament. Moreover, once people learned of the Núria program, adverse public opinion led to an anti-Catalan campaign that took the form of rallies, demonstrations, and a call to boycott Catalan products. Even with the proposed Statute of Núria heavily cut down, Catalan autonomy only received approval because of the crisis sparked by the failed coup attempt of General Sanjurjo in the preceding August. By September 1932, Prime Minister Azaña succeeded in shoring up a republican majority in parliament to pass Catalonia's first statute of autonomy in the twentieth century.

The new statutory framework prompted a number of adjustments in Catalan politics. As noted earlier, the Regionalist League adapted to the new political framework and the Christian democratic sectors of Catalan nationalism set in motion the Democratic Union of Catalonia [*Unió Democràtica de Catalunya*, or UDC], while ERC suffered its first splintering, when a group close to the daily *L'Opinió* split off to found the Republican Nationalist Party of the Left [*Partit Nacionalista Republicà d'Esquerra*, or PNRE] with such distinguished leaders as Josep Tarradellas, Joan Lluhí Vallescà, and Antoni Xirau.[87] Those who broke away criticized Macià's authoritarianism and ERC's lack of internal democracy. They also decried the violent acts being carried out by groups of ERC and Catalan State youth activists, members of *Joventuts d'Esquerra Republicana-Estat Català*, against CNT trade unionists, who accused their attackers of being "Catalan fascists."[88] The PNRE did not win any seats in the Spanish parliamentary elections of 1933, even though it stood with the Republican Catalan Nationalist Party of Nicolau d'Olwer; but it did wrest votes away from ERC, which suffered a clear setback at the polls.

As for the ideological direction of progressive Catalan nationalism in the spring of 1933, one noteworthy event was the revival of the alliance among the three historical nationalities. On this occasion, the initiative came from the Basque Country, which had remained on the sidelines, as had Galicia, during the Catalan nationalists' push for autonomy. The new process culminated in the Pact of Compostela on July 25, 1933, which represented the founding act of Galeusca (an acronym formed from Galicia, Euskadi [the Basque Country], and Catalonia). The new alliance won the backing of the Basques in the PNV, the young Galician Nationalist Party, and various Catalan nationalist parties, with ERC and the Regionalist League joining a week later in an event held in Bilbao. As noted earlier, however, the new alliance had no participation from the most ardent nationalist sectors because of its democratic character and its focus on regional autonomy.[89] When the Galicians and Basques visited Catalonia in August 1933, the writer and politician Antoni Rovira i Virgili captured the notion underpinning Galeusca when he wrote: "We Catalans and republicans realise perfectly well that we cannot count on much support from the republicans of Spain in the national aspect of our ideas. The Constitution of the Republic puts excessive limits on our ideal of Catalan nationalism. We often see how the imperialist and unitarist prejudices of historical Spain are very much alive in the spirit of many republicans and even of many on the Spanish left" ["*Nosaltres, catalans i republicans, ens adonem perfectament que, en l'aspecte nacional de les nostres idees, no podem recolzar-nos gaire en el conjunt dels republicans d'Espanya. La Constitució de la República posa límits excessius al nostre ideal de catalanisme. I sovint, veiem com els prejudicis unitaristes i imperialistes de l'Espanya històrica són ben vius en l'ànima de molts republicans I fins de molts esquerristes castellans*"]. For this reason, Antoni Rovira i Virgili defended the importance of the alliance with the Basques and Galicians, because only with them did the Catalans coincide "in affirming the authentic nations, in a desire to achieve the most sweeping freedoms for them on the basis of self-determination, [and] in the love of their own languages and cultures as a tool of spiritual independence" ["*en l'afirmació de les nacions autèntiques, en la voluntat d'assolir per a elles llibertats amplíssimes damunt la base de l'autodeterminació,*

*en l'amor a la llengua i a la cultura pròpies com a instrument d'inde-
pendència espiritual"*].⁹⁰ However, the reactionary turn of Spanish
politics undermined the foundations of the Galeusca Pact. This was
demonstrated in the elections of November 1933 when the proponents
of Galeusca did not succeed in forming any stable coalition and had to
look on as the deep political rifts that divided ERC and the Regionalist
League throughout 1934 made it impossible to achieve the unity dreamt
of by the Galeusca proponents.

The Events of October 1934
and the Divisions in Catalan Nationalism

In 1934, the thorniest problem in Catalan politics was the passage of the
Crop Contracts Law [*Llei de Contractes de Conreus*] by the *Generalitat
de Catalunya* and the law's subsequent suspension by the Court of
Constitutional Guarantees [*Tribunal de Garantías Constitucionales*].
The law was an agricultural reform put forward by ERC, which was now
led by Lluís Companys (1882–1940), who had succeeded to the post after
the death of Macià on Christmas Day in 1933, and it set out provisions
to help tenant farmers gain access to the land they were cultivating. The
tenant farmers, who belonged to the agricultural Union of Rabassaires,
represented a sector that was in direct confrontation with the landown-
ing elite, which mobilized in defense of its interests through the Catalan
League, the landowners' association *Institut Agrícola Català de Sant
Isidre*, and the Spanish Agrarian Party [*Partido Agrario Español*].⁹¹
Right-wing forces succeeded in getting the law in question suspended
by the Court of Constitutional Guarantees. This showdown between
the governments of the Spanish state and Catalonia posed major problems. Moreover, the Republic had faced dangerous instability since
the elections of November 1933, when the radical governments first of
Alejandro Lerroux and then of Ricardo Samper relied on the backing
of unstable majorities that forced them to garner external support from
the Spanish Confederation of Autonomous Rights party [*Confederación
Española de Derechas Autónomas*, or CEDA]. CEDA, which was led
by José María Gil-Robles, was regarded as a reactionary party that
could force the Republic to lurch toward becoming an authoritarian
and anti-democratic regime, since the CEDA leaders had expressed

clear sympathy for the totalitarian form of state that Italian fascism had been trying to establish for over a decade. In addition, contemporary Europe had already witnessed Hitler's rise to power in January 1933 and the crackdown on Austrian socialism carried out by the authoritarian government of Dollfuss in Vienna. In short, the jackboot of reactionary dictatorships menaced the whole of Europe, and Catalan and Spanish republicans felt the threat too.

Crisis broke out on October 4 when Lerroux formed a new government and named three CEDA cabinet ministers. This led to an uprising of Republican forces, particularly in Catalonia and Asturias. If an alliance of labor unions and miners in northern Spain unleashed a genuine revolution, the events in Catalonia were marked by the central role of President Companys, who proclaimed a Catalan Republic within the Spanish Federal Republic in order to create a new republican government to wage battle against Madrid institutions that had slid toward fascism. Companys had the support of the Workers' Alliance [*Aliança Obrera*], a coalition comprised of the UGT and the unions that had signed onto the Manifesto of the Thirty, but not the backing of the CNT. Companys' vulnerability became clear when the called general strike was partial and when, above all, he was unable to stop the army when it forced the *Generalitat de Catalunya* to surrender on day seven, threw the government into prison, and began hunting down Catalan republican politicians. If the Catalan rebellion was easily put down by the army, the revolt in Asturias took on the traits of a mass insurrection, thanks to the joint participation of the UGT and CNT, and it was crushed brutally by the colonial army of Francisco Franco.

The army stamped out Companys' proclamation in a matter of hours, and the subsequent peace led to the dismantling of Catalan institutions, including the *Generalitat de Catalunya* and the municipal governments that had lent their support to the initiative. Companys himself was thrown in prison, as were the members of his government and hundreds of ERC party members and leftists more broadly across all of Catalonia, with the final headcount totaling some three thousand individuals.[92] From that moment on, Catalan institutional politics was marked by the military and institutional intervention of the government of the Republic, which decided to appoint a governor-general to perform the functions that rightfully corresponded to the president of the *Generalitat* and his executive council. Catalonia's statute of autonomy was de facto suspended. Then, through a law of January 2, 1935, the suspension was given legal cover when it was established that any formerly devolved powers would remain suspended until the Republic's parliament, by proposal of the Spanish government, lifted the ban and allowed for a resumption of self-government.[93] The Spanish language was reestablished as the official working language of Catalonia, the reforms carried out under the Crop Contracts Law were abolished, the flying of the Catalan flag was banned, and the *Generalitat's* police academy [*Escola de Policia*] was disbanded. In short, the Spanish state took back a good many of the powers that it had granted to the Government of Catalonia.

Over the course of 1934 and 1935, the politics of the Catalan left revolved around demanding the restoration of the *Generalitat de Catalunya* and the suspended statute of autonomy and calling for amnesty and the release of those imprisoned in the wake of the October events. The Lerroux government's crisis precipitated early elections in February 1936 and led to a radicalization of positions. Sectors of left-wing Catalan nationalists and Galician nationalists joined the Popular Front coalition, which was called the Left Front in Catalonia [*Front d'Esquerres*], while the Regionalist League aligned itself with conservative forces in the Catalan Front of Order coalition [*Front Català d'Ordre*] and the PNV presented an independent list in the elections.

Epilogue: Civil War, Galeusca Solidarity, and Collective Defeat

The elections of February 1936 prompted a declaration of amnesty for those imprisoned after the October events of 1934, bringing the release of the Catalan government and its restoration. However, any institutional normality was cut short by the violent military coup and ensuing civil war of July 1936. For nearly three years, the Republic's authorities and the cultural and educational elites remained immersed in a state of emergency.[94]

Indeed, in the summer of 1936, the Government of Catalonia's authority collapsed. Formally, it carried on, but it was de facto supplanted by the Central Committee of Anti-Fascist Militias [*Comitè Central de Milícies Antifeixistes*].[95] This organization was led by anarchists and included all republican and labor forces, most notably the new political forces mentioned earlier, such as POUM, an anti-Stalinist Marxist party,[96] and PSUC, a pro-Soviet Marxist party.[97]

Over these months, Catalan society was shaken by an upsurge of revolutionary fervor. Enterprises were collectivized by the labor unions. Yet there was also persecution of anyone considered to be an enemy of the new order. In the autumn of 1936, the *Generalitat*, with a government led by Lluís Companys and including anarchists and communists, succeeded in retaking power and sought to bring the situation under control. These were the months when the *Generalitat* assumed a number of powers that corresponded to the state, such as creation of the People's Army of Catalonia [*Exèrcit Popular de Catalunya*], control of the Bank of Spain, and coordination of production and consumption activities throughout Catalonia.[98] However, the divisions between the revolutionaries of the CNT and POUM, who were in favor of consolidating the revolution, and the members of ERC and PSUC, who were in favor of halting the revolution to concentrate on the war effort, led to clashes in May 1937. Their confrontation turned into a small civil war within the larger civil war and led to the expulsion of POUM representatives from power. The next step was a crackdown on POUM party members and the more revolutionary wing of the CNT, which witnessed the power that it had acquired in July 1936 broadly cut back.[99]

The end of hostilities on the streets of Barcelona and other Catalan towns and cities prompted the formation of a new executive council of the *Generalitat*, which President Companys announced in late June. On the council, the CNT, PSUC, and ERC enjoyed the same representation. In addition, Companys' cabinet had a representative of the Farmers' Union of Rabassaires and a minister without portfolio, who went to the Republican Catalan Nationalist Party of Lluís Nicolau d'Olwer, specifically to the renowned historian and archaeologist Pere Bosch Gimpera, who was a moderate republican and rector of the Autonomous University of Barcelona. When the anarchists saw that their numbers would be reduced (from four to three ministers) and that the naming of the moderate Bosch Gimpera would tilt the balance of power toward the nationalists, they protested and rejected the moves. This led Companys as president of the *Generalitat* to exclude the anarchists from the new Catalan government. The CNT no longer had the strength to impose terms as it had done before the May street clashes, and all the visible leaders of anarcho-syndicalism disappeared from the Catalan government, never to return. At that point, the cabinet posts were divided up between ERC and PSUC party members, with one representative from the Union of Rabassaires and one from the PCR.[100]

The May Days also had consequences for the autonomy of the *Generalitat*, which was curtailed in significant ways: the new Spanish government, presided over by Juan Negrín, decided to restore the power of the Ministry of Public Order and to impose centralist policies that Catalonia had cast off first with the 1932 statute of autonomy and later in the new wartime setting. The points of tension between the Republic's government and the *Generalitat* were numerous and may be said to have begun before the May Days, when the murky "Revertés affair" burst into the open, embroiling the speaker of the Catalan Parliament Joan Casanova. Casanova, a prominent ERC leader, had fled Catalonia in November 1936. Voices in the PSUC and CNT rose up to denounce an attempt by some members of Catalan nationalism to arrest the most prominent members of the FAI and force President Companys, their chief defender, to step down. These actions seemed to suggest that there was possibly an international agreement to overthrow the government of the *Generalitat*, supposedly with the help of Italian fascism. That would have facilitated the conditions for a separate peace with the creation of a hypothetical Catalan Republic, which would have benefited from the diplomatic neutrality of France and Great Britain.[101] Late in 1936, the republican Andreu Revertés (whose name was lent to the entire "affair"), then serving as the head of the *Generalitat*'s security services [*Seguretat i Serveis de la Generalitat*], was dispatched violently. Apparently, Revertés had taken a favorable view of Casanova's negotiations, but word began to leak and he was unable to escape in time: he was murdered in a ditch between Manresa and Calaf in November of the first year of the civil war. In addition, the secretary general of the Catalan State party,

Joan Torres Picart, fled into exile shortly afterward, leaving the party in the hands of Joan Cornudella, who managed to secure the survival of the pro-independence organization through his good relations with the CNT at a time when anarchist patrols had taken power into their own hands.[102] This story was to have an epilogue after Joan Casanova returned to Catalonia in late May 1937: he was denounced by the Catalan Communists (August 1937). Casanova's response to the accusations, however, did not result in his resignation. A year later, in 1938, Negrín as prime minister of the Republic would dredge up these events again as an example of the Catalans' lack of loyalty to the Republic.

Against this backdrop of clashes, President Companys tried several times to get the Spanish government to return Catalonia's statutory powers from July 1937 onwards, but to no avail. Negrín decided to take control not only of public order but also of entertainments, the system of associations, the press, and any meetings taking place in Catalonia. In Companys' view, these powers were laid out in the fifth article of Catalonia's statute of autonomy, and there was no reason for the central government to exert control. The Catalan authorities called for faithful adherence to their statutory powers and demanded respect for Catalonia's unique character, but the Spanish government blithely ignored them. In addition to losing control over public order, which was taken on by the central government after the May Days of 1937, Catalonia also lost the Ministry of Supplies [*Departament de Proveïments*] in the *Generalitat*. Again, the central government assumed direct control after disbanding the Catalan ministry through the decree of January 6, 1938. As a result, the Catalan authorities were limited solely to responsibility for the distribution of provisions through the supplies councils of the ancient vegueries, established by the decrees of September 23 and 3 November 3, 1937. Not only was this loss of any genuine administration of supplies detrimental to the local organization of Catalonia's economy, but it also provided clear evidence of the reestablishment of the state's authority in all areas, a trend that became increasingly evident over the course of the war. Similarly, the central authorities worked to take control of wartime industries, unleashing a smear campaign against the purported Catalan refusal to develop the necessary productive apparatus.[103]

Juan Negrín's animus toward Catalan autonomy, like that of Manuel Azaña, president of the Republic who had been present in Barcelona during the May Days of 1937, is remarked on in the memoirs of Carles Pi i Sunyer, who wrote that it was "an undeniable fact that the government of the Republic was pursuing a deliberate and persistent policy of gradual centralisation, with the return of the old anti-Catalanism" ["*un fet innegable que el Govern de la República seguia una deliberada i persistent política de centralització progressiva, amb el retorn del vell anticatalanisme*"].[104]

The general tenor of the state's attitude toward Catalonia was clear enough. All of the subsequent negotiations of the *Generalitat* with the government of the Republic ended in failure. Catalonia's grievances filled a very long list, the most important items of which included the state's insolvency when it came time to pay its debts to Catalonia, the imposition of de facto censorship, the firing of all former officials in the *Generalitat*'s Ministry of Defence and Public Order, and a whole host of other affronts. This state of affairs only worsened when the capital of the Republic moved to Barcelona in late October 1937. At that point, the authority of Catalan institutions was utterly ignored by the agents of the central government, who operated without taking any account of the legality of local representative bodies. In this respect, the sessions of the Catalan Parliament devolved into mere routine. One highlight among the body's final assemblies was doubtless the session when the post of speaker of the parliament was offered to Josep Irla, with the backing of the vise presidents Antoni Rovira i Virgili and Manel Serra i Moret, both elected in the session of October 1, 1938. As holder of the post, Josep Irla would become, in exile, the new president of the *Generalitat* after Companys was assassinated in October 1940.[105]

In any event, the closing sessions of the *Generalitat* came to a complete standstill because of the serious political crisis that broke out in August 1938, when Juan Negrín replaced the Catalan representative in his cabinet with a member of the PSUC, Josep Moix. This occurred when the republican Jaume Aiguader resigned after clashing with the prime minister (as did the Basque Manuel de Irujo). Aiguader stepped down because of the passage of a decree that would, on one hand, confiscate and militarize the war industry and, on the other hand, militarize special courts for political crimes and crimes of high treason. The first part was voted for by all the cabinet ministers save Aiguader, while the second part was voted against not only by Aiguader but also by the other Spanish republican parties. In the end, the decree was not put into effect because Manuel Azaña, president of the Republic, viewed it as unconstitutional and refused to sign it. The fact that Moix became minister, however, had an immediate impact on the fragile ERC-PSUC coalition in power at the *Generalitat*. Companys accused the secretary of the Catalan Communists, Joan Comorera, of disloyalty, and this set off a whole series of accusations, recriminations, and disputes that were flung back and forth between the two main Catalan political parties and that would carry on even afterwards in exile. The front lines reached Catalonia in the spring of 1938, and the arrival of the war and military defeat served to maintain the state of emergency and soon forced the *Generalitat* into exile in France.

Amid these wartime contingencies, an example of Galeuska solidarity can be seen in the hospitality given by the *Generalitat* to Basque refugees and to the delegation of the Basque government in Barcelona, as well as in the week of assistance to the Basque Country in the spring of 1937.[106] Similarly, the *Generalitat* took in the few Galicians who were able to reach Catalonia and it threw its support behind the Galician statute of autonomy, which was presented in a session of the Republican Parliament held in Montserrat on February 1, 1938.[107]

Military collapse precipitated the fall of Catalonia. In early February 1939, Catalonia was entirely occupied by Franco's troops. Thousands of people were forced into exile, including the Catalan president Companys and the Basque president Irujo, who separated from one another with the idea of reviving the Galeusca Pact in exile. Lluís Companys was captured by the German Gestapo at the beginning of World War II, delivered to Spain, and executed by firing squad on October 15, 1940. Franco's vicious dictatorship took aim to close the door on a historical period in which Catalan nationalism had become the mainstay of Catalan society and had succeeded in spreading its symbolic imaginary to the whole of that society. To achieve this end, the new authorities engaged in a systematic persecution of any identity that was not Spanish, seeking to erase all traces of the Basque, Galician, and Catalan identities from public life, while also striving to impose a new Spanish identity that was unitarist, ultra-Catholic, illiberal, anti-Marxist, and anti-democratic. The dictatorship sought to entrench itself, and for nearly forty years it stifled each and every yearning for democracy.

Bibliography

Abelló Güell, Teresa. *El debat estatutari del 1932*. (Barcelona, Parlament de Catalunya, 2007).

Agirreazkuenaga, Joseba. "A reformulación do autogoberno dos vascos," in Beramendi, Justo; Diéguez, Uxío Breogan et al. *Repensar Galicia. As Irmandades da fala*. Santiago de Compostela: Xunta de Galicia/Museo de Pobo Galego, 2017, pp. 59–67.

Aisa, Ferran. *Una història de Barcelona. Ateneu Enciclopèdic Popular*, 1902–1979. (Barcelona: Virus, 2009).

Aisa, Ferran. *CNT. La força obrera de Catalunya*. (Barcelona: Base, 2013).

Almirall, Valentí. *Lo Catalanisme. Motius que 'l legitiman. Fonaments cientifichs i solucions practicas*. (Barcelona: Llibreria de Verdaguer and Llibreria de Lopez, 1886).

Álvarez Junco, José. *El emperador del Paralelo. Lerroux y la demagogia populista*. (Barcelona: RBA, 2012).

Anguera, Pere. *L'Onze de Setembre. Història de la Diada (1886–1938)*. (Barcelona: Publicacions de l'Abadia de Montserrat, 2008).

Anguera, Pere. *Les quatre barres. De bandera històrica a senyera nacional*. (Barcelona: Dalmau Editor, 2010).

Arrien, Gregorio; Goiogana, Iñaki. *El primer exili dels vascos. Catalunya 1936–1939*. (Barcelona-Bilbao, FRTF and FSA, 2000).

Avilés Farré, Juan. *Francisco Ferrer y Guardia*. (Madrid: Marcial Pons, 2006).

Ayats, Jaume. *Els Segadors. De cançó eròtica a himne nacional*. (Barcelona: L'Avenç, 2011).

Balcells, Albert; Pujol, Enric; Sabater, Jordi. *La Mancomunitat de Catalunya i l'autonomia*. (Barcelona: Proa, 1996).

Balcells, Albert; Pujol, Enric. *Història de l'Institut d'Estudis Catalans*. (Barcelona—Catarroja: Institute for Catalan Studies—Editorial Afers, 2002).

Balcells, Albert. *Llocs de memòria dels catalans*. (Barcelona: Proa, 2007).

Balcells, Albert. "L'Institut d'Educació General de Prat de la Riba. Higiene i civisme, 1914–1923," in *Cercles. Revista d'Història Cultural*, no. 12 (2009).

Balcells, Albert. *El pistolerisme*. (Barcelona, Pòrtic, 2009).

Balcells, Albert. *El projecte d'autonomia de la Mancomunitat de Catalunya del 1919 i el seu context històric*. (Barcelona: Parlament de Catalunya, 2010).

Balcells, Albert. "Catalanism and National Emancipation Movements in the Rest of Europe," *Catalan Historical Review*, no. 6 (2013), pp. 97–102.

Berger, Gonzalo. *El Comitè Central de Milícies Antifeixistes. Voluntaris per la llibertat.* (Vic: Eumo, 2018).

Bofill I Matas, Jaume. *Prat de la Riba i la cultura catalana* (ed. Jordi Casassas i Ymbert). (Barcelona: Edicions 62, 1979).

Bonamusa, Francesc. *El Bloc Obrer i Camperol (1930–1932).* (Barcelona: Ed. Curial, 1974).

Bonamusa, Francesc (ed). Generalitat de Catalunya. Obra de Govern 1931–1939. Vol I. (Barcelona: Departament de la Vicepresidència, 2006).

Bonamusa, Francesc. "El període de més gran autonomia (juliol 1936—maig 1937)," in *Història de la Generalitat de Catalunya: dels orígens medievals a l'actualitat, 650 anys* (ed. Teresa Ferrer i Mallol). (Barcelona: IEC, 2011), pp. 337–360.

Brañas, Alfredo. "El Regionalismo en el Norte de Europa," in La España Regional, Vol. XIV (1893), pp. 551–554.

Burgaya, Josep. *La formació del catalanisme conservador i els models "nacionals" coetanis. Premsa catalanista i moviments nacionalistes contemporanis, 1868–1901.* (Unpublished doctoral thesis. Autonomous University of Barcelona, 1999).

Cabo Villaverde, Miquel. "Solidaridad Gallega y el desafío del sistema de la Restauración," in *Ayer*, no. 64 (2006), pp. 235–259.

Casassas, Jordi. *Entre Escil·la i Caribdis. El catalanisme i la Catalunya conservadora de la segona meitat del segle XIX.* (Barcelona: La Magrana, 1990).

Casassas, Jordi. (ed). *L'Ateneu i Barcelona. Un segle i mig de cultura.* (Barcelona: RDBA, 2006).

Casassas, Jordi. *La nació dels catalans.* (Catarroja: Afers, 2014).

Casassas, Jordi. "What Made Catalonia Unique (1901–1939)," in *Historical Analysis of the Catalan Identity*, ed. Flocel Sabaté (Zurick, Peter Lang, 2015), pp. 301–328.

Casassas, Jordi. *La voluntat i la quimera. El noucentisme català entre la Renaixença i el marxisme.* (Barcelona: Edicions 62, 2017).

Castells, Víctor. *Galeusca. Un ideal compartit.* (Barcelona: Rafael Dalmau, 2008).

Cattini, Giovanni C. "La política de la Generalitat després dels Fets de Maig," in *La Guerra Civil a Catalunya.* Vol. III: *Catalunya, centre neuràlgic de la guerra* (edited by Solé i Sabaté, Josep Maria, and Villarroya i Font, Joan). (Barcelona: Edicions 62, 2004), pp. 30–39.

Cattini, Giovanni C. *Historiografia i catalanisme. Josep Coroleu i Inglada (1839–1895).* (Catarroja: Afers, 2007).

Cattini, Giovanni C. *Prat de la Riba i la historiografía catalana. Intel·lectuals i crisi política a la fi del segle XIX.* (Catarroja: Afers, 2008).

Cattini, Giovanni C. *El gran complot. Qui va trair Macià? La trama italiana.* (Badalona: Ara llibres, 2009).

Cattini, Giovanni C. "Los regionalistas catalanes en la España de la Restauración." *Bulletin d'Histoire Contemporaine de l'Espagne*, no. 45, 2010.

Cattini, Giovanni C., Santacana, Carles. "International Models of Catalan Nationalism (1882–1914)," in *Empires and Nations from the Eighteenth to the Twentieth*

Century, eds. Antonello Biagini, Giovanni Motta (Cambridge: Cambridge Scholars Publishing, 2014), pp. 327–336.

Cattini, Giovanni C. "The Advent and Politicisation of Distinct Catalan Identities (1860–1898)," in *Historical Analysis of the Catalan Identity*, ed. Flocel Sabaté (Zurick, Peter Lang, 2015), pp. 269–300.

Cattini, Giovanni C. "Myths and Symbols in the Political Culture of Catalan Nationalism (1880–1914)," in *Nations and Nationalism*, no. 21.3 (2015), pp. 445–460.

Comalada Negre, Àngel. *Catalunya davant al centralisme*. (Barcelona: Sirocco, 1984).

Culla, Joan B. *El catalanisme d'esquerra (1928–1936)*. (Barcelona: Curial, 1977).

Culla, Joan B. *El lerrouxisme a Catalunya (1901–1923)*. (Barcelona: Curial, 1987).

Culla, Joan B. *Esquerra Republicana de Catalunya. Una història política (1931–2012)*. (Barcelona: Columna, 2012).

De La Granja, José Luis. "Las alianzas políticas entre los nacionalismos periféricos en la España del Siglo XX," *Studia Historica. Historia contemporánea*, no. 18 (2000), pp. 149–175. Available at: http://revistas.usal.es/index.php/0213-2087/article/view/5907

De La Granja, José Luis. *El Oasis vasco. El nacimiento de Euskadi en la República y la Guerra civil*. (Madrid, Tecnos, 2007), pp. 217–246.

Diaz Fouces, Oscar. El primer galleguisme en el mirall català. (Barcelona, Llop Roig, 2020)

Ehrlich, Charles E. *Lliga regionalista: lliga Catalana 1901–1936*. (Barcelona: Editorial Alpha, 2004).

Espinet, Francesc; Tresserras, Josep Maria. *La gènesi de la societat de massa a Catalunya, 1888–1939*. (Bellaterra: Publicacions de la UAB, 1999).

Estévez, Xosé. *De la Triple Alianza al Pacto de San Sebastián*. (San Sebastián: Cuadernos Universitarios E.U.T.G.—Mundaiz, 1991).

Estévez, Xosé. *Galeuzca: la rebelión de la periferia (1923–1998)*. (Madrid: Entinema, 2009).

Ferrer I Pont, Joan Carles. *Nosaltres sols: la revolta irlandesa a Catalunya*. (Barcelona: Publicacions de l'Abadia del Montserrat, 2007).

Figueres, Josep M. *El primer diari en llengua catalana. Diari Català (1879–1881)*. (Barcelona, Institute for Catalan Studies: 1999).

Figueres, Josep Maria. *La Veu de Catalunya, 1899–1937*. (Barcelona: Editorial Base, 2014).

Gabriel, Pere. "Transicions i canvis de segle," in Historia de la cultura catalana. Vol. VI. El modernisme 1890–1906. (ed. by Pere Gabriel). Barcelona: ed. 62, 1995.

Gallego, Ferran. *Barcelona, mayo de 1937*. (Barcelona: Debate, 2007).

Galofré, J. *El Primer Congrés Catalanista (1880)*. (Barcelona: Rafael Dalmau, 1979).

González Calleja, Eduardo. *La España de Primo de Rivera. La modernización autoritaria 1923–1930*. Madrid: Alianza, 2005.

Gonzàlez Vilalta, Arnau; López Esteve, Manel; Ucelay Da Cal, Enric. *El 6 d'Octubre. La desfeta de la revolució catalanista de 1934*. (Barcelona: Editorial Base, 2014).

Izquierdo, Santi. *La primera victòria del catalanisme polític*. (Barcelona: Pòrtic, 2001).

Izquierdo, Santi. *República i autonomia: el difícil arrelament del catalanisme d'es-querres (1904–1931).* (Catarroja: Afers. 2006).

Lladonosa, Manel. *Catalanisme i moviment obrer: el CADCI entre 1906–1923.* (Barcelona: Publicacions de l'Abadia de Montserrat, 1988).

Llorens, Jordi. *La Unió Catalanista i els orígens del catalanisme polític. Dels orígens a la presidència del Dr. Martí i Julià (1891–1903).* (Barcelona, Publicacions de l'Abadia de Montserrat, 1992).

Llorens, Jordi. *La Lliga de Catalunya i el Centre Escolar Catalanista. Dues associa-cions del primer catalanisme polític.* (Barcelona: Rafael Dalmau, 1996).

Mañà, Teresa. *Les Biblioteques populars de la Mancomunitat de Catalunya: 1915–1925.* (Lleida: Editorial Pagès, 2007).

Lorenzo Espinosa, José María. "Influencia del nacionalismo irlandés en el nacio-nalismo vasco 1916–1936," in *Nuevas formulaciones culturales: Euskal Herria—Europa.* (Donostia, Eusko Ikaskuntza, 1992), pp. 240–247.

Marinello Bonnefoy, Juan Cristobal. *Sindicalismo y violencia en Cataluña. 1902–1919.* (Unpublished doctoral thesis. Autonomous University of Barcelona, 2014).

Maymí, Josep. *Josep Irla. La tenacitat d'un compromís.* (Barcelona: Publicacions de L'Abadia de Montserrat, 2003).

Mees, Ludger. "La Euskadi invertebrada: el País Vasco en tiempos de la Solidaridad Catalana," in VvAa., *Solidaritat Catalana i Espanya.* (Barcelona: Base, 2008).

Moreno Luzón, Javier. "De agravios, pactos y símbolos. El nacionalismo español ante la autonomía de Cataluña," *Ayer,* no. 63, 2006, pp. 131–135.

Nadal, Joaquim. *El memorial de Greuges i el catalanisme polític.* (Barcelona: Magrana, 1986).

Núñez Seixas, Xosé Manuel. "El mito del nacionalismo irlandés y su influencia en los nacionalismos gallego, vasco y catalán (1880–1936)," in *Spagna contemporanea* no. 2 (1992), pp. 25–58.

Pella I Forgas, Josep. "El regionalismo en España. Aragón y Galicia," in La España Regional, Vol. I (1886).

Pérez Francesch, J. L. *Les Bases de Manresa i el programa polític de la Unió Catalanista (1891–1899).* (Manresa: Fundació Caixa de Manresa, 1992).

Pich I Mitjana, Josep. *El Centre Català.* (Catarroja: Editorial Afers, 2002).

Pich I Mitjana, Josep. *Almirall i el Diari Català (1879–1881).* (Vic: Eumo Editorial, 2003).

Pich I Mitjana, Josep. *Federalisme i catalanisme: Valentí Almirall (1841–1904).* (Catarroja: Afers, 2004).

Pi Sunyer, Carles. *La República y la Guerra. Memorias de un político catalán.* (Mexico: Oasis, 1975).

Pradas Baena, M. A. *L'Anarquisme i les lluites socials a Barcelona 1918–1923: la repressió obrera i la violència.* (Barcelona: Publicacions de l'Abadia de Mont-serrat, 2003).

Prats, Josep. *Los anarquistas en la crisis política española.* (Buenos Aires: Editorial Alfa, 1964).

Puigsech Farràs, Josep. *Nosaltres, els comunistes catalans.* (Vic: Editorial Eumo, 2001).

Puigventós, Eduard. *Complot contra Companys. L'afer Rebertés i la trama catalanista per aconseguir la Generalitat durant la Guerra Civil.* (Barcelona: Societat Catalana d'Estudis Històrics, 2008).

Rodríguez Madriñán, Xavier. "A revolución irlandesa en A Nosa Terra. Unha crònica de ausencias, paixón e silencio (1916–1923)," in J. Beramendi, U.B. Diéguez et al., *Repensar Galicia. As Irmandades da fala.* Santiago de Compostela: Xunta de Galicia/Museo de Pobo Galego, 2017, pp. 201–216.

Roig I Rosich, Josep Maria. *La dictadura de Primo de Rivera a Catalunya: un assaig de repressió cultural.* (Barcelona: Publicacions de l'Abadia de Montserrat, 1992).

Roig I Rosich, Josep Maria. *Francesc Macià: de militar espanyol a independentista català.* (Barcelona: Esfera dels Llibres, 2006).

Roig I Rosich, Josep M. *Francesc Macià: polític, teòric, agitador. Documents (1907–1931).* (Barcelona: Generalitat de Catalunya, 2010).

Roig I Rosich, Josep M.; Cattini, Giovanni C. *El temps de les il·lusions.* Vol. I, of Jordi Casassas (ed.), *La Segona República a Catalunya* (Barcelona, Ara llibres, 2015).

Rovira I Virgili, Antoni. "Nacions d'Ibèria. Bascos, Gallecs i Catalans," in *La Humanitat,* 6/8/1933.

Rubiralta, Fermí. *Joan Cornudella i Barberà (1904–1985). Biografia política.* (Barcelona: Publicacions de l'Abadia de Montserrat, 2003).

Rubiralta, Fermí. *Una història de l'independentisme polític català.* (Lleida: Pagès Editors, 2004).

Rubiralta, Fermí. *Daniel Cardona i Civit 1890–1943. Una biografia política.* (Catarroja: Afers, 2008).

Santacana, Carles. "La configuració dels municipis perifèrics: l'impacte cultural i sociopolític," in Oyón, José Luis (ed), *Vida obrera en la Barcelona de entreguerras.* (Barcelona: CCCB, 1999).

Santacana, Carles. Un país en tensió, Vol II, of Jordi Casassas (ed.), *La Segona República a Catalunya* (Barcelona, Ara Llibres, 2015).

Tavera, Susanna. *Solidaridad Obrera. El fer-se i desfer-se d'un diari anarcosindicalista (1915–1939).* (Barcelona: Col·legi de Periodistes, 1992).

Termes, Josep; Colomines, Agustí. *Les Bases de Manresa de 1892 i els orígens del catalanisme polític.* (Barcelona: Generalitat de Catalunya, 1992).

Tona, Abelard. *Memòries d'un nacionalista català. Del nacionalisme radical al comunisme. Història menuda (1922–1932).* (Barcelona: Publicacions de l'Abadia de Montserrat, 1994).

Tosstorff, Reiner. *El POUM en la revolució espanyola.* (Barcelona: Base, 2009).

Ucelay Da Cal, Enric. *La Catalunya populista.* (Barcelona: La Magrana, 1982).

Ucelay Da Cal, Enric. "Daniel Cardona i Civil i l'opció armada del nacionalisme radical català (1890–1943)," in *La Batalla i altres escrits* (Enric Ucelay, ed.). (Barcelona: La Magrana, 1984).

Ucelay Da Cal, Enric. "La Mancomunitat de Catalunya i la Diputació de Barcelona," in *Història de la Diputació de Barcelona*. (Barcelona, Diputació de Barcelona, 1987), pp. 93–139.

Ucelay Da Cal, Enric; Gonzàlez Vilalta, Arnau; Núñez Seixas, Xosé Manuel. *El catalanisme davant del feixisme 1919-2018*. (Barcelona: Editorial Gregal, 2018).

Ullman, Joan Connelly. *La Semana Trágica*. (Barcelona: Ediciones B, 2009).

Vega Massana, Eulàlia. *Entre revolució i reforma. La CNT a Catalunya (1930-1936)*. (Lleida: Pagès Editors, 2004).

Velasco, Miquel Angel. *Manuel Serra i Moret (Vic, 1884-Perpignan 1963)*. (Vic: Patronat d'Estudis Ausonencs, 2009).

Villarroja, Joan. "La Generalitat del maig de 1937 al febrer de 1939," in *Història de la Generalitat de Catalunya: dels orígens medievals a l'actualitat, 650 anys* (ed. Teresa Ferrer i Mallol). (Barcelona: IEC, 2011), pp. 361–380.

Villarroya, Joan. Guerra i Revolució. 1936-1939, Volum III, of J. Casassas (ed). *La Segona República a Catalunya*, Barcelona, Ara Llibres, 2015.

Notes

1. Cattini, Giovanni C. "The Advent and Politicisation of Distinct Catalan Identities (1860–1898)," in *Historical Analysis of the Catalan Identity*, ed. Flocel Sabaté (Zurick, Peter Lang, 2015), pp. 269–300.

2. Casassas, Jordi. *La nació dels catalans*. (Catarroja: Afers, 2014).

3. Gabriel Pere. "Transicions i canvis de segle," in *Historia de la cultura catalana*. Vol. VI. *El modernisme 1890-1906* (ed. Pere Gabriel). Barcelona: ed. 62, 1995.

4. Espinet, Francesc; Tresserras, Josep Maria. *La gènesi de la societat de massa a Catalunya, 1888-1939*. (Bellaterra: Publicacions de la UAB, 1999).

5. Pich i Mitjana, Josep. *Federalisme i catalanisme: Valentí Almirall (1841-1904)*. (Catarroja: Afers, 2004).

6. Pich i Mitjana, Josep. *Almirall i el Diari Català (1879-1881)*. (Vic: Eumo Editorial, 2003); Figueres i Artigues, Josep M. *El primer diari en llengua catalana. Diari Català (1879-1881)*. (Barcelona, Institute for Catalan Studies: 1999).

7. Pich i Mitjana, Josep. *El Centre Català*. (Catarroja: Editorial Afers, 2002), p. 31.

8. Galofré, J. *El Primer Congrés Catalanista (1880)*. (Barcelona: Rafael Dalmau, 1979).

9. Nadal, Joaquim. *El memorial de Greuges i el catalanisme polític*. (Barcelona: Magrana, 1986).

10. Almirall, Valentí. *Lo Catalanisme. Motius que 'l legitiman. Fonaments cientifichs i solucions practicas*. (Barcelona: Llibreria de Verdaguer and Llibreria de Lopez, 1886).

11. Cattini, Giovanni C. *Historiografia i catalanisme. Josep Coroleu i Inglada (1839-1895)*. (Catarroja: Afers, 2007), pp. 195–206.

12. Llorens, Jordi. *La Lliga de Catalunya i el Centre Escolar Catalanista. Dues associacions del primer catalanisme polític*. (Barcelona: Rafael Dalmau, 1996).

13. Comalada Negre, Àngel. *Catalunya davant al centralisme*. (Barcelona: Sirocco, 1984), pp. 127–229.

14. Cattini, Giovanni C. *Prat de la Riba i la historiografía catalana. Intel·lectuals i crisi política a la fi del segle XIX*. (Catarroja: Afers, 2008).

15. Llorens, Jordi. *La Unió Catalanista i els orígens del catalanisme polític. Dels orígens a la presidència del Dr. Martí i Julià (1891–1903)*. (Barcelona, Publicacions de l'Abadia de Montserrat, 1992).

16. Termes, Josep; Colomines, Agustí. *Les Bases de Manresa de 1892 i els orígens del catalanisme polític*. (Barcelona: Generalitat de Catalunya, 1992); Pérez Francesch, J. L. *Les Bases de Manresa i el programa polític de la Unió Catalanista (1891–1899)*. (Manresa: Fundació Caixa de Manresa, 1992).

17. Casassas, Jordi. *Entre Escil·la i Caribdis. El catalanisme i la Catalunya conservadora de la segona meitat del segle XIX*. (Barcelona: La Magrana, 1990), p. 274ff.

18. Casassas, Jordi (ed). *L'Ateneu i Barcelona. Un segle i mig de cultura*. (Barcelona: RDBA, 2006).

19. Burgaya, Josep. *La formació del catalanisme conservador i els models "nacionals" coetanis. Premsa catalanista i moviments nacionalistes contemporanis, 1868–1901*. (Unpublished doctoral thesis. Autonomous University of Barcelona, 1999); Cattini, Giovanni C., Santacana, Carles. "International Models of Catalan Nationalism (1882–1914)," in *Empires and Nations from the Eighteenth to the Twentieth Century*, eds. Antonello Biagini, Giovanni Motta (Cambridge: Cambridge Scholars Publishing, 2014), pp. 327–336.

20. Pella i Forgas, Josep. "El regionalismo en España. Aragón y Galicia," in *La España Regional*, Vol. I (1886), p. 161.

21. Cattini, Giovanni C. "Los regionalistas catalanes en la España de la Restauración." *Bulletin d'Histoire Contemporaine de l'Espagne*, no. 45, 2010, pp. 19–42.

22. S.N. "Els Jocs Florals de 1893," in *La España Regional*, Vol. XIV (1893), p. 282.

23. Brañas, Alfredo. "El Regionalismo en el Norte de Europa," in *La España Regional*, Vol. XIV (1893), pp. 551–554.

24. Estévez, Xosé. *De la Triple Alianza al Pacto de San Sebastián*. (San Sebastián: Cuadernos Universitarios E.U.T.G.—Mundaiz, 1991), pp. 63–70.

25. Izquierdo, Santi. *La primera victòria del catalanisme polític*. (Barcelona: Pòrtic, 2001).

26. Culla, Joan B. *El lerrouxisme a Catalunya (1901–1923)*. (Barcelona: Curial, 1987); Álvarez Junco, José. *El emperador del Paralelo. Lerroux y la demagogia populista*. (Barcelona: RBA, 2012).

27. Ehrlich, Charles E. *Lliga regionalista: lliga Catalana 1901–1936*. (Barcelona: Editorial Alpha, 2004).

28. Figueras, Josep Maria. *La Veu de Catalunya, 1899–1937*. (Barcelona: Editorial Base, 2014).

29. Casassas, Jordi. *La voluntat i la quimera. El noucentisme català entre la Renaixença i el marxisme*. (Barcelona: Edicions 62, 2017).

30. Cattini. Giovanni C. "Myths and Symbols in the Political Culture of Catalan Nationalism (1880–1914)," in *Nations and Nationalism*, no. 21.3 (2015), pp. 445–460.
31. Anguera, Pere. *Les quatre barres. De bandera històrica a senyera nacional.* (Barcelona: Dalmau Editor, 2010).
32. Ayats, Jaume. *Els Segadors. De cançó eròtica a himne nacional.* (Barcelona: L'Avenç, 2011).
33. Anguera. Pere. *L'Onze de Setembre. Història de la Diada (1886–1938).* (Barcelona: Publicacions de l'Abadia de Montserrat, 2008); Balcells, Albert. *Llocs de memòria dels catalans.* (Barcelona: Proa, 2007).
34. Cabo Villaverde, Miquel. "Solidaridad Gallega y el desafío del sistema de la Restauración," in *Ayer*, no. 64 (2006), pp. 235–259.
35. Mees, Ludger. "La Euskadi invertebrada: el País Vasco en tiempos de la Solidaridad Catalana," in VvAa., *Solidaritat Catalana i Espanya.* (Barcelona: Base, 2008).
36. Ullman, Joan Connelly. *La Semana Trágica.* (Barcelona: Ediciones B, 2009).
37. Marinello Bonnefoy, Juan Cristobal. *Sindicalismo y violencia en Cataluña. 1902–1919.* (Unpublished doctoral thesis. Autonomous University of Barcelona, 2014).
38. Culla, Joan Batista. *El republicanisme lerrouxista a Catalunya . . .* cit.
39. Tavera, Susanna. *Solidaridad Obrera. El fer-se i desfer-se d'un diari anarcosindicalista (1915–1939).* (Barcelona: Col·legi de Periodistes, 1992).
40. Avilés Farré, Juan. *Francisco Ferrer y Guardia.* (Madrid: Marcial Pons, 2006).
41. Aisa, Ferran. *CNT. La força obrera de Catalunya.* (Barcelona: Base, 2013).
42. Izquierdo, Santi. *República i autonomia: el difícil arrelament del catalanisme d'esquerres (1904–1931).* (Catarroja: Afers. 2006).
43. Balcells, Albert; Pujol, Enric; Sabater, Jordi. *La Mancomunitat de Catalunya i l'autonomia.* (Proa, Barcelona: 1996).
44. Balcells, Albert; Pujol, Enric. *Història de l'Institut d'Estudis Catalans.* (Barcelona—Catarroja: Institute for Catalan Studies—Editorial Afers, 2002).
45. Mañà, Teresa. *Les Biblioteques populars de la Mancomunitat de Catalunya: 1915–1925.* (Lleida: Editorial Pagès, 2007).
46. Balcells, Albert. "L'Institut d'Educació General de Prat de la Riba. Higiene i civisme, 1914–1923," in *Cercles. Revista d'Història Cultural*, no. 12 (2009).
47. Bofill i Matas, Jaume. *Prat de la Riba i la cultura catalana* (ed. Jordi Casassas i Ymbert). (Barcelona: Edicions 62, 1979).
48. Balcells, Albert; Pujol, Enric; Sabater, Jordi. *La Mancomunitat de Catalunya i l'autonomia*, cit., pp. 108–178; Ucelay da Cal, Enric. "La Mancomunitat de Catalunya i la Diputació de Barcelona," in *Història de la Diputació de Barcelona.* (Barcelona, Diputació de Barcelona, 1987), pp. 93–139.
49. Moreno Luzón, Javier. "De agravios, pactos y símbolos. El nacionalismo español ante la autonomía de Cataluña," *Ayer*, no. 63, 2006, pp. 131–135.
50. Balcells, Albert: *El projecte d'autonomia de la Mancomunitat de Catalunya del 1919 i el seu context històric.* (Barcelona: Parlament de Catalunya, 2010).

51. Beramendi, Justo; Diéguez, Uxío Breogan et al. *Repensar Galicia. As Irmandades da fala*. Santiago de Compostela: Xunta de Galicia/Museo de Pobo Galego, 2017.
52. Estevez, Xosé. *De la Triple Alianza al Pacto de San Sebastián*, cit., p. 190ff.
53. Agirreazkuenaga, Joseba. "A reformulación do autogoberno dos vascos," in J. Beramendi, U.B. Diéguez et al., *Repensar Galicia*, cit., pp. 59–67.
54. Balcells, Albert. *El pistolerisme*. (Barcelona, Pòrtic, 2009).
55. Pradas Baena, M. A. *L'Anarquisme i les lluites socials a Barcelona 1918–1923: la repressió obrera i la violència*. (Barcelona, Publicacions de l'Abadia de Montserrat, 2003).
56. Roig i Rosich, Josep Maria. *Francesc Macià: de militar espanyol a independentista català*. (Barcelona: Esfera dels Llibres, 2006).
57. Casassas, Jordi. "What Made Catalonia Unique (1901–1939)," in F. Sabaté (ed.), *Historical Analysis of the Catalan Identity*, op. cit., pp. 301–328.
58. Lorenzo Espinosa, José María. "Influencia del nacionalismo irlandés en el nacionalismo vasco 1916–1936," in *Nuevas formulaciones culturales: Euskal Herria—Europa*. (Donostia, Eusko Ikaskuntza, 1992), pp. 240–247; Núñez Seixas, Xosé Manuel. "El mito del nacionalismo irlandés y su influencia en los nacionalismos gallego, vasco y catalán (1880–1936)," in *Spagna contemporanea* no. 2 (1992), pp. 25–58; Ferrer i Pont, Joan Carles. *Nosaltres sols: la revolta irlandesa a Catalunya*. (Barcelona: Publicacions de l'Abadia del Montserrat, 2007); Rodríguez Madriñán, Xavier. "A revolución irlandesa en *A Nosa Terra*. Unha crònica de ausencias, paixón e silencio (1916–1923)," in J. Beramendi, U.B. Diéguez et al., *Repensar Galicia*, cit., pp. 201–216.
59. Ucelay da Cal, Enric. "Daniel Cardona i Civil i l'opció armada del nacionalisme radical català (1890–1943)," in *La Batalla i altres escrits* (Enric Ucelay, ed.). (Barcelona: La Magrana, 1984); Rubiralta, Fermí. *Daniel Cardona i Civit 1890–1943. Una biografia política*. (Catarroja: Afers, 2008); Velasco, Miquel Angel. *Manuel Serra i Moret (Vic, 1884-Perpignan 1963)*. (Vic: Patronat d'Estudis Ausonencs, 2009).
60. Roig i Rosich, Josep M. *Francesc Macià: polític, teòric, agitador. Documents (1907–1931)*. (Barcelona: Generalitat de Catalunya, 2010).
61. Tona, Abelard. *Memòries d'un nacionalista català. Del nacionalisme radical al comunisme. Història menuda (1922–1932)*. (Barcelona: Publicacions de l'Abadia de Montserrat, 1994), pp. 33–34.
62. Roig i Rosich, Josep Maria. *Francesc Macià: de militar espanyol a independentista català*, op. cit., pp. 225–226.
63. Estévez, Xosé. *De la Triple Alianza al Pacto de San Sebastián*, cit., pp. 228–239 and 353–360; Castells, Víctor. *Galeusca. Un ideal compartit*. (Barcelona: Rafael Dalmau, 2008), pp. 43–54.
64. [A.R.V], "Galicia, Bascònia i Catalunya," La Publicitat, 8/7/1923, p. 1.
65. Estévez, Xosé. *De la Triple Alianza al Pacto de San Sebastián*, cit., p. 363ff.
66. Tona, A. *Memòries d'un nacionalista català*, cit., pp. 36–37.

67. González Calleja, Eduardo. *La España de Primo de Rivera. La modernización autoritaria 1923–1930.* (Madrid: Alianza, 2005).

68. Aisa, Ferran. *Una història de Barcelona. Ateneu Enciclopèdic Popular, 1902–1979.* (Barcelona: Virus, 2009).

69. Lladonosa, Manel. *Catalanisme i moviment obrer: el CADCI entre 1906–1923.* (Barcelona: Publicacions de l'Abadia de Montserrat, 1988).

70. Roig i Rosich, Josep Maria. *La dictadura de Primo de Rivera a Catalunya: un assaig de repressió cultural.* (Barcelona: Publicacions de l'Abadia de Montserrat, 1992).

71. Estévez, Xosé. *De la triple alianza al Pacto de San Sebastián . . .*

72. Cattini, Giovanni C. *El gran complot. Qui va trair Macià? La trama italiana.* (Badalona: Ara llibres, 2009).

73. Roig i Rosich, Josep M. *Francesc Macià: polític, teòric, agitador. Documents (1907–1931),* cit., pp. 466–467.

74. Estévez, Xosé. *Galeuzca: la rebelión de la periferia (1923–1998).* (Madrid: Entinema, 2009).

75. Rubiralta, Fermí. *Una història de l'independentisme polític català.* (Lleida: Pagès Editors, 2004), p. 57.

76. Bonamusa, Francesc. *El Bloc Obrer i Camperol (1930–1932).* (Barcelona: Ed. Curial, 1974).

77. Rubiralta, Fermí. *Daniel Cardona i Civit 1890–1943. Una biografia política.* (Catarroja: Afers, 2008), p. 117ff.

78. Roig Rosich, Josep M.; Cattini, Giovanni C. *El temps de les il·lusions.* Vol. I of *La Segona República a Catalunya* (coord. per Jordi Casassas) (Barcelona, Ara llibres, 2015).

79. Santacana, Carles. "La configuració dels municipis perifèrics: l'impacte cultural i sociopolític," in Oyón, José Luis (ed), *Vida obrera en la Barcelona de entreguerras.* (Barcelona: CCCB, 1999), pp. 85–98.

80. Culla, Joan B. *Esquerra Republicana de Catalunya. Una història política (1931–2012).* (Barcelona: Columna, 2012).

81. Ucelay da Cal, Enric. *La Catalunya populista.* (Barcelona: La Magrana, 1982).

82. Balcells, Albert. "Catalanism and National Emancipation Movements in the Rest of Europe," *Catalan Historical Review,* no. 6 (2013), pp. 97–102.

83. Ehrlich, Ch. E. *Lliga regionalista. Lliga catalana (1901–1936),* cit.

84. Prats, Josep. *Los anarquistas en la crisis política española.* (Buenos Aires: Editorial Alfa, 1964), p. 85.

85. Vega Massana, Eulàlia. *Entre revolució i reforma. La CNT a Catalunya (1930–1936).* (Lleida: Pagès Editors, 2004).

86. Abelló Güell, Teresa. *El debat estatutari del 1932.* (Barcelona, Parlament de Catalunya, 2007).

87. Culla, Joan Baptista. *El catalanisme d'esquerra (1928–1936).* (Barcelona: Curial, 1977).

88. Ucelay, Enric; Gònzalez Vilalta, Arnau; Núñez Seixas, Xosé Manuel. *El catalanisme davant del feixisme 1919–2018.* (Barcelona: Editorial Gregal, 2018).

89. De la Granja, José Luis. "Las alianzas políticas entre los nacionalismos periféricos

en la España del Siglo XX," *Studia Historica. Historia contemporánea*, no. 18 (2000), pp. 149–175. Available at: http://revistas.usal.es/index.php/0213-2087 /article/view/5907; ídem, *El Oasi vasco. El nacimiento de Euskadi en la República y la Guerra civil.* (Madrid, Tecnos, 2007), pp. 217–246.

90. Rovira i Virgili, Antoni. "Nacions d'Ibèria. Bascos, Gallecs i Catalans," in *La Humanitat*, 6/8/1933, p. 3.

91. Santacana, Carles. *Un país en tensió*, Vol II, of J. Casassas (coord.) La Segona República a Catalunya . . . cit.

92. Gonzàlez Vilalta, Arnau; López Esteve, Manel; Ucelay da Cal, Enric. *El 6 d'Octubre. La desfeta de la revolució catalanista de 1934.* (Barcelona: Editorial Base, 2014).

93. Bonamusa, Francesc. *Generalitat de Catalunya. Obra de Govern 1931–1939.* Vol I. (Barcelona: Departament de la Vicepresidència, 2006), pp. 47–55.

94. Villarroya, Joan. *Guerra i Revolució. 1936–1939*, Volum III, of J. Casassas (coord). *La Segona República a Catalunya* . . ., cit.

95. Berger, Gonzalo. *El Comitè Central de Milícies Antifeixistes. Voluntaris per la llibertat.* (Vic: Eumo, 2018).

96. Tosstorff, Reiner. *El POUM en la revolució espanyola.* (Barcelona: Base, 2009).

97. Puigsech Farràs, Josep. *Nosaltres, els comunistes catalans.* (Vic: Editorial Eumo, 2001).

98. Bonamusa, Francesc. "El període de més gran autonomia (juliol 1936—maig 1937)," in *Història de la Generalitat de Catalunya: dels orígens medievals a l'actualitat, 650 anys* (ed. Teresa Ferrer i Mallol). (Barcelona: IEC, 2011), pp. 337–360.

99. Gallego, Ferran. *Barcelona, mayo de 1937.* (Barcelona: Debate, 2007).

100. Villarroja, Joan. "La Generalitat del maig de 1937 al febrer de 1939," in *Història de la Generalitat de Catalunya: dels orígens medievals a l'actualitat, 650 anys* (ed. by Teresa Ferrer i Mallol), cit., pp. 361–380.

101. Puigventós, Eduard. *Complot contra Companys. L'afer Rebertés i la trama catalanista per aconseguir la Generalitat durant la Guerra Civil.* (Societat Catalana d'Estudis Històrics, Barcelona, 2008).

102. Rubiralta, Fermí. *Joan Cornudella i Barberà (1904–1985). Biografia política.* (Barcelona: Publicacions de l'Abadia de Montserrat, 2003).

103. Cattini, Giovanni C. "La política de la Generalitat després dels Fets de Maig," in *La Guerra Civil a Catalunya. Vol. III: Catalunya, centre neuràlgic de la guerra* (edited by Solé i Sabaté, Josep Maria, and Villarroya i Font, Joan). (Barcelona: Edicions 62, 2004), pp. 30–39.

104. Pi Sunyer, Carles. *La República y la Guerra. Memorias de un político catalán.* (Mexico, Oasis, 1975).

105. Maymí, Josep. *Josep Irla. La tenacitat d´un compromís.* (Barcelona: Publicacions de L'Abadia de Montserrat, 2003).

106. Arrien, Gregorio; Goiogana, Iñaki. *El primer exili dels vascos. Catalunya 1936–1939.* (Barcelona-Bilbao, FRTF and FSA, 2000).

107. Estévez, Xosé. *Galeuzca: la rebelión de la periferia (1923–1998).* Madrid, 2009.

Nationalism and Nation Building in Galiza (1891–1950).

UXÍO-BREOGÁN DIÉGUEZ CEQUIEL

The late modern period in Galiza represented a continuation from the end of the early modern period; there was little industrialization and the population—which was predominantly rural and with little growth for some decades—was widely dispersed across the region,[1] with no real central powerhouse. With no national bourgeoisie, nor any wide-reaching workers' movement or cultural movement (with the exception of the members of the so-called *Rexurdimento*, as we will see) to bring society together and with a high level of migration—primarily to Latin America—the leaders of this nation were to be found in the rancorous peasants' movement that had come about to defend the legitimate claims of the peasantry within the framework of the Spanish state and against the local and supra-local authorities (but without a program of modernization for the country as a whole, meeting the demands of this movement at a local level). The latter situation was framed against a backdrop of an end-of-century agrarian crisis and large-scale changes taking place in the current system, which was faced with the emerging global market as opposed to the traditional, local model.[2] In the early twentieth century, this movement gave rise to large-scale organizations, of which two should be highlighted, Solidariedade Galega and Acción Galega.

The Underpinning of a New Galiza

From Solidariedade Galega and Acción Galega to the Asociación Rexionalista Galega

Solidariedade Galega was set up in A Coruña in early 1907, in response to the Agricultural Unions Law that had been enacted the previous year, and remained in existence until 1912. This was a profoundly pro-Galician organization that had been motivated strongly by the Solidaritat Catalana movement and its electoral success in 1907. Solidariedade Galega thus stood in the elections, winning 258 local councilmember seats in 1910; this was quite a good result. Acción Galega, for its part, burst onto the scene with great force from its center in Ourense (although it was managed from Madrid), and mobilized thousands of peasant workers against the socage system. Although he died in 1914, its leader, the priest Basilio Álvarez, was a true figurehead until his death.[3] Both associations published homonymous journals through which they disseminated their ideology, which proclaimed the empowerment of the Galician peasantry (understood as the "Galician people" by antonomasia, as they formed the overwhelming majority of the population and the perseverance of traditional Galician society in the rural regions of the Atlantic coast). The demand for civil and political rights, in popular terms and in defense of the peasants, was ever-present in the pages of these journals, along with a declaration in favor of Galician culture and language, thereby asserting Galiza as a political entity.

The forerunner of these mass-agrarian organizations in terms of their Galician-focused strategy was the creation of the Asociación Rexionalista Galega (ARG) in the city of A Coruña in the last decade of the nineteenth century. With a brief, primarily symbolic existence (1890–92), this group was sponsored and led by the historian Manuel Murguía. Without doubt, this cadre organization was the operational high-point of Galicianism of the time.

Between the creation of the ARG and the aforementioned organizational articulation of the agrarian masses, institutions would be established in Galiza without which the subsequent evolution of this nation cannot be understood. This was the case with the (Real) Academia Galega, founded in 1906 under the presidency of none-other than Manuel Murguía and supported by emigrant Galicians, especially from Havana (Cuba). Migration is one of the defining traits of contemporary Galiza, with hundreds of thousands of Galician men and women spread out across the globe, especially in the Americas. (In Europe, the only other country with similar levels of migration is Ireland.) This was a migrant mass that systematically gave rise to an overseas social network, which in turn sought to alleviate the suffering in Galiza by sending funds from the countries in which these people had settled (one should highlight that it was not just the setting up of cultural institutions but also—and prior to these—the creation of schools and professional training centers). It was this Galician diaspora that made the Galician flag[4] a national symbol; and that interpreted what would become the Galician national anthem.[5]

The historian Manuel Murguía (along with the writer Rosalía de Castro) was a central figure, as the reader can see, in that late nineteenth and early twentieth-century pro-Galicia movement. Throughout his life, he was instrumental in promoting the history of Galiza and the construction and socialization of a national Galician imaginary, a dynamic to which the historians Benito Vicetto, first, and Francisco Tettamancy, sometime later, also contributed. This work was carried out in parallel to the start of a scholarly study of the Galician language, an attempt by the Academia Galega to establish some "standardization rules" of the nation's language. The Galician language, although spoken by the majority of the people of Galiza, was totally marginalized in comparison with Spanish as it clashed with the process of Spanish nation building. This was a situation against which the famous *Rexurdimento*[6] had been organized in the previous century; the backdrop to which was the proclamation of 1846.[7]

I now turn my attention to another important late nineteenth-century pro-Galician figure, Alfredo Brañas Menéndez. A professor of political economics since 1888, he had recently returned from the University of Oviedo, where he had earned a professorship in natural law, and was a councilmember in Santiago de Compostela between 1890 and 1891. He was an active member of the Asociación Rexionalista Galega, writing vociferously in its gazette, *La Patria Gallega*. He was the leader of the Catholic sector of this movement, with the liberal sector led by Manuel Murguía.[8] During this time, Brañas authored the *Bases generales del regionalismo y su aplicación a Galicia* (General Principles of Regionalism and their Application in Galiza), among other works, and he maintained close ties with the pro-Catalan movement of the time. In this regard, one should mention that he attended the *Jocs Florals* in Barcelona in 1893, as a member of the jury, and was decisive in attracting Francesc Cambó—who was, according to him, the co-founder and leader at the time of the Lliga Regionalista[9]—to the cause of Catalanism, and thus he was also influential in the role of the other promoter of the Lliga, Enric Prat de la Riba. Brañas died in Santiago de Compostela in 1900 at the age of just forty-one. He had been one of the most prestigious and influential pro-Galician intellectuals up until that point (and in the later history of Galician nationalism, until the late 1930s) but his death meant that the pro-Galician-leaning agrarian movement mentioned earlier[10] never counted on his support.

After the time of these Galician agrarian organisations, a new organisation burst onto the scene with great force in 1916, born under the name *Hirmandade dos Amigos da Fala* [Brotherhood of Friends of the Language], a situation which we will look at next.

As Irmandades da Fala
(The Brotherhood of the Language), 1916–1931

In early 1916, Antón Vilar Ponte returned to Galiza from his emigration to Cuba some years earlier, almost coinciding with the arrival of Fuco Gómez in Havana. Vilar Ponte would play a major role in modernizing the political framework, with a pro-Galician organization, as we will see. His figures of reference included the Galician lawyer and journalist Aurelio Ribalta, working from Madrid, and Rodrigo Sanz of Ferrol, the alma mater of the Universidade Popular da Coruña, and co-founder of the already defunct Solidariedade Galega (with time he became a central figure in the "Secretariado de Galicia" in Madrid), as well as Manuel Lugrís Freire, director of the Escola Rexional de Declamación and co-founder of the Real Academia Gallega; also the founder of the agrarian Solidariedade Galega, which, along with its homonymous publication, also released *A Nosa Terra* in 1907. They were responsible for various writings that theorized about the need to grant autonomy to Galiza in an attempt to bring the level of wellbeing that the social majority in Galiza were lacking (given that the Spanish centralist system focused only on the problems and miseries of Galiza). These demands were made in the context of the differential situation in Galiza, starting with the language as the most visible element of this. These proclamations would be repeated by the eldest of the Vilar Ponte siblings.

In this order of things, he published a short work entitled *Nacionalismo Gallego. Nuestra "afirmación" regional (Apuntes para un libro)* (Galician Nationalism: Our Regional "Affirmation" (notes for a book)) on January 5, 1916. In this pamphlet, the intellectual and journalist reaffirmed the demands of Aurelio Ribalta in favor of the Galician language and Galician autonomy, presenting a need to create a "League of Friends of the Language." He explained to the editor of *La Voz de Galicia* newspaper the need to articulate a movement that would defend the Galician language, starting with a recognition of Galiza as a "natural homeland" and its inhabitants "a free people with a historic character" as well as the great necessity to create a strong pro-Galician platform that would bring together all the forces with which this ideology resonated.

The text cemented a large part of the existing pro-Galician tradition, adding some new elements, especially the term "nationalism" as an updated synonym of what had previously been termed "regionalism" by the movement led (as already mentioned) by the historian Manuel Murguía.

On May 18, 1916, just four months after its publication, Antón Vilar Ponte called the constitutional meeting of what would be formally named the Hirmandade dos Amigos da Fala, at the offices of the Real Academia Gallega in Rúa Rego d'Auga, no. 38–1ª, seemingly at the suggestion of Ramón Vilar Ponte.[11] This was fifty-three years after Rosalía de Castro published the poem "Cantares Gallegos," a symbol of the nineteenth-century Galician *Rexurdimento*.

This meeting at the premises of the Academia Galega was attended by the acclaimed intellectuals and activists Manuel Lugrís Freire, Francisco Tettamancy, Uxío Carré Aldao, Uxío and Leandro Carré Alvarellos, Florencio and César Vaamonde Lores, Xosé Baldomir, Xosé Iglesias Roura, and Micaela Chao Maciñeira, as well as Antón and Ramón Vilar Ponte; moreover, it received the support of figures including Victoriano Taibo, Lois Porteiro Garea, and Xesús Culebras, in addition to the tangential welcoming of the initiative of Manuel Murguía, who had, by then, turned eighty-three.

The Hirmandade that was created at this meeting soon became known as the Irmandade da Fala, spreading across the entire Galician region in the coming months and years. The organization would renew the pro-Galician politics of the time, broadening the horizon from a local or regional to a Galician national framework; it became the hegemonic reference in all of Galiza, bringing together the men and women who saw (and thought of) Galiza as their real land/nation and concerned about the devaluing of the Galician language and culture, a situation to which they sought a political solution.

Expansion of Irmandiño Nationalism: The Nationalist Press, Patriotic Youth, and Electoral Struggle

One of the first initiatives promoted by the Irmandades da Fala was the publication of a newspaper with an editorial line that connected with early twentieth-century Galician agrarianism: *A Nosa Terra*. This is an extraordinary source for studying Galician nationalism in the first third of the twentieth century.

The first edition was published on November 14, 1916, with a full-length article by Antón Vilar Ponte, part diatribe, part declaration of principles, entitled "Coa Bandeira Ergueita" (With the flag raised). In the text, Vilar Ponte stated that the paper would arouse the "feelings and thoughts" of Galician youth, who would "start to join the fight," and described Galiza as a "Natural Homeland with its own language."[12]

The social awareness that this would give to the Irmandades, in terms of their agenda and ideology, gave rise to the (re)launch of *A Nosa Terra* (after its original publication as a voice of the Galician agrarian movement, Solidariedade Galega, in 1907), under the direction of the treasurer of the Irmandades, Xosé Iglesias Roura.

This media outlet contained articles by Irmandade activists who set out their political ideology, issue after issue. Through this paper, the militants of the Irmandades postulated their ideas theorizing and theorized on the problem of Galician nationhood (from economics to institutional politics, via literature, language, folklore, and urban planning and architecture). It attracted—and instructed—new recruits to swell the nationalists' ranks to face the future. However, the linguistic-cultural-identity issue was the main issue that filled its pages.

From the outset, *A Nosa Terra* (ANT) would celebrate initiatives, acts, and ideas in its "*Cadro Branco*" (White Box) while denouncing the opposite in a "*Cadro Mouro*" (Dark Box). In the first edition of ANT, the *Cadro Branco* contained a eulogy to Rodrigo Sanz: "a cultured, austere man, highly admired by us and at the Ateneo de Madrid, where they have him as a teacher [who] has always spoken in Galician." The *Cadro Mouro* tells of a "regionalist party(!) in honor of Rosalía de Castro, which took place in the Theater of A Coruña. The only ones to speak in Galician were a few, highly cultured speakers of our language—and only in short phrases. Everyone else expressed themselves in Castilian".

Alongside this binomial, other sections of the ANT included "*Peneirando*"—(which focused on general current affairs) and "*Novas da Causa*", which chronicled the evolution of the "Galician Cause" and Galicianism that the Irmandades were generating and promoting. Gradually, new features appeared in the eight-page paper, such as "*Tribuna Libre*" and "*Follas Novas*", to give space to articles on collaboration and reviews of newly published books, respectively.

This active defense of the Galician language and homeland brought together, in the Irmandades, members of different political parties and others with no political affiliation, united in the ideal of Galiza being recognized (and respected) for its national personality. This new, patriotic grouping brought together late nineteenth-century regionalist cadres together with new recruits born in the late-nineteenth- and early-twentieth centuries, who would rejuvenate pro-Galician politics. These groups held wildly differing opinions on religious, social, and—to a large extent—political questions but the issue of Galician nationalism acted as a common denominator. Therefore, it should be remembered that we are not talking about a political party, but rather a local grouping with a patriotic ideal in which the binding force was the question of Galician nationalism, distilled into the defense of the Galician language and "identity" —exclusively to begin with—and that culminated in the fight for the normalization and legalization of the language, as well as a vindication of the *fact* of Galician nationhood and the existence of the nation of Galiza evidenced by a (long) history.

From the outset, the Irmandades da Fala sought to increase the number of young cadres to their cause, as was evident with their assertions printed in ANT, with an intense proselytist tone in this respect. The Galician philosopher Johán Vicente Viqueira would become one of these members, one of the most important in the nascent Irmandades movement and one of the hardest working in this sense. He theorized and called for a "Galician School" as a patriotic necessity. Shortly after the creation of the Irmandades da Fala, he claimed that Galician youth needed to be more "idealistic" and "romantic" in order to reclaim their Galician heritage).[13]

In the pages of ANT, one could constantly find various articles and editorials that insisted on this idea. They claimed that Galician youth had an obligation to join the Irmandades da Fala as a way of committing to their homeland and its development in all areas of life. This was a highly pro-Galician political commitment that opposed Spanish centralism, which was defined as the main impediment to the country and as the root of each and every one of the problems that Galiza had faced throughout a long, secular historical process.

There is no doubt that the work of political agitation carried out by the Irmandades da Fala from its inception brought its rewards. Hundreds of people joined up and took them as a reference, channeling their concerns through the Irmandades. Immediately after the success in A Coruña, in cities and towns such as Santiago de Compostela and Monforte, and in the following months and years in Pontevedra, Ourense, Vilalba, Ferrol, Betanzos, Lugo, Melide, and A Estrada, how well Beramendi studied (2008), together with representations in Madrid, Porto, Buenos Aires, and Havana—among many other places, a total of twenty-eight groups—the Irmandades da Fala saw men and women joining up in search of better times for Galiza.

The Irmandades also attracted other pro-Galician organizations that already existed in the aforementioned places, such as the Irmandade Rexionalista Galega, of which the journalist Antonio Valcárel was an active militant. He was also a member of the A Coruña branch of the Irmandades da Fala and was that organization's candidate for the A Coruña constituency in the Spanish elections of 1918. The Irmandades da Fala showed keen interest in these elections, as they had in the municipal elections of the previous year,[14] encouraging the candidacy of Antonio Valcárcel (who could not, eventually, stand), as well as Rodrigo Sanz in Pontedeume (who also was unable to stand), Antón Lousada Diéguez in A Estrada, Lois Porteiro in Celanova, and Francisco Vázquez in Noia, as the historian Justo Beramendi writes. Despite their failure in the elections, the electoral work that the Irmandades da Fala had done at the time (together with the previously mentioned municipalities in 1917) gave rise to an important socialization and growth of the Irmandades da Fala.

Building on their electoral experience in 1918, they started to socialize their systematic criticism of the lack of parliamentarians in the Spanish system that could defend the interests of Galiza and started to highlight the need to have a Galician parliament in the nation. This criticism was designed to raise awareness among Galician society of the need for Galician representatives in Spanish institutions and for a legal, political, and administrative framework of their own, respectively. From then on, the Irmandades membership promoted the idea that, despite not having any institutional representation, it was the Irmandades that could influence Spanish politics, an influence that would be greater if they could count on pro-Galician parliamentarians who subscribed to their ideals, as stated by the lawyer Lois Peña Novo.[15]

Two years after the Irmandades were founded, by the end of 1918, they had some seven hundred members and twenty-one local groups. In addition, they had also created a critical mass in favor of Galician representation with a nationalist agenda in Spanish government, which would continue to grow throughout the 1920s.[16]

In this way, the Irmandades da Fala also managed to obtain a political and institutional presence that meant the country had its own voice. They promoted electoral work that resulted in the investiture of the first nationalist councilmember in history, Lois Peña Novo. The Galician lawyer was elected to the city council of A Coruña in the municipal elections of February 1920. Antón Vilar Ponte became the second electoral success for Galician nationalism, also in the city in which the Irmandades movement was born. The debate regarding the electoral struggle and the results of this in the elections appeared in *A Nosa Terra* (nos. 111 and 112, 1920), presenting Peña Novo as a "historic councilmember, as he has become the first nationalist councilmember we have ever had in our homeland."

These magnificent results were representative of how the Irmandades were swelling their ranks, with the support of some of the most highly respected intellectuals in the country. They included the Vilar Ponte brothers, Manuel Lugrís Freire, Vicente Risco, Manuel Banet Fontenla, Manuel Iglesias Roura, Ramón Cabanillas, Salvador Cabeza de León, Francisco Tettamancy, Galo Salinas, Antón Lousada Diéguez, Lois Peña Novo, Ramón Otero Pedrayo, Uxío Carré Aldao, Uxío and Leandro Carré Alvarellos, Xosé Lesta Meis, Alfredo Somoza, Federico Zamora, Daniel Rodríguez Castelao, Armando Cotarelo, Victoriano Taibo, Arturo Noguerol, Xaime Quintanilla, Evaristo Correa Calderón, Gonzalo López Abente, Víctor Casas, Florentino and César Vaamonde Lores, María Miramontes, Ánxel Casal, Camilo Díaz Baliño, Roberto Blanco Torres, Bernardino Varela, Elvira Bao Maceiras, Eleuterio González Salgado, Amparo López Jean, Carmen Chao and Mercedes Vieito Bouza, and the deceased Lois Porteiro Garea and Johán Vicente Viqueira. The leading theorist was Vicente Risco, from Ourense, the author of *Teoría do Nazonalismo Galego* (1920). *A Nosa Terra* disseminated this work prior to its publication, promoting it among its readers.

The First Galician Nationalist Assembly

In early 1917, the Irmandades da Fala organized their first large-scale event, calling it "glorious and patriotic." It consisted of a horse ride between A Coruña, Lugo, Monforte, and Vilalba on January 28. The promoters claimed that they were developing an "Event for those who will sow the blessed idea of Galician redemption. An event of sun, youth, patriotism, and altruism. The first ride of the new Quixotes".[17]

Participants in this event included the veterans Manuel Lugrís Freire, Manuel Banet Fontenla, Francisco Tettamancy, and Xenaro Mariñas González (father of Jenaro Marinhas del Valle),[18] as well as Antón and Ramón Vilar Ponte, Alfredo and Lois Somoza Gutiérrez, Ricardo Carballal Lafourcade, Lois Peña Novo, and a young Evaristo Correa Calderón, among others.

From then on, the members of the Irmandades da Fala organized a continuous series of public events and, in the spring of 1918, around the second anniversary of the Irmandades da Fala, Antón Vilar Ponte wrote a review of the work they had done, attributing the creation of the Irmandades da Fala to his brother Ramón and calling the Galician language the "soul of the people," a key element in the pro-Galician political fight, and calling the Portuguese language a "brother tongue".[19]

Immediately after this remembrance by Antón Vilar Ponte the "regulations" of the Irmandades were redacted and legalized. Specifically, on June 12, 1918, this document, which standardized the structure, functions, and purpose of the various local groups of the Irmandades, was presented to the civil government. The purpose of this, according to Vilar Ponte, was that the regulations would be "the aggrandizement of our lands in all aspects" under the heading "All by Galicia and for Galicia," working to achieve "a wide-reaching autonomy for Galicia in all ambits."[20]

In this document the *irmandiños* stated that they would work for the dissemination of the "scientific, literary, and artistic culture of Galiza," and for the study of the "economic, legal, and social questions"; with the "agrarian question being the most important," they would pay special attention to the study of the "organization of the peasant workers." Thus, under these regulations, the Irmandades set out four sections: Culture and Language; Economy and Social Studies; Agriculture; and, lastly, Politics. They created a national "Directory" for the practical management of the federation of all the Irmandades established (in which the "presidents" of each local group were included; the organizational framework named a "president," "vice-president," "general secretary," and four "board members").

When this document was being legalized, the Irmandades da Fala envisaged a national-level meeting to bring together its activists to discuss its consolidation and to create a route map. The initial date was October 24 but the outbreak of the Europe-wide flu epidemic forced the postponement of the event which was to focus on "all the significant elements of Galicianism," an exchange of ideas, and, as reported in *A Nosa Terra*, a canon with which to govern. The location chosen for the event was Lugo, the result of its historic significance, as well as for its central location.[21]

They kept the walled city as the location and set a new date. Hence, the event was held between Sunday, November 17 and Monday,

November 18, 1918. Titled the "*I Asambreia Nazonalista Galega*" or the "*Asambreia de Lugo*," its aim was to achieve the "Integral autonomy of the *Nazón Galega* and set out a concrete program to find solutions to the problems that deeply affect national life in Galicia".

Thus, the members of the Irmandades da Fala present at this assembly approved a program-manifesto that would guide pro-Galician politics for the coming decades, formally and explicitly inaugurating Galician nationalism (surpassing the previous regionalism, without any subtle distinctions) with the manifesto itself calling the pro-Galician cadres present at that assembly "today and forever Galician nationalists".[22]

In the same document, they demand the constitution of an "Autonomous Galician Power" and a "Xuntoiro" or Galician parliament; of a "Federation of Iberia" consisting of the existing states in this framework, Portugal included; of a Galician taxation regime; they affirm the equality of rights for women with respect to men, including the demand for universal suffrage; the management of education in Galiza; and that the Galician language should be co-official, along with Castilian, in Galiza, among other points. Moreover, they proclaimed the "aesthetic sovereignty in the Nation of Galicia," which would govern over urban and rural constructions, enacting a law that would oblige the owners to maintain the aesthetic standards or each region of Galiza.

This document was signed by figures from the Galician movement including Antón Lousada Diéguez, Vicente Risco, Arturo Noguerol, Xaime Quintanilla, Manuel Banet Fontenla, Ramón Cabanillas, Afonso Daniel Rodríguez Castelao, Antón Vilar Ponte, Lois Peña Novo, Johán Vicente Viqueira, Roberto Blanco Torres, Lois Ares, Salvador Mosteiro, Xosé Faraldo, Carlos Monasterio, Ramón Oxea, Ánxel Casal, and Federico Zamora. It emphasized that all the Irmandades da Fala were represented by these activists, together with delegations from sixty-seven agrarian societies and five cultural centers; support was received from five agrarian societies, eleven councils, more than forty-nine associations, and numerous personalities from Galiza at the time.

After this first assembly a second was held in Compostela in November 1919 and a third in Vigo in April 1921, prior to the break-up that would take place around the fourth Nationalist Assembly. This last one took place in Monforte in February 1922. It saw the birth of the Ourense-based Irmandade Nazonalista Galega (ING), parallel to and a breakaway from the Irmandades da Fala. The ING was led at the Galician level by the writer and philosopher Vicente Risco, together with Antón Lousada Diéguez (plus Antón Vilar Ponte as a leader in the region of A Coruña).

In March 1923, the Fifth Nationalist Assembly was held, sponsored by the ING. This meeting was held six months prior to the Spanish military coup of September, led by General Miguel Primo de Rivera; this was, naturally, a defining point in the history of Galician nationalism and the Spanish state as a whole, as the general implemented a pro-Spanish, right-wing, totalitarian dictatorship.

Language, Education, the Collective Imaginary, and the Social Question in the Galician Nationalism of the Irmandades

Among the activities of the Irmandades throughout their history, the importance of their social agitation in favor of the language and the sovereignty of Galiza through meetings in plazas, meeting rooms, and theaters cannot be over-emphasized. Furthermore, the Irmandades also published fervently. As well as publishing *A Nosa Terra*, they also created a "Galician-Castilian Vocabulary" in instalments, with a large glossary and a series of traditional sayings, many of which were no longer in widespread use. Along with this vocabulary, one should also highlight the concern shown (and the debate generated) about the norms of the standardization of the Galician language, which were finally published a decade and a half after the founding of the Irmandades, after attempts throughout the 1920s. The fruit of this intense labor was *Celtiga*, a publishing house and journal promoted by the Irmandade da Fala in Ferrol in 1921. This initiative was closed down by Primo de Rivera in 1923 and replaced by the publishing house and journal *Lar*, which was backed by the Irmandade da Fala of A Coruña from 1924 onward. Directed by Leandro Carré Alvarellos and Ánxel Casal, the journal persisted until 1926 and the publishing house until 1927 when a new entity was established: Nós. Pubricacións galegas e imprenta. This project was headed by Ánxel Casal and María Miramontes and they would take on the publishing of *A Nosa Terra*.

In this work of recovering the Galician language for all areas of use and the fight for its legalization, a majority current would be in favor of the unification of Galician and Portuguese (which would have a direct link with the proposal for the Federation of Galiza with Portugal; the Irmandades seeing these two regions as historically being part of a whole, from the root of the old Suebi Kingdom of Galiza). Along these lines, the Irmandades da Fala promoted monolingual education in Galician which gave rise to the Escolas do Insiño Galego (Galician Education Schools) in April 1924, led by María Miramontes and Ánxel Casal, as well as other pro-Galician initiatives launched in the field of education, as has been excellently explored by Sabela Rivas Barrós and Ernesto Vázquez Souza.[23] These schools were created on the basis of a well-argued critique of the prevailing educational system in Galiza, in which teachers came from outside Galiza and marginalized the country's own language, imprinting on the collective Galician imagination a feeling of clear inferiority with regard to the Spanish language (and culture) that these teachers standardized in the country, as a higher language, and as a language for transmitting knowledge and science.

The schools run by María Miramontes and Ánxel Casal taught and/or influenced young people who would soon become new cadres for the Galician nationalism, as was the case with Pedro Galán Calvete and Jenaro Marinhas del Valle. It was in these schools that the future Galiza was shaped: "The Galician Education Schools will be the fulcrum on which rests the future of the Galician movement; they are the foundation of the true Galician 'rexurdimento'" (renaissance).[24]

Under the wing of the Irmandades da Fala, various nationalist student groups were also formed. One of these was the Xuventú Escolar Nazonalista (sic), formed in Santiago four years before the above-mentioned schools, out of the activism of a university student, Valentín Paz Andrade.

In this same order of things, university students started the Seminario de Estudos Galegos in 1923, which had the aim of promoting scientific knowledge in Galiza and in Galician (which was not guaranteed by the University of Santiago de Compostela at that time). The members of the Irmandades were fully behind this initiative, legitimizing it and the leaders of the Irmandades appointed the professors

Armando Cotarelo Valledor (1923) and Salvador Cabeza de León (1925) as the first and second presidents of the *seminario* (the post was later occupied by Luís Iglesias Iglesias and Ramón Otero Pedrayo).

At the same time, the Irmandades were working to establish (and socialize) some special dates in the (national) Galician calendar: April 26 (*mártires de Carral* (Martyrs of Carral)); July 25 (Galiza Day); and the 17th December 17 (*"perda das liberdades gallegas"* (Loss of Galician Liberties), in honor of the murdered Galician nobleman and marshal Pero Pardo de Cela, killed on the orders of Isabella of Castile in 1483). Galiza Day or "Día da Patria" was approved at the Second Nationalist Assembly of the Irmandades da Fala, held in Santiago de Compostela in November 1919, with the date of the celebrations set as July 25.[25]

These dates were chosen to favor the creation of a patriotic collective imaginary and a Galician national (collective) consciousness. Part of this patriotic Galician imaginary of the time was Celtism (and Atlanticism),[26] which played an important role in the national identity in opposition to the Mediterranean identity of Spain. In this respect, one should underscore the work of the archaeologists Florentino López Cuevillas and Fermín Bouza Brey, as well as that of writer Plácido Castro in the late 1920s; they revitalized the discourse, in this sense, that was started by the historian Manuel Murguía in the latter part of the nineteenth century.[27]

This consciousness and imaginary defended and valued the rural world and the lower classes that lived there (as opposed to the Castilianized urban areas). The very fact of using *A Nosa Terra*— which had been an organ for agrarian expression of Solidariedade Galega back in 1907—as a means of spreading the message became a real declaration of principles. A large part of the initial membership of the Irmandades da Fala had, in fact, been figureheads in the agrarian movement (Manuel Lugrís Freire, Uxío Carré Aldao, and Galo Rodríguez Salinas, for example). They joined the "Galician Cause" with the recognition of a rich rural world in which Galician was the commonly spoken language. Likewise, they valued the monolingual, Galician speaking factory workers who were fighting for their rights in the urban world (the majority of whom came from the rural, peasant world). With this situation, it should come as no surprise that there was a close relationship between the Galician lawyer Lois Porteiro Garea and the workers' leader José Pasín, an anarchist from Santiago who had been a founding member of the Irmandade da Fala of Santiago; Porteiro had been his lawyer, along with many other unionists.[28]

The Irmandades da Fala put great emphasis on their sensitivity toward the working poor and even some of their own cadres noticed this class consciousness especially in their anti-cacique fight and against socage. It is no coincidence that, later, Lois Porteiro Garea would advise and defend various labor union activists from Santiago, including Pasín, specifically before and after the 1917 *Folga Xeral* (General Strike); nor that in 1918 Ramón Vilar Ponte would drive the creation of the Sindicato da Construción (Construction workers' union) in Viveiro, together with Agapito García Atadell, as happened in A Coruña with Calviño, a notable anarchist activist, and with the socialist Xaime Quintanilla, a member of the Irmandades da Fala in Santiago initially and later in Ferrol. This reality gave rise to the agreement, at the aforementioned Fifth Nationalist Assembly, of the Irmandades da Fala in 1923, to create an umbrella organization for Galician unions, the Confederation of Galician Workers. Responsibility for this fell to Ramón Vilar Ponte, César Parapar Sueiras, Xosé María Calviño, and Xaime Quintanilla, the speakers on the proposal presented at the meeting.

At that time, the Irmandades da Fala were also cultivating international relationships, especially in the Iberian context. The Irmandade Nazonalista Galega and the Irmandades da Fala signed a "Triple Alliance" pact with pro-Basque and Catalan sovereignty organizations on September 11. This was a meeting and a pact that resulted from a Catalan initiative, specifically from Acció Catalana, whose paper *La Publicitat* called together the Catalan, Basque, and Galician nationalists, as has been explored thoroughly by the historian Víctor Castells.[29]

The Irmandades da Fala sent a delegation consisting of Federico Zamora and Alfredo Somoza to the signing of this tripartite pact; and the ING sent a telegram in support.[30] Yet the military coup of September 13 that same year headed by General Miguel Primo de Rivera, two days after the National Day of Catalonia, meant that the agreement did not give rise to any political action; it was, however, a reference upon which the Galeuzca alliance was built in 1933 between nationalists from the three countries, a situation studied in minute detail by Xosé Estévez [31] and Castells.

Galician Nationalism in the Last Years of the Primo de Rivera Dictatorship: The Founding of ORGA and the Constitution of the Partido Galeguista, 1929–1931

The Irmandades da Fala continued to publish *A Nosa Terra* and remained active during the dictatorship of Miguel Primo de Rivera, for whom they initially had partial sympathy for his (false) anti-cacique discourse and in favor of "regional" identities, as can be seen on the pages of the *irmandiño* paper itself. At the start of the dictatorship, the A Coruña branch of the Irmandades focused on launching the Escolas do Insiño Galego, the Seminario de Estudos Galegos, and the Escola Dramática Galega (Galician School of Dramatic Arts), primarily educational and cultural activities. They also continued holding conferences and printing publications; however, when these had a substantive political content they were shut down, as was the case with *Céltiga* at the start of the dictatorship, which was totally revised by military censors, and the highest profile example being that of *A Nosa Terra*. Meanwhile, the Irmandade Nazonalista Galega was dying out with some of its most important members being initially active in the structure of the Rivera dictatorship.

In any event, by the end of the 1920s, Primo de Rivera's rule was in its death throes and the Spanish monarchy that had supported it would not survive either. Most of the pro-Galician activists that had previously been part of the ING now converged once more with the Irmandades da Fala. With the collapse of Primo de Rivera and his system, around 1929, the republican left (and others beside) ramped up their actions, seeking a new era. The pro-Galician activists considered creating a political party for this new, republican-leaning era they sensed was coming. Thus, a large part of the active members of the Irmandades da Fala, together with republican federations from A Coruña, participated in the creation of the Organización Republicana Gallega Autónoma (ORGA) in the fall of 1929, which was led by Santiago Casares Quiroga and with Antón Vilar Ponte, Ánxel Casal, and Victor Casas among the cadres of Galician nationalism who were most active in this party.

In March 1930, during the so-called *Dictablanda*, important representatives of the A Coruña Irmandade and members of ORGA were enthusiastic participants in the "Lestrove Pact" and the launch of the Federación Republicana Gallega (FRG), including Antón Vilar Ponte, Federico Zamora, and Alfredo Somoza. The remaining Irmandades da Fala did not form part of either of these. The majority of the Irmandades did not trust republicanism, including activists such as Victor Casas and Ánxel Casal, leaving the Galician nationalist Antón Vilar Ponte practically alone in ORGA with just his closest allies from the Coruña Irmandade, including the economist Lois Peña Novo. In September 1930, in opposition to tyranny and centralism, several prominent figures in Galiza signed the "Barrantes Pact". These included the agrarian cleric Basilio Álvarez and the nationalists Daniel Rodríguez Castelao, Ramón Otero Pedrayo, Álvaro de las Casas, Florentino López Cuevillas, and Lois Peña Novo.

Thus, in April 1930, members of the Irmandades da Fala met up in A Coruña, including a good number of those who had been part of the ING and who were part of ORGA and the FRG. The Sixth Nationalist Assembly was held and it led—not without tensions—to the construction of a new political organization, into to which the Irmandades da Fala would reconvert, ahead of what appeared could be a new Spanish Republic. In the month of July, coinciding with the National Day of Galiza, Galician nationalists organized a series of events including one known as the "Xantar da Barxa" (Lunch at Barxa). Here, they appeared to be reorganizing the political-organizational relaunch of the pro-Galician ideology before the new era, in which new nationalist groups were formed for the coming Galician landscape, the most important of these being the Partido Galeguista de Pontevedra, led by Alexandre Bóveda and Pedro Basanta.

Republicanism and the Pro-autonomy Movement

The Galician nationalism that was still centered around the Irmandades da Fala affirmed the following, before the fall of the dictatorship of Primo de Rivera, the *dictablanda*, and the Bourbon monarchy, in an especially optimistic tone:

The eight years of dictatorship that prevented us from being in contact with our beloved Galician people were of great profit as they created in us Galicians a consciousness of our true value and of the need for Galicia to control its own destiny, as it was demonstrated blatantly that the centralist regime was an obstacle to the development of our own lives.[32]

Galician nationalism agreed with the republican solution, especially if it opted for a federal solution for the state; and when it came to setting a date for establishing the constitutional parliament, pro-Galician sympathizers believed strongly in the backing that the Republic would give to an autonomous Galician jurisdiction. The leaders of the Irmandades understood that, "The Republic has come to put the problem on the road to a clear solution and thus we cannot lose a moment to call Galicia to join this patriotic crusade so that we do not miss this chance to win our autonomy."[33]

Thus, ORGA called a mass, pro-autonomy assembly on the June 4, 1931, the culmination, according to the Irmandade nationalists, of fifteen years of work carried out by that pro-Galician brotherhood, one of whose central aims was to finally achieve a federal Galician state before the aforementioned constitutional parliament that would be a "truly extraordinary achievement in the political life of Galicia."[34]

This was a context in which, therefore, all attention was focused on June 28, 1931, the date of the constitution of those new parliament of what would be the Second Spanish Republic, in charge of modelling the new legal-administrative system, in a federal or centralist key, in which the pro-Galician sympathizers hoped to gain several members of parliament from within their ranks, or who were at least in favor of their ideology. This representation took the form of two nationalists in the Spanish parliament, Daniel Rodríguez Castelao and Ramón Otero Pedrayo;[35] they were labelled by the press as Galicianists, as opposed to other recently elected representatives of Galician constituencies, making clear the lack of trust that existed in the ranks of the Galician nationalist movement toward ORGA.[36] The leadership of the Irmandades affirmed that the work of Castelao and Pedrayo in the constitutional parliament would be committed to the "Galician cause" and emphasized the political importance of the two men.[37] This historic event—two explicitly nationalist representatives in the chamber of the Republic—was preceded by another unique event: the proclamation of the Galician state.

From the Proclamation of the Galician State to the Split with ORGA and the Creation of the Partido Galeguista

On June 27, 1931, in the run-up to the elections to the constitutional parliament, hundreds of workers, of the more than twelve thousand workers on strike over the construction of the Zamora–A Coruña railroad, marched through the streets of Santiago calling for a Galician state. Various reports in the next day's press emphasize the importance of this event. *El Pueblo Gallego* reported on how the mass-event developed on that Saturday with workers demonstrating on the streets of Santiago de Compostela, marching to the Pazo de Raxoi, the location of the Council headquarters, in the Praza do Obradoiro:

> *Raising the blue and white flag on the building and proclaiming the Galician State. All the authorities resigned immediately.* The people demanded that Alonso Ríos be installed as president of the Revolutionary Council. He, in turn stated that he was "of the people" and that he would die rather than surrender.[38]

In Santiago, the same thing happened as the previous day in Ourense, where Antón Alonso Ríos along with Pedro Campos Couceiro, both newly returned from decades in Argentina, to where they had emigrated, would be the acclaimed figures representing the new "Galician Republican State" and the driving force behind the demonstration in Santiago.

As well as the two aforementioned activists, the *irmandiño* pro-Galician sympathizers, without the necessary social force and mobilizing capacity, and in the process of reorganization, had been, for practical purposes, on the periphery of that proclamation. They did not have a political platform to issue directives to their members in an unequivocal manner—either for or against this—and so, according to various veteran cadres of the movement (specifically, those with a more intellectual profile who were focused on the ideas) the country was not sufficiently mature for an initiative such as this to take hold (although, as they indicated, it had great scope and they were in favor of it). This is how Salvador Cabeza de León,[39] sitting president of the Seminario de Estudos Galegos, would express that proclamation. This was because he favored not forcing the creation of a Galician state within the framework of a Spanish Republic under construction and understood that it was necessary to support from Galiza a federal Spanish Republic, in which Galician autonomy could be developed with greater popular support.[40]

Now, pro-Galician sympathizers were fully confident that, in the medium term, the historic moment when full Galician liberties would be won was near. One month after that significant event, coinciding with the Day of Galiza in 1931, they stated that it was they who had created "the Galicianist atmosphere that Galiza breathes today. *We were the ones who imagined and who built a new and free Galicia. And so now our patriotic ideal has the chance to become real.*"[41]

However, the positions that ORGA would adopt after this assembly in favor of the statute of autonomy and, above all, the lack of transfer of powers at the institutional and governmental level of what had been agreed at that meeting—(among other things) weeks after it was held, was not to the liking of the *irmandiño* nationalists. Surprisingly, that organization did not take the steps in line with those agreed at that large-scale event, in contrast with majority organizations in the Basque Country and Catalonia that were closely tied to the approval of their respective statutes of autonomy. In the same issue of *A Nosa Terra* in which they disseminated the statutes, the Galician nationalists made their criticism known with respect to non-Galician nationalist republicanism, for not taking firm action in favor of the Galician statute.[42]

Thus, nationalists in the Irmandades da Fala, together with a majority of the most active members of ORGA, worked on the idea of creating a new party structure that would stand for a Galician statute, with all that that implied, starting with a Galiza-wide plebiscite.[43]

The Partido Galeguista and the Fight for "Autonomy"

The republican era would be seen by pro-Galician activists as a clear opportunity to create a strong Galician autonomy within the framework of the Spanish federal state. This was explained in the *Anteproyeito de Estatuto de Autonomía da Galiza* (Draft on the Statute of Galician Autonomy), published by the Seminario de Estudos Galegos in May 1931: namely, that of A "free Galician state" within a federal Spanish Republic, which would increase in favor of an Iberian-level federation of republics wherein Galiza, the Basque Country, and Catalonia were independent states alongside Spain and Portugal and any other countries that may wish to join.

To prepare for this new political landscape, that is, the Second Spanish Republic, it was urgently necessary to reshape the organization of the pro-Galician movement for the coming times. And so, on December 5 and 6, 1931, a new, national-level assembly was held in Pontevedra by the Irmandades da Fala: The Seventh Galician Nationalist Assembly. All the local groups of the Irmandades da Fala attended, along with small nationalist parties that had been set up immediately prior to this assembly[44] Figures including Daniel Rodríguez Castelao, Alexandre Bóveda, Manuel Lugrís Freire, Ramón Otero Pedrayo, Víctor Casas, Ánxel Casal, Ramón Vilar Ponte, Xosé Filgueira Valverde, Plácido Castro, Salvador Mosteiro, and Álvaro de las Casas attended. The importance of this meeting stems from the fact that those present took the decision to create the Partido Galeguista (PG): the organization that was formed, with leadership and responsibilities chosen democratically at this event, including the Consello Nacional (national council) and the executive committee of the party. The PG was, in practice, a structural reconversion of the Irmandades da Fala; at the outset, however, Antón Vilar Ponte would not form part of the party, despite his backing for it.

The central work of the PG would be, in accordance with the above, that which the Irmandades da Fala had set out as a tactical objective at the First Nationalist Assembly in 1918: the creation of an "Autonomous Galician Authority." The struggle in favor of a statute of autonomy in the republican era started there, backing the constitution of a "Galician State within a Federal Spanish Republic." And, as they had at that first nationalist assembly, they would fight for a Federation of Free Iberian States that would bring together all those states that would be created through a constitutional process, as was the case with the Galician state.

At the head of the Partido Galeguista was Alexandre Bóveda Iglesias, the secretary general of this new organization that would be at the forefront of Galician nationalism[45] from late 1931 on. According to many of the handwritten notes from that and previous meetings,[46] there is no doubt that this represented a new generation of Galician nationalists taking over from the old cadres. To this end, they needed to overcome differences among the Galician nationalist membership— made up of thirty-two local or supra-local pro-Galician groups[47]— to create the greater pro-Galician party that the PG would become. Joining these were "many allied Galicianists, nuclear cells that had been created, Galician artists spread all across our land, devoted brothers who, far from here, have worked for a better Galicia."[48]

From the founding of the PG, this new generation of activists and nationalist cadres played an important role. Alexandre Bóveda, specifically, and the Pontevedra group as a whole, would be the focal point for the modernization of Galician nationalism as represented by the gestation of the PG, a proper political party with statutes to be followed and respected. This made the party incompatible, in contrast to situation with the Irmandades da Fala, with parallel partisan activist groups. They were faithful to the program and structure of the new organization, which aspired to the "political self-determination of Galicia within the republican government structure."[49] This was stated in the second point of the declaration of principles of the party, the headquarters of which were in Tetuán Street, Pontevedra.

In this sense, first as secretary of the organization and, shortly after, as secretary general,[50] Bóveda would be in charge of the party's public representation and its expansion, as well as of internal cohesion; he represented the activist cadre that gave the party a common body and, as secretary general, he clarified positions and the theories that helped the training of other party members.[51]

He represented a new form of management, which would be backed by the old one, on seeing his potential. Important figures in the party's proselytism, based in Pontevedra, included the brilliant artist Daniel Rodríguez Castelao and the teacher and philosopher Antón Lousada Diéguez.[52] They moved the nerve center of Galician nationalism from A Coruña and Ourense to Pontevedra. This meant that, for example, the voice of political pro-Galician ideas, *A Nosa Terra*, just fifteen years after its founding in the city of the Tower of Hercules as the voice of the Irmandades, would be published in Pontevedra from 1932 onward, under the leadership of Victor Casas, another distinguished member of the new, brilliant cadres of Galician nationalism.[53] These included an extraordinary team of women and men, such as Castelao; Ánxel Casal;[54] María Miramontes;[55] Lois Tobío; Ramón Otero Pedrayo; Johan Carballeira; Ricardo Carvalho Calero; Plácido Castro; and Francisco Fernández del Riego.

They promoted a variety of initiatives aimed at introducing Galician nationalism to the common people through talks, seminars, rallies, and social gatherings. This dynamic, which was sponsored by the Irmandades da Fala, included meetings in the Café Moderno in Pontevedra and the Derby and Café Español in Santiago de Compostela. The latter of these was mentioned years later by the designer and artist Luís Seoane, who recalled that "in the meeting at the Café Español in Santiago, where students, writers, and artists got together, [we were the ones who] dreamed of a proud and dignified Galicia, governed by its people."[56]

This nationalism would grow its sphere of influence and popular appeal, in the heat of the social consciousness and strong activist mindset of a large part of the party's leadership at local and national level, expanding the ideological and political scope of the PG as it developed. In this way, the nationalism of its cadres acted as a common denominator with various tendencies working together to expand the project of this political organization.[57]

Likewise, the PG would increase the presence of nationalism in areas in which it had been barely present, as is the case in academia wherein the Seminario de Estudos Galegos, in the heat of the new republican era, could carry out its important work,[58] substantially increasing its collection of publications. Furthermore, overseas, they created entities including the Institución Cultural Galega, with headquarters in the centrally located Avenida de Mayo, no. 11370, Buenos Aires. This presented itself as a "representative of the Seminario de Estudos Galegos of San-Iago de Galiza, the most evident and clearest source of the coming Galician Culture."[59] This entity[60] had the

Organización Republicana Nacionalista Autónoma Galega (ORNAG), which had been founded in Buenos Aires in 1931, parallel to the creation of the PG, as its immediate political reference point. In practice, it was the Argentine arm of the PG itself, headed by Rodolfo Prada Chamocín and with Manuel Meilán Martínez[61] as its secretary.

However, in terms of the essential activities of political pro-Galician thought of the time, it was clearly that which would lead to the approval of a statute of autonomy for Galiza. All pro-Galician activities were leading to this tactical objective, in line with that mentioned above, namely, the start of a process to give the Galician nation official status. The particular ideology of various people within the pro-Galician movement had as a common anchor the belief in a statute of autonomy. However, it is true that what I term the left-wing of the pro-Galician movement was gaining ground within the movement and spreading to the whole of the membership. As the republican era went on, this situation led to a split on the right, breaking the movement into two groups. The first was led by Vicente Risco and the second by Xosé Filgueira Valverde. This had been coming since the start of the republican era; the most conservative-leaning veteran cadres (as regards social issues) were leaving the PG as they no longer felt represented. This was the case with Risco, and with Manuel Banet Fontenla and Filgueira, among others.[62]

The Struggle for the Statute of Autonomy: From the Assembly of Councils to the Plebiscite of 1936

Following the failure of Galician nationalism after having channeled its political aspirations toward Galician autonomy through the ORGA, the PG would be tasked with calling for a statute for Galiza that would lead to an "Autonomous Galician Authority." In the spring of 1932, the foundations were set in place for the first steps in this push for Galician autonomy. On April 19, under the initiative of Alexandre Bóveda (secretary of the recently formed Partido Galeguista) and Enrique Rajoy Leloup (a pro-Galician conservative and member of Santiago city council[63]), Raimundo López Pol, the mayor of Santiago, was seen as having the legitimacy to relaunch the project for a statute of autonomy. As such, on April 27, the city council of Santiago approved the calling of a meeting of all Galician town councils to debate what would become the definitive text of the statute of autonomy.

After this call and the positive response from the majority of the town councils in Galiza to the initiative from Santiago, the date was set for a preparatory meeting that would be known as the Asemblea de Concellos de Galiza Pro-Estatuto (Pro-Statute Assembly of Galician Councils). This meeting represented the first step in the drafting of the articles of the statute. This preparatory meeting, which was representative of the political, administrative, economic, and cultural elements that made up Galician life at the time, took place on July 3, 1932 at the assembly rooms of the University of Santiago de Compostela.

Out of the various proposals for articles of the statute of autonomy for Galiza put forward, there was agreement on a consensual text for the statute of autonomy. It was a transactional text that brought together the various tendencies and was in accordance with the republican statute of autonomy constitution, collating the parliamentary experiences accumulated with the Catalan statute. For this work, a joint committee from this assembly was appointed. The committee tasked with writing this new statute was made up of Salvador Cabeza de León, president, Enrique Rajoy Leloup, secretary, and members Manuel Iglesias Corral, Eladio Rodríguez González, Manuel Lugrís Freire, Jacobo Arias, Avelino López Otero, Rodrigo Sanz López, Santiago Montero Díaz, and Alexandre Bóveda. The committee finished its work on September 4, 1932. This new text had some necessary changes from the project of maxims pushed by the nationalists, especially by Alexandre Bóveda, at that meeting. It no longer referred to Galiza as a "Free State within the Federal Spanish Republic" but rather as an "autonomous region within the Spanish state." Likewise, other changes included the equality of the Spanish and Galician languages and the indispensable knowledge of the latter to work in the state civil service, which had been in the SEG project, becoming merely a recommendation in the newly redrafted text.

It must be borne in mind that these concessions were deemed necessary for the objective of a statute for Galiza in the view of the PG. This organization, although present across all Galiza, knew perfectly well that adopting a maximalist position on its claims for autonomy would only result in either the approval of a statute that would definitively reference the centralism of the state, supported by a minimum of administrative autonomy, or the definitive paralysis of the process within the framework of the new legal-administrative system that was still being consolidated. The PG, choosing a more pragmatic approach, opted for the consensus document, to which amendments could be tabled.

On November 1, the mayors of Santiago, Ferrol, A Coruña, Lugo, Ourense, Pontevedra, Vigo, Betanzos, Mondoñedo, Noia, Tui, O Carballiño, Lalín, and Sarria called all the town councils of Galiza to the assembly wherein the articles of statute would be approved prior to be put to a plebiscite of the Galician people.[64]

The Pro-Statute Assembly of Councils

On December 10 and 11, 1932, the PG held the Second Assembly in Santiago de Compostela. Various points were discussed at this assembly but the question of the statute occupied most of the debating time; in the conclusions collated by the PG in a notebook, it stated that, "The Statute is the greatest concern in these critical hours." The PG assumed responsibility in this aspect.

On Saturday, December 17, 1932, at around 12:30, after a delay of an hour and a half, the inaugural session of the Pro-Statute Assembly of Councils got underway. Over the next three days they would debate the statutory text that would be put to the public in a referendum. Xaime Quintanilla, the socialist mayor of Ferrol, who had been appointed president of the assembly, could not take on the role due to illness and was substituted by Bibiano Fernández Osorio Tafall. He was tasked with opening the assembly with Enrique Rajoy Leloup acting as secretary. In a press release issued in the early hours of December 17 in Santiago, it was highlighted that in Santiago de Compostela, "in almost all the streets there were banners welcoming the assembly members and extolling their love for Galicia."[65]

It was a spirit that seemed to foreshadow a favorable outcome to the question of autonomy. In general, it was an assembly of great debate, in terms of theme and duration, in which Galiza, represented through its town councils (227 out of a total of 319) was playing for its statute.

Only two issues particularly raised the tone of the assembly: one was the co-officiality of the Galician and Spanish languages; the other was the future capital of the autonomous region.[66]

Be that as it may, on December 19, 1932, the statute of autonomy was approved by the Assembly of Councils with the support of 209 of the 227 town councils present at the meeting. After the assembly, newspapers, pamphlets, and posters, among other means, were used to express the historical importance of the result of that summit in favor of the Galician statute of autonomy. One newspaper of the time stated that, "We now have a Statute. Galicia has taken its first steps in its liberation from the centralist yoke and is ready to put the Statute to a plebiscite."[67]

From Political Repression to the Autonomy Plebiscite

As required by the Spanish law of the time, after the assembly of town councils, the articles of association agreed on would have to be submitted to a plebiscite at the Galician level. The central autonomy committee stated that it would take place in the fall of 1933. However, the desired plebiscite, set for the symbolic date of December 17,[68] would be frozen *sine die* as a result of the electoral victory in November of that year of a constellation of pro-Spanish organizations that would come to rule the Spanish Republic. These organizations, centered around the CEDA (Spanish Confederation of Autonomous Rights), made any normal running of the already existing autonomies impossible governmentally, as was the case with Catalonia, which had had a statute since 1932, or those still in the process of attaining autonomy, as was the case with Galiza and the Basque Country.

This situation emerged when the PG tried to raise awareness among the Galician population of the need for sovereignty, as a result of everyday problems. It denounced the agreements between Spain and Uruguay to import meat, which marginalized and seriously damaged the Galician cattle industry. The representative Rodríguez Castelao stated in *A Nosa Terra*, "Galicia needs to be free . . . If it is only through absolute separation that we can save our homeland from central oppression, then we call for absolute separation."[69]

Castelao's stance here was the same as most of the cadres of the PG: ever-more left-leaning and toward explicit pro-sovereignty positions.

In the words of Victor Casas, it was never so "necessary as it is now . . . for Galicia to have political independence or, at least, an ample autonomy."[70]

The first year of government under the Second Republic was particularly belligerent for Galician, Basque, and Catalan nationalism, as well as for the left in general in Spain. This was evident, for example, in the response of the CEDA government to the Asturian Revolution and the proclamation of the Catalan State,[71] and the democratic reactions against the ultra-pro-Spain, right-wing government. This government forced the two most important pro-Galician activists, Castelao and Bóveda, to be banished from their roles as civil servants in late 1934.[72] This was obviously the response of the markedly pro-Spain, right-wing government to the decisive contributions of these two pro-Galician figures in the process of constructing the Galician nation and their important social profiles. To this we need to add the numerous detentions that nationalist cadres suffered, as was the case of Ramón Suárez Picallo and Álvaro de las Casas. Furthermore, we can add the closure, between October 6 and February 9, 1935, of the nationalist mouthpiece, the newspaper *A Nosa Terra*.

At the end of the first four months of 1935, pro-Galician activists held the Fourth Nationalist Assembly, on April 20 and 21 in Santiago and the Federación de Mocedades Galeguistas (FMG), created one year earlier, held its second national-level plenary.[73] The PG would ratify the line of action and work developed throughout the previous year and there would be no changes in the composition of its executive secretariat, renewing the positions of the architect Manuel Gómez Román, as secretary general of the PG, Castelao in the political secretariat,[74] and Bóveda in area of organization, along with Xerardo Álvarez Gallego, propaganda secretary, Plácido R. Castro, secretary of (international) relations, and Sebastián González García, technical secretary. The pro-Galician activists were decidedly following a path of necessary social growth, albeit under the conditions of a semi-clandestine state. Their central campaign was the struggle for the statute of autonomy in a newly left-leaning republic. In this sense, they promoted various meetings with several left-wing Spanish organizations in favor of a new, progressive government at the state level, in order to define a common denominator from which to work with some level of coordination against the ultra-pro-Spain right-wing.

The ratification by the PG of the line of action that it had started at the assembly held the previous January, when it committed to seek broad republican alliances with other left-wing organizations, would provoke the split of the Ourense based Dereita Galeguista, led by Vicente Risco.[75]

It was decided, firmly, to extend the alliance with the Catalan and Basque nationalist organizations, but also with the Spanish left. This alliance came together in the coalition named the Frente Popular (Popular Front), established on the June 2, 1935. It was made up of, among others from beyond the PG, the Partido Socialista Obrero Español (PSOE), Unión Republicana (UR), Partido Comunista de España (PCE), Izquierda Republicana (IR), Esquerra Republicana de Catalunya (ERC),[76] and the Partido Obrero de Unificación Marxista (POUM). The integration agreement in this coalition conditioned the PG—in the hypothetical case of the now allied left forces coming into government—to immediately enable such a government to legalize the work favorable to the statute of autonomy and to set a date, consequently, for the plebiscite on autonomy that had been postponed since November 1933, after the successful 1932 Assembly of Councils. The coalition, which was interested in joining forces, approved and settled the demands of the pro-Galician elements that the PG be part of it.

Meanwhile, toward the end of 1935 and after a year in exile, Bóveda and Castelao, returned to Galiza, coinciding almost with the fall of the pro-Spanish right-wing government responsible for their expatriation. From this moment on, the campaign for autonomy was resumed publicly, in line with the mandate given to Galician Manuel Portela Valladares to create a provisional government in the impasse created until the formation of a new government, for which he would call elections for February 1936. This new set of elections obliged the PG to call its second Special National Assembly. It needed to choose candidates and present the PG to Galician society with proven unity after the biennial rule of the CEDA. Alexandre Bóveda, as the PG's organizational secretary, held various meetings around the country to standardize a course of action and to take stock of the internal state of the organization.

The Second Special National Assembly was held with great success in the Salón Ideal in Santiago de Compostela, at the end of January 1936. As its central point, integration within the Popular Front in the electoral lists would be resolved, and to this end there were internal votes on candidates for the party in which Castelao gained 1,785 votes and Bóveda 1,735; Ramón Suárez Picallo gained 1,775 votes and Antón Vilar Ponte 1,771, among others.[77] After this special assembly, the members of the Frente Popular alliance held hundreds of events. The PG held numerous meetings, with entertainment by traditional Galician musical groups such as the famous *Os Dezas* bagpipers, which had all joined the Partido Galeguista one year earlier. The researcher Manuel Igrexas highlights this event in one study.[78]

The Frente Popular, primarily backed within the PG by Bóveda, Castelao, and Suárez Picallo, gained in the elections called for February 16, 1936 to the state parliament, with the PG winning three seats, namely: Daniel R. Castelao for Pontevedra and Ramón Suárez Picallo and Antón Vilar Ponte for A Coruña.[79] The seats won and the votes that gave rise to these results—over 400,000 in these three constituencies for Galician nationalism—were a great success; to this can be added the appointment of Alexandre Bóveda, a pro-Galician candidate in Ourense who was not officially elected. Everything pointed to clear tricks on the part of the local right-wing, such as fraudulent voting "by the dead, the absent, and the sick,"[80] given that they did not have direct relations with the pro-Galician presence in the province and the pull of Bóveda himself with the 25,000 votes that he won, according to official scrutineers; José Calvo Sotelo, the Spanish right-wing, leader prevented his confirmation. The PG, naturally, tried to challenge the result but there was little that it could do.

The joy of the overall result would be short-lived with the death of one of the newly elected representatives: Antón Vilar Ponte. Together with his brother Ramón, he had been, twenty years earlier, one of the driving forces behind the Irmandades da Fala. He died on March 4, 1936, having only joined the PG half a year earlier. He had, however, in some way, always effectively belonged,[81] moving ever further from its founding principles. In a circular from the organization's secretary, the PG recommended that for one month, from March 15 on, all male members should wear a black tie.

The Plebiscite on the Statute of Autonomy

Once the new, progressive Spanish government had been installed, after the elections of February 1936, Galician nationalism managed to get a date set for the autonomy plebiscite. At the insistence of the nationalists, the date was set for June 28 for the populace to approve or reject the articles of association. Thus, from March until June there was an intensive campaign, overseen by the leadership of the PG, in favor of the "liberties of Galiza," as can be seen in numerous publications from the time, in which Galician nationalism would be at the forefront. Members traveled thousands of kilometers to hold meetings, conferences, and events of all types at which they would stress the importance for the country of a statute of autonomy. Several speeches by various pro-Galician leaders were captured on film that was distributed to movie theaters across Galiza.[82] Dozens of Galician nationalists contributed to spreading the pro-statutory message locally. One of these was Avelino Pousa Antelo, an activist in the Federación de Mocedades Galeguistas, who acted with absolute clarity. They had little financial support, surviving on their activist will and the dreams that guided them.[83]

It was a huge campaign, as noted in the press and in the official results of the polling day, June 28. Despite the controversy surrounding the election, official results showed that there was a 75 participation rate with 993,351 votes for the statute and 6,161 against, with 1,451 spoiled or blank ballots. In truth, the result was not substantially different to those that, for representation, had been held at the Pro-Statute Assembly of Councils in 1932. Then, 70 percent of Galician town councils approved the statute proposal. The generation of young Galicians born after the turn of the century was decisive in that success, along with the newest activists and the veteran cadres of Galician nationalism.

After the plebiscite, it only remained, according to the republican founding charter, for the Spanish parliament to give it parliamentary status and approve the statutory document. For this, a delegation was

sent to Madrid to present the document to the president of the parliament. It was headed by Daniel Rodríguez Castelao and included
Ánxel Casal, Lois Tobío Fernández, and Manuel Gómez Román. The
Galician articles of association did not gain parliamentary status at that
time despite being presented to the president of the parliament on July
15, as a result of the military coup on July 18, 1936.[84]

Faced with the fascist uprising, Galician nationalism positioned
itself with democracy, with the republic, and the local PG groups
that took part in the republican resistance. The main pro-Galician
leaders were assassinated, jailed, and/or purged; hundreds of activists
went into exile to escape the terror. The scale of the calculated terror
inflicted on Galician nationalism is obvious: the secretary of the PG,
Alexandre Bóveda, was assassinated in the summer of 1936, as was the
mayor of Santiago (and great editor), Ánxel Casal, and the leader of
the A Coruña branch of the Federación das Mocedades Galeguistas,
Pedro Galán Calvete, who was just nineteen years old; in the fall, the
activist Victor Casas was executed and in 1937 various cadres of the PG
were killed, including the pro-Galician mayor of Bueu and a respected
journalist. For each of the activists that are named here, hundreds of
pro-Galician activists, along with anarchists, communists, socialists,
and others who were active in Galiza in the republican era, were killed,
tortured, or imprisoned. Then there were the thousands who were
forced into exile.

Galician Nationalism Abroad

From the late nineteenth century on, patriotic Galician demonstrations were held overseas. This was quite natural given that the Galician
emigrant communities, as noted, were made up of hundreds of thousands of people.[85] At that time, the epicenter of the Galician expatriate
community was in Cuba. In Argentina, thousands of Galicians arrived,
overtaking the preeminence of Cuba in Galician emigration. The
Xuntanza Nazonalista da Habana was founded in Cuba in 1920 and
the Sociedade Nazonalista Pondal[86] established in Argentina in 1927,
after the Irmandade Nazonalista Galega had been created in Buenos
Aires in 1923.

From the Xuntanza Nazo(n)alista Galega da Habana [87]
to the Comité Revolucionareo Arredista Galego d'Habana [88]

In 1913, a figure central to Galician nationalism in that Caribbean country arrived in the Cuban capital. His influence extended over more than the first half of that century due to his immense activism and creative capacities. I am referring to the thinker, prolific writer, and humanist, Francisco Gómez Gómez. He was self-taught, having been—like many of his generation—illiterate. He settled in the Cuban capital at just eighteen years of age and lived there until his death. His activism gave rise to various entities and publications that became a point of reference for Galician *arredismo* (independence) in Cuba.[89]

At the end of the 1900s, Francisco Gómez Gómez, known as "Fuco Gómez," played an active role in the activities of the Galician collective in Cuba, writing in newspapers and magazines including *Heraldo de Galicia*, *Galicia*, and *Ecos de Galicia*, and managing to organize his fellow countrymen and women politically.

In 1920 he was the co-founder of the Xuntanza Nazoalista/Nazonalista Galega da Habana, together with César Parapar Sueiras, Sinesio Fraga, and Tomás Rodríguez Sabio, among others. The Xuntanza formed part of the Irmandades da Fala and by 1921 had around a hundred members, according to the organization itself. Fuco Gómez was a member of the board of writers of the first publication by the organization, *Nós*, Órgano da Xuntanza Nazonalista Galega d'Habana, of which eight editions are known, and which would be followed around one year later by *Terra Gallega*,[90] a continuation of the previous publication. With a clear *arredista* (pro-independence) ideology, both journals, as can be seen it their editorials and articles, referenced the political thinking of Fuco Gómez and of all the men and women who made up the Galician sovereigntist organization; they were influenced strongly by the secessionist proclamations of the Cuban activist José Martí, but also by the pro-Catalan sympathizers who had settled on the Caribbean island.

This change of title was the result of the government's closing down of *Nós*, a publication that was censured, thus obliging the promoting group to launch *Terra Gallega*, of which Fuco Gómez was the administrator. Shortly after the launch of this publication, a serious crisis hit the Xuntanza Nazonalista da Habana, after Fuco Gómez denounced the business of

Fernández Doallo, a known man of letters in Havana, Galician journalist, and owner of the newspapers *Ecos de Galicia* and *Heraldo de Galicia* (on which, as indicated, Gómez had worked), ending with the closure of the Xuntanza in 1925 as a result of the fractures produced by that process.[91]

However, given that in 1921, in parallel to the creation of the Xuntanza, Fuco had created his own partisan project, the Comité Revolucionareo Arredista Galego d'Habana, subsequent to the existence of the Xuntanza—which he saw as a broader front on which the committee should keep the lead—Gómez would continue with his strong political activism as normal. From 1925 on, that committee was the platform for action of this activist thinker on Galician independence, together with a small group of Galician separatists. At the beginning it was a secret organization with a discourse and purported practice favorable to the fall of the Spanish monarchy and the military dictatorship of Miguel Primo de Rivera (which had just begun in September 1923) as well as in favor of the establishment of a Galician state.[92] In 1925, two years from publication of his *Grafia Galega*,[93] with the break-up of the Xuntanza, Fuco Gómez continued with the same idea that he had has since the outset: to set up in Cuba the logistical apparatus of Galician independentism with the aim of coordinating various action groups in Galiza that would carry out specific actions of various types, along the line of the patriotic Irish movement and its support groups in the United States.[94] The ramifications of this even reached the Spanish capital, thanks to Fuco Gómez's relationship with Fermín Penzol.[95] At the time, Penzol was part of the Mocidade Céltica. It had been created in Madrid as a Galician youth organization that also included Rof Carballo and Carlos Maside, among other figures who would play important roles in the culture, economy, and politics of Galiza decades later. The group was made up of, primarily, fervently pro-Galician students.[96] In 1929, it was renamed Acción Galega Radical Autonomista (AGRA),[97] and its objective was to improve Galician society via a government of its own, represented by the proclamation of a Galician state. The group was relaunched, like much of the organized pro-Galician political activity in Galiza before the fall of Miguel Primo de Rivera, and the entry of the brief *Dictablanda* (1929–1931), the immediate prelude to the proclamation of the Second Spanish Republic.

For that reason, Fuco Gómez returned from Cuba to Galiza to seek the establishment of a Galician state. His return was quite successful as it coincided with the ideology and support of other activists returning from emigration to the Americas, including Pedro Campos Couceiro,[98] a member of the Sociedade Nazonalista Pondal, and Antón Alonso Ríos, an agrarian activist from the Federación de Sociedades Galegas. The latter would be the visible figure of an ephemeral, but symbolic, Galician state that would be proclaimed in June 1931, leveraging the strike of twelve thousand workers on the Zamora–A Coruña railroad line construction in the summer of that year.[99] The tireless activist and prolific writer Fuco Gómez tried to implement the CRAG throughout the Galician national territory, which had kept the Galician state alive, after its proclamation in the summer of 1931. To this end, he sought collaboration with young pro-Galician activists, sympathizers of the Irmandades da fala, including Ramón Pineiro, whom he had met during the pro-autonomy campaign carried out around the Pro-Statute Assembly of Councils discussed earlier.[100]

That same year, Fuco Gómez published *Naciones Ibéricas*,[101] a compilation of texts written since 1923; therein he openly expressed his patriotic and social ideals, with women's rights playing a central role. The following year, in fall of 1933, he published a pamphlet titled "Absolute Independence, the only salvation for Galicia." After the publication of this manifesto, Fuco Gómez had to escape arrest, with the civil governor of A Coruña opening a case against him and ordering the complete withdrawal of the document.[102]

There was almost no support for Fuco Gómez's work and proclamations from most of the backers of the Partido Galeguista (PG). Likewise, he received little backing from the supposedly pro-independence pro-Galicia movement in Galiza, as represented by Álvaro de las Casas, who launched Vanguarda Nazonalista Galega in July 1933. This initiative had little intention, it must be said, of articulating a political-organizational framework for Galician Independentism in Galiza.[103] Fuco Gómez and his proposals only connected with Galician youth during his time on Galician soil. Yet, in any case, he had little practical success and returned to Cuba in 1935.

The Juntoiro Patria Galega

After 1935, Fuco Gómez worked on what would become the publication *Patria Galega*, back in Havana, and the group that revolved around him, the Juntoiro Patria Galega (with him as its first director and second "effective spokesman"). With the reactionary military coup of July 1936, various cadres of Galician nationalism went into exile in Cuba, including Xerardo Álvarez Gallego and, although for just a short time, Lois Tobío and Xohán López Durá.[104] They did not have a relationship with Fuco Gómez through the manifest lack of understanding between them and Gómez, who hoped his patriotic project would be supported by those in the PG. His pro-independence position was irreconcilable with their pro-autonomy ideals.[105] The *Patria Galega* journal reveals Fuco Gómez's militancy in Cuba as well as pro-Galician independence sympathies that revolved around it on the Caribbean island, between 1941 and 1961, when the publication would finally collapse.

Whatever the case, Galician nationalism abroad would have other organizational centers from 1941 with Buenos Aires as its new capital. The arrival of republican exiles after 1936 (and especially after 1939) to Latin America gave rise to large, active Galician communities in countries where previously there had been just a small presence. Alongside Argentina, this is true for Uruguay, Mexico, Chile, and Brazil. Buenos Aires was the destination for most Galician nationalists escaping from the Franco dictatorship, such as Daniel Rodríguez Castelao. One of the leading cadres of Galician nationalism since the early years of the Irmandades da fala, he was instrumental rebuilding Galician nationalism in exile, as we will see.

The Sociedade Nazonalista Pondal

In 1923, the Irmandade Nazonalista Galega de Bos Aires was created, with the help of the writers Eduardo Blanco Amor and Ramiro Illa Couto.[106] They would work in line with the program of the Irmandades da Fala[107] among the Galician community in the Argentine capital, publishing *Terra. Boletín da Cultura Galega*, a publication that would have a short life. In 1927, the entity adopted the name of Sociedade d'Arte Pondal, but was transformed shortly into the Sociedade Nazonalista Pondal (SNP), which was very active.[108]

The organization was active in ideological-political campaigning among the expatriate Galician community, denouncing the mistreatment that Galician men and women received as immigrants in the Americas. From the outset, the SNP had its journal, *A Fouce* (previously published by the predecessor of the SNP), which was presented as a "paper for the Nationalist Youth in the Americas," which evinced an explicitly pro-independence ideology in every edition.[109]

The group was made up mainly of self-taught youths with great intellectual and professional abilities. They were immigrants or second-generation immigrants. As Bieto Cupeiro observed, the *Pondalians* were not "men of money, rather they are almost all workers with more or less qualifications."[110]

The Sociedade Nazonalista Pondal remained active until 1938, keeping *A Fouce* as a means of expressing and disseminating its ideology until that time. The publication reappeared between 1941 and 1944,[111] giving a new lease of life to the SNP, albeit with little activity. In 1941, the organization took a new path; it was still firmly pro-independence but now it was also anti-fascist and pro-communist, highly influenced by current international affairs, namely World War II.

Through the editions of *A Fouce* in this new period, we can see this tactical change of direction after the start of Francoist repression in Galiza and the arrival in the Americas of Galician exiles. During this period, the publishers of this referential paper were influenced by communism in its fight against fascism, and also by Daniel Rodríguez Castelao. This did not mean that the group—whose flag was the blue and white flag of Galician independentism—had abandoned its strategic plans for Galiza; quite the opposite. The group would now start to slide into a more explicitly communist position, which was something that had been present in a mild form in the group previously; anarchism was also present. Its sympathizers joined together with like-minded Galician and Spanish exiles and this contributed to the dissemination of Galician nationalism among them.[112]

After the military coup of 1936, the Sociedade Nazonalista Pondal (SNP) entered into a profound debate about its position in relation to its priorities and policy of alliances.[113] After the military coup had been condemned, against the background of the harshness of the context, the SNP split between those in favor of a common cause with the pro-Galician forces operating in Argentina, namely those affiliated in the PG from Buenos Aires, and those who were opposed to this position.[114] This debate had been growing since 1939, the year in which a large number of pro-Galician sympathizers—those who had not been detained or had not already left—went into exile, mainly to the Americas, and became members of the overseas Galician society. As recounted to me by Bernaldo Souto and Ricardo Flores,[115] the position defended by the latter and initially attacked by the former (among others) triumphed: namely, to carry out joint work between "autonomists" and pro-independence *arrdistas*. Fundamental to this was the arrival of Daniel Rodríguez Castelao in Argentina in July 1940. He settled in Buenos Aires, a city with an estimated 400,000 Galicians at the time.[116] Castelao was the focal point around which pro-Galician forces regrouped and reorganized. He founded the Irmandade Galega and relaunched its paper, *A Nosa Terra*, as we will see. As regards the case under study here, the importance of the *Pondalian* activists in this reorganization should be noted; most participated in the creation of the Irmandade Galega and, above all, in the increased pro-Galician nature of the Federación de Sociedades Galegas (FSG). Many of these activists were leaders of this organization and responsible for its propaganda organ, *Galicia*, the successor to *El Despertar Gallego*, its journal during the 1930s. It was a new stage in which they had to work and to pool their efforts to achieve this.

In this context, some months before the relaunch of *A Nosa Terra*, *A Fouce*, the voice of pro-Galician independence feeling in Argentina, was also re-founded. It returned to the presses on August 15, 1941, for a second, brief run, claiming that the journal was the "sincere expression of Galician feeling, intransigent mouthpiece of the most absolute Galicianism in its first incarnation, [and it] starts this second period to continue the sermon aimed at awakening in the Galician people a national pride."[117]

The group that would launch this new stage was initially formed by Moisés da Presa, Antón Castro, Vicente Barros, Santiago Nolla, Xohán González, and Bernaldo Souto, according to what the latter communicated to me; publishing fourteen issues of *A Fouce* in the two and a half years of its new incarnation. To a large extent, the relaunch was thanks to those who had taken refuge with the pro-Galician sympathizers already there in the face of the Spanish military coup; the ideology of class was prioritized over patriotic sentiment when it came to forging alliances. However, these did not prosper, given the profoundly patriotic feelings they held. Thus, in the early 1940s, a large part of that group met up at the headquarters of the Irmandade Galega with old comrades from the SNP who were still active, as was the case of Ricardo Flores. Both sides were sure that they were now in another new period in which the dynamics of the past were no longer valid. They had to maintain their ideology but also introduce new dynamics of interrelations with the expatriate community and, more than anything, with pro-Galician independence organizations. In this respect, the *Pondalian* Antón Castro stated that this "change of circumstances calls for a change of tactics. The procedures which were once effective are today inadequate."[118]

Most of the Pondal activists integrated into the Irmandade Galega and they, along with other pro-Galician sympathizers, promoted various projects. In the mid-1940s there was another publication alongside *A Fouce*. Only five editions were published under the name *Loita*, as told to me by the *Pondalian* Bernaldo Souto.[119]

Thanks to this new era of the SNP, and to the context in the Iberian Peninsula and Europe, the separatists' presence would grow moderately in Argentina, beyond its capital city. For example, in Rosario, a new group of separatists was formed, under the inspiration of the Irmandades da fala and the masonic creed, which gave rise to the Irmandade Galeguista Manuel Curros Enríquez, with which Castelao collaborated.[120]

Galician Nationalism in Exile: From the Irmandade Galega to the Consello de Galiza,[121] 1941–1944

In the 1940s, some 400,000 people made up the Galician community in Buenos Aires—known as the "fifth province of Galiza"—and it had around 250 different societies;[122] this community procured for Castelao the place in which he would set up residence from June 1940 on, along with his wife Virxinia Pereira. It was from here that he spread his Galician nationalist ideology. The Galician businessman, Manuel Puente,[123] acted as his patron.

Castelao would be the undisputed leader of pro-Galician political organization and the central nexus for exiled militants (and sympathizers) of that nationalism. This movement underwent a clear radicalization as a logical response to the military repression happening back home. This was a context in which, as noted, there were clear ideological differences between left and right, but above all, and for our case, between Galician nationalism (progressivism) and totalitarian Spanish nationalism (fascism). This would lead to the strengthening the nationalist claims of the pro-Galician forces, and Castelao in particular, with clearly pro-independence statements.[124]

The Irmandade Galega

Castelao's workrate while in exile in the Americas was dizzying. He was there for nine years and he was extraordinarily and especially productive during that time. A central concern during his time in exile was the political-organizational relaunch of the pro-Galician movement, albeit from beyond Galician territories. Wherever there were Galicians, Castelao understood the need to organize unitarily those who declared themselves nationalists and to proselytize among the Galician emigrant community.

In these circumstances, and after breaking off relations with the Casa de Galiza, which was already sliding toward Francoism, the bulk of Buenos Aires-based Galician nationalist forces, which were grouped together in the Grupo Galeguista and the Agrupación Artística e Cultural Ultreya of Buenos Aires as well as in the Sociedade Nazonalista Pondal (SNP), and which, as noted, were all active within the framework of a new era, met up at the Centro Ourensán in Buenos Aires. From this moment on, he worked on the creation of a party "of a cultural and patriotic character" that would combine its forces and efforts[125] under the name Irmandade Galega. This entity was created out of an assembly held on December 13, 1941, with a board of directors initially chaired by Antón Alonso Ríos, who was experienced in these struggles and was highly respected among the Galician community based in Latin America; one should recall that he had been sent from the Americas to Galiza during the Second Republic as a representative of the Federación Galega de Sociedades Agrarias (the Galician Federation of Agricultural Societies);[126] the vice-president was the doctor Ramón Rey Baltar and Daniel Rodríguez Castelao assumed the position of leadership (and honorary presidency), which was formally the responsibility of the Cultural Commission.[127] Among the members of the Irmandade Galega, as well as Castelao and Alonso Ríos, there were significant pro-Galician figures from the republican era, such as Xosé Núñez Búa, a secondary school teacher and the initially controversial Eduardo Blanco Amor.[128] He had been director of the *Galicia* seminary[129] since the summer of 1936, together with new recruits. These included the musicologist and antifascist Rodolfo Kubik, originally from Czechoslovakia. Although he was totally uninvolved with Galician nationalism prior to his time in exile, he joined up as a result of the close friendship he had with Castelao in the context of Buenos Aires-based antifascist circles.

Among the Irmandade's first and primary activities was the reorganization of pro-Galician activities overseas, creating a type of Partido Galeguista in exile.[130] And it was created out of the reunion of some of the cadres of the pre-coup nationalism and thanks to the implication of the anti-Franco part of the Galician collective already settled in Buenos Aires. They started coordinating from Buenos Aires with pro-Galician groups from Montevideo, Santiago de Chile, Havana, New York, and Mexico; they all came under the name of the Irmandade Galega and acted as local groups in a process that we would today term "viral." As well as these groups, they maintained relations with nuclei of pro-Galician sympathizers from Rosario, Mendoza, and La Plata, envisaging a plan "to do joint work that can reach transcendental importance for the future of the Galician Homeland."[131]

Thus, at that assembly in December 1941, the Irmandade Galega, with the aim of reconstructing Galician nationalism, approved its principles as well as the board that would implement these ideals and govern the new organization. This board was made up of Antón Alonso Ríos, president; Ramón Rey Baltar, vice-president; Xosé Abraira, secretary; Daniel Nogueira, Vice-secretary; Alfonso Fernández Prol, treasurer; Eduardo López, sub-treasurer; and members Vicente Barros,

Pedro Campos Couceiro, and Xohán González. The latter three were veteran activists from the Sociedade Nazonalista Pondal.

Furthermore, and no less important, that Irmandade agreed that on the date of the assassination of Alexandre Bóveda (the ex-secretary general from the republican-era PG) they would establish the "Día dos Mártires Galegos" (Galician Martyrs Day]),[132] re-socializing the ideology and patriotic program of the PG among the overseas Galician collective. The establishment of the Galician Martyrs Day was one of the first activities carried out by those exiled Galicians, in memory of all those men and women who had been assassinated for their belief in liberty for Galiza.[133]

The Relaunch of Galeuzca and the Creation of the Consello de Galiza

From early 1941 on, exiled Galician, Basque, and Catalan nationalists would try to recreate the pact that had united them under the name Galeuzca since 1933. It is true that it was specifically Castelao who made the greatest effort to relaunch the pact (as clearly explained in the wonderful study of the subject by Xosé Estévez), together with the Basque president José Antonio Aguirre, with whom Castelao had a close relationship. On May 9, 1941, representatives of the three countries of the Spanish State[134] republished that patriotic document, agreeing to work together in every ambit that they saw as jointly beneficial. The Galician delegates to the pact were Castelao, Alonso Ríos, and Lino Pérez. The Basques were represented by the Basque Nationalist Party (PNV) party members Ramón María Aldasoro, José María de Lasarte, and Franscisco Basterrechea, together with the pro-Catalan activists Manuel Serra i Moret, Josép Escolá i Marsá, and Pere Más. That agreement did not lead to much activity until late 1944, when it was ratified at a meeting in Mexico on December 22.[135] The delegates of the three countries of the Spanish State, as well as the representatives of their patriotic organizations, renewed that tripartite agreement to fight for their rights of "freedom, sovereignty, and self-determination," standing against "international fascism" and intensifying "the efforts being made against the tyrannical and totalitarian regime of General Franco, until the complete overthrow of that regime is achieved."[136]

Galician activists in America would work to create an unofficial Galician government in exile. They would be legitimized by the
results of the autonomist plebiscite of 1936, as well as by the elections
of February of that year. Likewise, they would feel pressured by the
Catalan nationalists and, particularly, by the Basque nationalists, since
both would have functioning governments in that exile. The Consello
de Galiza came into being on November 15, 1944 in Montevideo.[137]
The initiative for its creation came, once again, from Daniel Rodríguez
Castelao, following an idea of Manuel de Irujo, the ex-minister and
parliamentary representative of the Basque Nationalist Party (PNV)
who had promoted the Consejo Nacional de Euzkadi[138] three years
earlier, before which the Consell Nacional de Catalunya[139] had been
expanded. And in this way, on his own merits, Castelao became the
first president of the Consello Galego, which also included at the outset
the representatives Antón Alonso Ríos, Ramón Suárez Picallo, Elpidio
Villaverde, and, shortly thereafter, Alfredo Somoza.[140]

According to the minutes of the constitution of the Consello de
Galiza, its signatories were "the only Galician representatives living
in exile in South America, and, by a spontaneous decision of all of
them, they agree to join in a single body of political direction to save,
uphold, and defend the final will of Galiza, howsoever long this dis-
ruption should last, in which the people are deprived of all democratic
expression."[141] These representatives acted as "trustees of the legalized
will of their people," according to the text of the founding document,
and symbolized the political direction of Galiza in line with the exiled
Basque and Catalan governments to work for the reinstatement of
democracy in Spain.

According to the memoirs of lawyer Lois Tobío Fernández, who
was in exile in Montevideo at that time and central to the technical
advice when designing the Consello de Galiza, this body "signified the
keeping alive of the idea of the liberty of Galicia in the years of exile."[142]

Months prior to pushing for that Galician government-in-exile,
Castelao had finished and published his most important book, *Sempre
en Galiza*[143] on March 10, 1944 by the *Centro Ourensán* of Buenos
Aires. There was an initial run of several thousand copies with a few
hundred copies reserved for distribution in Galiza as soon as that

would be possible,[144] as stated by Castelao himself. *Sempre en Galiza* was a compilation of Castelao's writings about the problems of the Galician nation, in the past, present, and future and through the use of fine humor and sharp criticism, reminiscent of his journalism in pre-republican times. Castelao organized the work into three "books" brought together in one volume, some of which had been published previously in *A Nosa Terra*.[145] The genial writing and argument of the author of *Sempre en Galiza*, a book of almost four hundred pages containing numerous biographical notes, perfectly outlined the nationalist argument in the face of the tough situation it found itself in, explaining the history of their homeland to thousands of Galicians. The interest in this book meant it would be republished many times, right up to the present day.

At that time, pro-Galician activists, together with Basque and Catalan nationalists, promoted the *Galeuzca* journal, their mouthpiece for the twelve months between August 1945 and July 1946 in twelve editions, after the signing of the aforementioned tripartite pact;[146] the period of greatest visibility of this agreement in exile. The publication, initially supported by the Consello de Galiza, as confirmed by Xosé Estévez,[147] presented itself as a historical source of great interest, reflecting a large part of the activities of those activists at that time and their nationalist ideas regarding economics, politics, territorial design, and so on. It managed to give the greatest possible backing to the Galician, Basque, and Catalan nationalists and Galeuzca and its homonymous journal served to amplify this message; the Consello became a respected body throughout *Galeguidade* (literally, "Galicianality")— a term that was used profusely during Castelao's time in exile to refer to the entirety of Galicians exiles—and total opposition to Francoism. To this effect, Castelao made various efforts to get Manuel Portela Valladares, originally from Pontevedra, to join the Consello de Galiza. The ex-president of the government of the Second Republic, he was a highly respected politician despite the defamatory campaign waged against him by the Francoist regime. Finally, months after its founding, Portela joined the Consello de Galiza.[148]

When Portela Valladares spoke in this context, the San Francisco Conference[149] had just begun. Some exiles placed great faith in the event, such as the *lehendakari* José Antonio Aguirre, but the pro-Galician faction showed little interest.[150] It is true that this meeting, which resulted in the United Nations Charter,[151] did not result in any variation to the "Spanish problem," meaning it would be necessary to keep all fronts open. At the time, Castelao attempted to normalize the relationship between proponents of the pro-Galician ideology that had developed freely overseas and that which was evolving inside the Galician country, seeking political dialogue between the two sides through the epistolary genre, closely watched by the censors, played a central role. Sympathizers of the domestic variant of this ideology, which was reconstructed in 1944 around the central figure of Ramón Piñeiro, were not at all pleased with Portela Valladares[152] integration in the *Consello de Galiza*. Nor were they happy with the creation of the body itself and Castelao's initiative as a whole, given that they saw that any pro-Galician leadership at the time should come from within the country itself. This lack of legitimacy of the Consello was also shared by other pro-Galician elements in exile, as was the case for example of those settled in Mexico and led by Luís Soto. Nevertheless, Castelao attempted to strengthen the prestige and work of the Consello de Galiza, establishing communications with all the pro-Galician groups that existed in exile in an arduous campaign, giving the Galeuzca alliance a foothold. In the end, the greatest achievement of the Consello de Galiza was the negotiation with Spanish republicanism regarding Galician autonomy, which led to the approval in the republican parliament, meeting in Mexico, of the statute of autonomy within the framework of exile, in the fall of 1945.[153]

Epilogue

The unsatisfactory resolution of World War Two as regards the Francoist dictatorship, which remained unscathed by the Allied victory, gave rise to great frustration within Galician nationalism, together with Basque and Catalan nationalism and the whole of Spanish republicanism. The pro-Galician movement in exile was coming to the end of its first great era. It ended abruptly with the death of Castelao in January 1950, after his acceptance as a minister (without portfolio) in the government of Giral. He held this post between 1946 and 1947, moving his home to the French capital.

After 1950, Galician nationalism in exile would be led by Antón Alonso Ríos, who declined to become president of Consello de Galiza, working instead as its secretary general. From overseas, he attempted to reorganize nationalism in Galiza, in contrast to those pro-Galician activists who, after the arrest of Ramón Piñeiro and the lack of resources with which to combat Francoism in secret, decided at the turn of 1950 to focus their efforts in the cultural field. They founded the publishing house Galaxia, in defense of the Galician language through cultivating the use of the language among the younger generations. This reorganization of Galician nationalism on Iberian soil would have to wait another decade until the Consello da Mocidade (Youth Council) and the key work of Antón Moreda;[154] from this moment on, Galician nationalism entered into a new (and very productive) era in Europe.

Bibliography

Alvajar López, Javier (1988), "Apuntes sobre la Delegación del Consejo de Galicia en Europa," *Anuario Brigantino* n°11, Betanzos, Concello de Betanzos, pp. 125–136.

Beramendi, Justo (1985), *Losada Diéguez. Obra completa*, Vigo, Xerais/Museo do Pobo Galego.

Beramendi, Justo (2008), *De Provincia a Nación. Historia do galeguismo político*, Vigo, Xerais.

Beramendi, Justo e Roca Cendán, Manuel (1996), *Lois Peña Novo. Obra completa. Compostela*, Universidade de Santiago de Compostela.

Beramendi, Justo; Diéguez Cequiel, Uxío-Breogán; Fernández Pérez-Sanjulián, Carme; García Negro, Mª Pilar; and González Reboredo, Xosé Manuel (2017), *Repensar Galicia: as Irmandades da Fala*, Santiago de Compostela, Xunta de Galicia/Museo do Pobo Galego.

Biscainho Fernandes, Carlos Caetano e Lourenço Módia, Cilha (2002), *O Ideario teatral das Irmandades da Fala : estudio e antoloxía*, Sada, Ediciós do Castro.

Brañas, Alfredo (1889), *El Regionalismo. Estudio sociológico, histórico y literario*, Barcelona, Jaime Molinas.

Cabo Villaverde, Miguel (1998), *O agrarismo*, Vigo, A Nosa Terra.

Castells, Víctor (2008), *Galeusca. Un ideal compartit*, Barcelona, Dalmau.

Costa, Lluís (2006), *El nacionalismo cubano y Cataluña*, Barcelona, Publicacións de l'Abadia de Montserrat.

Cupeiro, Bieito (1989), *A Galiza de alén mar*, Sada, Ediciós do Castro.

Diaz Fouces, Oscar (2016), "Pequenas achegas para uma história da revista As Roladas," in *Murguía, Revista Galega de Historia*, n°34, pp. 37–57.

Diéguez Cequiel, Uxío-Breogán (2002), *A Asemblea de Concellos de Galiza Pro-Estatuto*, Pontevedra, Fundación Alexandre Bóveda.

Diéguez Cequiel, Uxío-Breogán (2003), Álvaro de las Casas. Biografía e documentos, Vigo, Galaxia.

Diéguez Cequiel, Uxío-Breogán (2010), *Alexandre Bóveda nos seus documentos*, Ourense, Cátedra Alexandre Bóveda/Difusora de Letras, Artes e Ideas.

Diéguez Cequiel, Uxío-Breogán (2015), *Nacionalismo galego aquén e alén mar Desarticulación, resistencia e rearticulación (1936–1975)*, Compostela, Laiovento.

Diéguez Cequiel, Uxío-Breogán (Coord., 2016), *As Irmandades da Fala (1916–1931). Reivindicación identitaria e activismo socio-político-identitario na Galiza do primeiro terzo do s.XX*, Compostela, Laiovento.

Diéguez Cequiel, Uxío-Breogán / Ríos, Lois (2020), *A viaxe ás illas Blasket de Plácido Castro (1928)*, Compostela, Instituto Galego de Historia.

Estévez, Xosé (2002), *Castelao e o Galeuzca*, Compostela, Laiovento.

Estévez, Xosé (2009), *Galeuzca: la rebelión de la periferia (1923–1998)*, Madrid, Entinema.

Fernández Del Riego, Francisco (1983), Ánxel Casal e o libro galego, Sada, Ediciós do Castro.

González Tosar, Luís (1991), "Forxa de escritores," in *Homenaxe a Ramón Piñeiro*, A Coruña, Caixa Galicia, pp. 247–252.

Igrexas, Manuel, "Apuntamentos sobre a biografía de Ramón de Valenzuela," in Ferreiro, Charo and Pena, Inmaculada (Coord., 2006) *Homenaxe a Antón Alonso Ríos e Ramón de Valenzuela*, Compostela, Xunta de Galicia, pp. 9–16.

Ínsua López, Emilio Xosé and Nuevo Cal, Carlos (2003), *O primeiro Antón Villar Ponte: achegamento ao período de formación do fundador das Irmandades da Fala (1881–1908)*, A Coruña, Fundación Caixa Galicia.

Ínsua López, Emilio Xosé (2004), *Antón and Ramón Villar Ponte : unha irmandade alén do sangue*, Compostela, Centro Ramón Piñeiro para a Investigación en Humanidades.

Ínsua López, Emilio Xosé (2016), *A Nosa Terra é nosa! A xeira das Irmandades da Fala (1916–1931)*, A Coruña, Baía.

Maceira Fernández, Xosé Manuel (2007), *O nacionalismo cívico: interpretación do contributo da Irmandade da Fala da Coruña*, Ames, Laiovento.

Magariños, Alfonso (2003), *A demografía na Galicia contemporánea*, Noia, Toxosoutos.

Máiz, Ramón (1983), *Alfredo Brañas. O ideario de rexionalismo católico tradicional-ismo*, Vigo, Galaxia.

Máiz, Ramón (1984), *O Rexionalismo galego : organización e ideoloxía: (1886–1907)*, Sada, Ediciós do Castro.

Núñez Seixas, Xosé Manoel (1991), "La 'Sociedade Nazonalista Pondal': el separatismo gallego en la emigración," in Justo G. Beramendi and Ramón Máiz (comps.), *Los Nacionalismos en la España de la II República*, Santiago de Compostela/México, Consello da Cultura Galega/Siglo Veintiuno, pp. 171–193.

Núñez Seixas, Xosé Manoel (1992), *O Galeguismo en América : 1879–1936*, Sada, Ediciós do Castro.

Núñez Seixas, Xosé Manoel, and Cagiao Vila, Pilar (Ed. 2006), *O exilio galego de 1936, política, sociedade, itinerarios,* Sada, Ediciós do Castro.

Pastoriza Rozas, Xosé Luis (2017), "Ramiro Isla Couto: pioneiro do nacionalismo alén mar," in Justo Beramendi, Uxío-Breogán Diéguez et al. *Repensar Galicia: as Irmandades da Fala,* Xunta de Galicia/Museo do Pobo Galego, pp. 309–324.

Rodríguez Fer, Claudio (1997), "Emigración, Exilio e Guerra Civil," in *Jornadas de la Emigración gallega a Puerto Rico,* Sada, Ediciós do Castro, pp. 63–77.

Rivas Barrós, Sabela (2002), *O ideario educativo no galleguismo: escolma de textos e fontes bibliográficas,* Sada, Ediciós do Castro.

Rodríguez Castelao, A. (1944), *Sempre en Galiza.* Buenos Aires, Edicións As Burgas.

Santos, Antom, and Diéguez, Uxío-Breogán (2011), *Antón Moreda. Memoria do exilio,* Santiago de Compostela, Instituto Galego de Historia.

Tayadella, Antònia (1992), "La Renaixença: els certàmens literaris," *Jornadas de Lengua y Literatura catalana, gallega y vasca,* II. (Ed. P. Urquizu et al.). Madrid: UNED, pp. 50–55.

Urquizu, Patricio (1991), "Antoine d'Abbadie y el resurgir literario vasco en la segunda mitad del siglo XIX." *Conferences on Catalan, Galician and Basque languages and literature.* Madrid: UNED, 1991, pp. 85–97.

Vázquez Souza, Ernesto (2003), *A Fouce, o Hórreo e o Prelo. Ánxel Casal ou o libro galego moderno,* Sada, Ediciós do Castro.

Velasco Souto, Carlos (2000), *Galiza na II República,* Vigo, A Nosa Terra.

Velasco Souto, Carlos (2002), *O agrarismo galego,* Santiago de Compostela, Laiovento.

Notes

1. In 1900, Galicia has a total of 1,950,515 inhabitants (almost the same number as in 1860 when there were 1,799,224 inhabitants, and little more than in 1826 when there were around 1,600,000), representing 10.5 percent of the total Spanish population (11.5 percent and 11.2 percent in 1860 and 1826, respectively). See Alfonso Magariños, *A demografía na Galicia contemporánea* (Noia: Toxosoutos, 2003).

2. In the case of Galicia, this situation has been studied in detail by Miguel Cabo Villaverde, *O agrarismo* (Vigo: A Nosa Terra, 1998).

3. He died in the United States in 1943, one of the thousands of exiled republicans opposed to the establishment of the Franco regime.

4. In 1898, the *Eco de Galicia* newspaper explained that the Galician flag would have a white background and a sky-blue diagonal stripe from top-left to bottom-right (and which later had a shield added, symbolizing the seven provinces of the old Kingdom of Galicia, prior to its breaking up by the Spaniard Javier de Burgos in 1833).

5. It was interpreted in the Centro Gallego in Havana on December 20, 1907, with words by Eduardo Pondal (from the poem "Os Pinos," composed in 1890) and music by Pascual Veiga.

6. As part of the movement in defense and promotion of the Galician language as a superior framework for collective identity, the literary, cultural, and especially political movement known as the *Rexurdimento* began in the mid-nineteenth century. The Galician *Rexurdimento* coincided with the Catalan and Valencian *Renaixença*. As in Catalonia, so the *Xogos Florais* were organized in Galicia; the first *Jocs Florals* were held in 1859 and just two years later, in early 1861, the first *Xogos Florais* were held. In turn, in Euskadi there is evidence of these literary meetings from almost a decade before, specifically, since 1851. In 1853 they were called the *Phertxuetaco Gudua* ("War of verse") and, beginning in 1880, *Joko loretuak* ("Floral Games"). See Patricio Urquizu, "Antoine d'Abbadie y el resurgir literario vasco en la segunda mitad del siglo XIX," in *Jornadas de Lengua y Literatura catalana, gallega y vasca* (Madrid: UNED, 1991), 85–97; Antònia Tayadella, "La Renaixença: els certàmens literaris," in *Jornadas de Lengua y Literatura catalana, gallega y vasca II*, ed. P. Urquizu et al. (Madrid: UNED, 1992), pp. 50–55.

7. On April 2, 1846, Colonel Miguel Solis headed a liberal-progressive uprising, centered in Lugo against the Absolutist General Ramón María Narváez, commander of the Spanish government at the time, as president and minister of state and war; the pro-democracy uprising was supported by the Galician *provincialistas* (pro-Galicians of the period), who supported a decentralization of the Spanish state that would favor the political, economic, and cultural claims of Galicia against Spanish centralism and uniformity.

8. Brañas was referred to as "the most fervent of the Galician regionalists" in his 1889 work *El Regionalismo. Estudio sociológico, histórico y literario* (Barcelona: Jaime Molinas, 1889), 200.

9. Something that Cambó confessed to Wenceslao Fernández Flórez in an interview for the *El Noroeste* newspaper in the summer of 1916: "It was a Galician who was the decisive influence in launching me into nationalist politics . . . I heard his speech. That same day I signed up in the Catalanism Party and since then I haven't stopped working for it!"

10. See Ramón Máiz, *Alfredo Brañas. O ideario do rexionalismo católico tradicionalismo* (Vigo: Galaxia, 1983).

11. See Justo Beramendi, *De Provincia a Nación. Historia do galleguismo político* (Vigo: Xerais, 2007); Emilio Xosé Ínsua, *A Nosa Terra é nosa! A xeira das Irmandades da Fala* (A Coruña: Baía, 2016); Xurxo Martínez, *Común temos a patria. Biografía dos irmáns Villar Ponte* (Vigo: Xerais, 2018).

12. *A Nosa Terra* 1, 1916.

13. *A Nosa Terra* 45, 1918.

14. Beramendi, *De Provincia a Nación*, 439–446

15. *A Nosa Terra* 50, 1918.

16. Beramendi, *De Provincia a Nación*, 645 ff.

17. *A Nosa Terra* 9, 1917. It is to be expected that the review in the paper linked the event to the fight to regain freedoms in Galicia, referring to them being lost after

the murder of the medieval lord Pero Pardo de Cela in 1483 on the orders of Queen Isabella I of Castile (along with her husband Ferdinand II as the Catholic Monarchs): "for the first time, since Galician liberties were lost at Frouseira, the great and blessed dream of creating for Galicia, our homeland, enslaved but not dead, a nationality with its own character, natural and historic, filled with glory and power in that golden century of Xelmírez, until then the flag of our sacred redemption will not be consciously raised."

18. The reminder of that pro-Galician movement until his death, in 1999.

19. "If we want to ourselves, we have to cultivate ourselves in Galician . . . Of our language that magnanimously and fruitfully opens the doors to the hearts of many millions of souls who express themselves in Portuguese, our brother tongue." *A Nosa Terra* 56, 1918.

20. Regulations of the Irmandade da Cruña, Irmandades da Fala, A Coruña, 1918. Capitalization as per the original.

21. The Irmandades stated that they chose the city of Lugo "as it is the most central point for all of Galicia. *And Lugo, also, [is] the ideal target audience of this meeting.* It is where the historic events took place with Antolín Faraldo's call for independence for our nation which was defeated by a vote (*A Nosa Terra* 70, 1918).

22. *A Nosa Terra* 73–74, 1918.

23. Sabela Rivas Barrós, *O ideario educativo no galleguismo* (Sada: Ediciós do Castro, 2000); Ernesto Vázquez Souza, *A Fouce, o Hórreo e o Prelo. Ánxel Casal ou o libro galego moderno* (Sada: Ediciós do Castro, 2003).

24. *A Nosa Terra* 197, 1924.

25. The date of July 25 had competition at the assembly from those in favor of December 17, symbolic in the fight against the Castilian centralism of the Catholic Monarchs.

26. See Uxío-Breogán Diéguez Cequiel, "Irlanda e o celtismo para o galeguismo. De Manuel M. Murguía á revista Nós," in *A propósito da viaxe de Plácido Castro ás Illas Blasket (Irlanda, 1928)* (Santiago de Compostela, Instituto Galego de Historia, 2020).

27. See Uxío-Breogán Diéguez Cequiel, "As *Irmandades da fala*, a historia e a construción do contemporáneo imaxinario (nacional) galego," in *As Irmandades da Fala cen anos despois,* ed. Carme Fernández Pérez-San Julián (A Coruña: Universidade da Coruña, 2016), 59–71 and Giovanni Conrad Cattini, "Mitos y tradiciones en la configuración de los nacionalismos. Un debate historiográfico internacional y una aproximación galaico-vasca-catalana (1970/2015)" *Murguía, Revista Galega de Historia* 37 (2018), 125–39

28. *A Nosa Terra* 19, 1917.

29. Víctor Castells, *Galeusca. Un ideal compartit* (Barcelona: Rafael Dalmau Editor, 2005).

30. *A Nosa Terra* 190, 1923.

31. See Xosé Estévez, *Galeuzca: la rebelión de la periferia (1923–1998)* (Madrid, Entinema, 2009).

32. "Ao decorrel-os dias," *A Nosa Terra* 284, June 1, 1931.

33. Ibid.

34. N.R., "Ao decorrel-os dias," *A Nosa Terra* (front page), July 1, 1931.

35. On Daniel Rodríguez Castelao, see Uxío-Breogán Diéguez Cequiel, "Castelao 1886–1950," Political Lives #3, Coppieters Foundation, 2019. Available online at https://ideasforeurope.eu/activity/paper/political-lives-3-castelao/. Castelao was elected to represent the Partido Galeguista de Pontevedra and Ramón Otero Pedrayo for the Partido Nazonalista Republicano de Ourense.

36. As we will see, exceptions were made in the ORGA group, namely for representative Ramón Suárez Picallo, elected by the Organización Republicana Gallega Autónoma de Bos Aires, and for Antón Alonso Ríos, representative for the Federación de Sociedades Galegas Agrarias e Culturais da República Arxentina; to these can be added Antón Vilar Ponte for the ORGA of A Coruña. These three would become members of the PG, although not until 1934 in the case of Vilar Ponte.

37. N.R., "Otero Pedrayo e Castelao no Parlamento" *A Nosa Terra*, October 1, 1931, 3.

38. Antón Alonso Ríos was, at the time, president of the Commission for the Statute of the Galician State. The day before he had been in Ourense at a meeting of this commission that had discussed the course of pro-sovereignty claims and the facts relating to the construction of the Zamora–A Coruña railroad. "No decrece la energía de la reclamación de Galicia" *El Pueblo Gallego*, June 27, 1931, 7; "Alonso Ríos es nombrado presidente de la Junta Revolucionaria de la República Gallega" *El Pueblo Gallego* (front page), June 28, 1931. See Uxío-Breogán Diéguez Cequiel, *Nacionalismo galego aquén e alén mar. Desarticulación, resistencia e rearticulación* (Santiago de Compostela: Laiovento, 2015), 178–82.

39. Professor of international law at the University of Santiago, he was a member of the Asociación Rexionalista Galega (1891) and co-organizer of the first *Xogos Florais*, as well as being president of the Seminario de Estudos Galegos from 1924 on.

40. Salvador Cabeza de León, "Encol do Galeguismo," *A Nosa Terra*, July 25, 1931, 5.

41. N.R., "Ao decorrel-os dias" *A Nosa Terra* (front page), July 25, 1931.

42. N.R., "Ao decorrel-os dias" in *A Nosa Terra* (front page), September 1, 1931.

43. N.R. "Ao decorrel-os dias" in *A Nosa Terra* (front page), November 1, 1931.

44. Beramendi, *De Provincia a Nación*, 847–68.

45. Alexandre Bóveda soon became the head of the accounts section at the Pontevedra headquarters of the Spanish Public Revenue Service. Immediately prior to the founding of the PG, he was General Secretary of the Partido Galeguista de Pontevedra.

46. Uxío-Breogán Diéguez Cequiel, *Alexandre Bóveda nos seus documentos* (Ourense: Difusora de Artes, Letras e Ideas, 2011).

47. Referenced in issue 22 of the publication sponsored by the PG. Documents from the First and Second Assemblies, 1931–1932, Santiago, pubricacións galegas e imprenta, 1933 (author's own archive).

48. Ibid.

49. Ibid.

50. Before the First Assembly of the PG, the secretary general of the new organization was Pedro Basanta, Alexandre Bóveda being the organization's secretary. At the Second National Assembly of the party, held in Santiago in 1932, Bóveda became secretary general and Plácido Castro the secretary of the organization. Bóveda left the role in 1935, going into exile. He continued with organizational responsibilities and Manuel Gómez Román assumed the role of general representative of the party.

51. Conversation between Uxío-Breogán Diéguez and Francisco Fernández del Riego, Vigo, September 24, 2003.

52. Both met Bóveda in Pontevedra in 1928, contributing to its formal integration into the *Irmadiño* movement via the economics department of the Seminario de Estudos Galegos.

53. Víctor Casas was born in 1900 and Bóveda in 1903, in contrast to Daniel Castelao and Antón Lousada Diéguez, born in 1886 and 1884, respectively.

54. Casal, biographically, is part of the 1900 generation; now though, we group him with those born before the turn of the century because he was chronologically. The majority of pro-Galician thinkers and ideologists, then, in Castelao's time either died before the dawn of the Second Republic (in the case of Manuel Murguía, Lois Porteiro Garea, Johán Vicente Viqueira, and Antón Lousada Diéguez) or they had distanced themselves from pro-Galician politics by that time, represented only slightly by the PG as they did not feel sufficiently represented by the party; some of these were members of ORGA, as is the case of one of the focal points and founder of the Irmandades da Fala and ORGA itself, Antón Vilar Ponte. He would go on to join the Partido Galeguista around the turn of 1934.

55. An active member of the Irmandades da fala and its female section, she was the co-founder, together with her husband Ánxel Casal, of the Escolas de Primeiro Ensiño (Primary education schools). She went into exile in 1936.

56. Luís Seoane, "O decorado e a máscara na obra de Castelao" *Galicia Emigrante* 1 (Buenos Aires, 1954), 20.

57. Ramón Suárez Picallo, for example, was a socialist. He became a representative for the PG in 1936. His brother, Xohán Antón Suárez Picallo was an anarchist and in 1935 held the position of secretary in the local group of Sada, where he worked as a teacher. He became secretary general of this group in 1936, the year he was assassinated after being tortured, as Avelino Pousa Antelo would state later (Os Verxeles, Teo, November 21, 2001). Alexandre Bóveda can be classed as a Christian Democrat with socialist leanings, and Castelao would evolve politically from having socialist sympathies to holding more pro-communist views. Ramón Otero Pedrayo held a conservative ideology and Filgueira Valverde and Vicente Risco were explicitly right-wing.

58. Workshops or study campaigns in the open air, normally held over several days.

59. As can be read in an advertisement placed in various news outlets of the Galician diaspora in Argentina. See, for example, *Alalá*, published by the Os Rumorosos choir, Buenos Aires, May 1935, 23.

60. With a majority managerial presence and driving force of the architects of the Sociedade Nazonalista Pondal (SNP), an organization to which I will refer later.

61. Meilán attended the *I Asemblea Nazonalista Galega* in 1918. He arrived in the Argentine capital in the spring of 1922, escaping from compulsory military service and Spain's war in Morocco. In 1934 he went to Uruguay, settling in Montevideo where there was a very active, well financed pro-Galician group that included the Canabal brothers. He maintained a close relationship with Daniel Rodríguez Castelao and was a nationalist activist until his death.

62. This was not the case with Ramón Otero Pedrayo; he never left the PG. Conversation with Nelson Regueiro, Montevideo, Uruguay, August 11, 2008.

63. Chosen by the monarchist coalition in the elections of April 1931, he would profess openly republican and pro-Galician positions, being a close friend of Alexandre Bóveda, a pivotal figure in his evolution.

64. See Uxío-Breogán Diéguez Cequiel, *A Asemblea de Concellos de Galiza Pro-Estatuto* (Pontevedra: Fundación Alexandre Bóveda, 2002).

65. *El Eco de Santiago*, December 17, 1932, 1.

66. Diéguez Cequiel, *A asemblea de Concellos de Galiza*, 15.

67. *Faro Vilalbés*, January 16, 1933, 2.

68. The first anniversary of the Assembly of Councils, as well as, one year previously, the anniversary of the assassination of the Galician noble Pero Pardo de Cela, on the orders of Queen Isabella "the Catholic" in 1483.

69. Daniel Rodríguez Castelao, "Novo aldraxe á Galicia a sempre aldraxada," *A Nosa Terra*, 1932, 1.

70. Víctor Casas, "Do momento," *A Nosa Terra* 292, February 1, 1932, 5.

71. The Asturias Revolution was a workers' insurrection between October 5 and 9, 1934 in Asturias on the Cantabrian coast. Moreover, the Catalan State was proclaimed between October 6 and 7, with Lluís Companys at its head. Both were put down violently by the Spanish military, on the orders of the president of the Spanish government, Alejandro Lerroux.

72. Castelao was forced to leave for Badajoz and Bóveda to Cádiz.

73. From its inception, the PG would promote a youth organization. In 1932, it formed the Mocedades Galeguistas, which became the FMG in 1934,

74. Álvaro Xil Varela acted as "interim political secretary" through the first half of 1936, in Pontevedra. See "Circular da Segredaría Política" *A Nosa Terra*, April 17, 1936, 2.

75. In February 1936, under the same name, a small group of pro-Galician activists from Pontevedra and led by Filgueira Valverde, would leave the PG, as was the case in April of that year in Santiago. In total, less than thirty affiliates left the party in these three places. See "A Dereita Galeguista," *A Nosa Terra*, April 10, 1936, 2.

76. It supported the Frente Popular after its participation to this effect, along with other organizations of the Catalan left, in the Front d'Esquerres of Catalonia.

77. Manuel Gómez Román received 1,683 votes, Xerardo Álvarez Gallego 1,639, Plácido R. Castro 1,498, Ricardo Carvalho Calero 1,416, Ramón Otero Pedrayo 1,354, Valentín Paz Andrade 1,304, and Manuel Peña Rei 1,219. All other candidates won less than 1,000 votes.

78. See Manuel Igrexas, "Apuntamentos sobre a biografía de Ramón de Valenzuela," in *Homenaxe a Antón Alonso Ríos e Ramón de Valenzuela*, ed. Charo Ferreiro and Inmaculada Pena (Compostela: Xunta de Galicia, 2006), 12.

79. Castelao was first on the list of candidates for the Frente Popular in Pontevedra, Súarez Picallo was fourth, and Vilar Ponte eighth in A Coruña.

80. "Ante a próisima anulación das actas de Ourense," *A Nosa Terra* (front page), March 13, 1936.

81. Despite his commitments to ORGA, which had joined the Republican Left and which he had co-founded with other pro-Galician activists.

82. A 1933 recording, after the Pro-Statute Assembly of Galician Councils of December 1932, titled *Por unha nova Galicia*. It was the work of the brothers Juan Enrique (1899–1984) and Ramón (1908–1981) Barreiro Vázquez, and paid for by the Partido Galeguista. It is known that there were two copies that were burned in 1936 before the military coup, as noted by Francisco Fernández del Riego and Avelino Pousa Antelo.

83. You pro-Galician activists, as mentioned by Díaz Pardo, had help from some JSU members. They took advantage of the context to paint graffiti in Santiago de Compostela said that proclaimed "Viva Russia" and "Viva a URSS." One of these graffiti was in the Praza do Obradoiro. It was a large red star containing a Galician flag with a white background and diagonal blue stripe. Conversation with Avelino Pousa Antelo, Os Verxeles, Teo, November 21, 2001.

84. It was debated and approved in exile, not without various vicissitudes, in the republican parliament that met in Mexico in November 1945. I do not cover these events in detail here. See Diéguez Cequiel, *Nacionalismo galego aquén e alén mar*, 117–38.

85. Vid. Núñez Seixas, Xosé Manoel (1992), *O Galeguísmo en América: 1879-1936*, Sada, Ediciós do Castro.

86. Collective that pay homage to the Galician writer Eduardo Pondal, from whom the poem *Os Pinos* (= *The pines*) published in 1886, would be taken to give rise to the Galician anthem.

87. Galician Nationalist Union of Havana.

88. Galician Revolutionary Independence Committee of Havana.

89. In Latin America, pro-Galician sovereignty sympathizers coined the term *arredista* to refer to *independentismo* or independentism (in contrast to the term *galleguista* or pro-Galician, which they would associated with a lighter form of autonomy).

90. Subtitled *paladín do honor da Raza Céltica*.

91. Fuco Gómez claimed that Doalla was trafficking Galician women into prostitution.
92. Closely linked to the pro-Catalan independence activists, the main driving forces of pro-Catalan ideas in the peninsula. For more information on pro-Catalan thought and nationalism in Cuba, see Lluís Costa, *El nacionalismo cubano y Cataluña* (Barcelona: Publicacións de l'Abadia de Montserrat, 2006).
93. Fuco Gómez, *Grafía galega* (Habana: Emprenta e Papeleiría de Rambla, Bouza y Ca., 1927).
94. Xurxo Martínez González, *Fuco Gómez* (Vigo: AGER, 2007), 19.
95. Together with Ramón Cabanillas, he was a backer at that time (1922) of the first children's magazine in Galician, founded and published in Madrid, titled *As Roladas. Follas dos rapaciños galegos.* See Oscar Diaz Fouces, "Pequenas achegas para uma história da revista As Roladas," *Murguía, Revista Galega de Historia* 34 (2016), 37–57.
96. This was not the first or the last case of a Galician nationalist organization being created in the Spanish capital, by means of young Galicians who worked or studied in Madrid as a result of the scarcity of opportunities in their homeland.
97. Formally presented on April 1, 1930 in Madrid, its birthplace.
98. Campos Couceiro, an activist with great theoretical training and forced into emigration to Latin America, was given the moniker "the Galician Macià." In one of his speeches, he highlighted the secular economic underdevelopment of Galicia. See "Alonso Ríos es nombrado presidente . . ." *El Pueblo Gallego*, June 28, 1931.
99. There are two complete articles that appeared in *El Pueblo Gallego* and *La Voz de Galicia* on June 28, 1931, referring to the proclamation of the Galician state, in which Alonso Ríos was a kind of provisional president. In *El Pueblo Gallego* it was stated how, on June 27, a large demonstration on the streets of Santiago "marched on the city hall, raising the blue and white flag on the building and proclaiming the Galician State". "Alonso Ríos es nombrado presidente" *El Pueblo Gallego*, June 28, 1931, 50–52.
100. Luís González Tosar, "Forxa de escritores," in *Homenaxe a Ramón Piñeiro* (A Coruña: Caixa Galicia, 1991), 247–52.
101. It was followed by *O idioma dos animás. Opúscaro de enxebreza*, published in 1937.
102. See Fuco Gómez, "Dend'o meu escondrixo perseguido pol-o delito de ser arredista," *A Fouce* 8, February 1934, 4.
103. In the elections of November 1933, its founder, Álvaro de las Casas, stood as an independent candidate rather than as a representative of the VNG. See Uxío-Breogán Diéguez Cequiel, Álvaro de las Casas. Biografía, obra e epistolario (Vigo: Galaxia, 2003), 67–74.
104. Lois Tobío initially went into exile in Cuba, as did López Durá, where he had Cuban nationality on account of having been born in Havana. Both were in the Cuban capital between 1939 and 1940. In September 1939, they cofounded the Escuela Libre de la Habana, set up in a house owned by a backer of the initiative,

María Luísa Gómez Mena, at 961 San Lázaro, Havana. The research by Dania Vázquez Matos on the Escuela Libre de la Habana is worth reading. See Dania Vázquez Matos, "La escuela libre de La Habana: vivero de inquietudes y desvelos renovadores" in *La Literatura y la Cultura del exilio republicano español de 1939: Actas del IV Coloquio Internacional* (La Habana, Cuba, Editorial Unicornio, 2002).

105. It is worth noting that Fuco Gómez would not change his ideas about pro-Galician activists after July 1936; he had an extraordinary opportunity to add, faced with this period of exile, those cadres who had been radicalized in their nationalism and their position against the Spanish state as a result of the fascist military coup.

106. There have been few studies on Ramiro Illa Couto. However, he was enormously influential in pro-Galician sovereignty activities in the Americas. See Xosé Luis Pastoriza Rozas, "Ramiro Isla Couto: pioneiro do nacionalismo alén mar," in Justo Beramendi, Uxío-Breogán Diéguez et al., *Repensar Galicia: as* Irmandades da fala (Santiago de Compostela: Xunta de Galicia/Museo do Pobo Galego, 2017), 309–24.

107. Although prompted by the split that Vicente Risco provoked in 1922, under the name *of* Irmandade Nazonalista Galega, as already mentioned.

108. See Bieito Cupeiro Vázquez, *A Galiza de alén* (Sada: Ediciós do Castro, 1989); Xosé Manoel Núñez Seixas, "La "Sociedade Nazonalista Pondal": el separatismo gallego en la emigración," in *Los Nacionalismos en la España de la II República*, ed. Justo G. Beramendi and Ramón Máiz (Santiago de Compostela/México: Consello da Cultura Galega/Siglo Veintiuno, 1991), 171–93.

109. "Fachada" *A Fouce* (front page) 1, 1926.

110. Cupeiro Vázquez, *A Galiza de alén*.

111. As the veteran *Pondalian* told me, at the turn of the century.

112. Cupeiro Vázquez, *A Galiza de alén*, 57–58.

113. Until this time, it had been critical of the Partido Galeguista as it was seen as very conservative in social issues and, above all, the PG's position was far from its own pro-independence stance.

114. Split, in turn, into those favorable to autonomy over any other organizational structure, as they had been prior to the military coup, and those who aligned in favor of communist-leaning Galician and Spanish exiles.

115. The former a member of the SNP from 1929 on, interview in Mar de Plata in 2008; the latter a member of the SNP from 1927 on, as mentioned in a conversation between Uxío-Breogán Diéguez and Ricardo Flores on October 20, 2001.

116. Between the mid-nineteenth and the mid-twentieth century, 600,000 Galicians would settle in Argentina (of which, including their descendants, there are currently 168,263 inhabitants). On this topic, see Alberto Vilanova Rodríguez, *Los Gallegos en la Argentina* (Buenos Aires, Centro Gallego de Buenos Aires, Ediciones Galicia, 1966); Xosé Manoel Núñez Seixas, ed., *La Galicia austral: la inmigración gallega en la Argentina* (Buenos Aires, Ed. Biblos, 2001); Ruy Farías comp., *Inmigración, pasado y presente* (Buenos Aires: Ministerio de

Cultura del Gobierno de la Ciudad de Buenos Aires/Ed. Buenos Aires Gallega, 2007); Alejandro P. Vázquez González, *Emigrantes galegos, transportes e remesas (1830–1930)* (Santiago de Compostela: Consello da Cultura Galega/Fundación Pedro Barrié de la Maza, 2015).

117. "De Novo na loita" *A Fouce* 1 (front page), II Xeira, August 15, 1941.

118. Antón Castro, "¿Qué facer? Motivos para unha polémica," *A Fouce* 1, July 15, 1941, 2–3. With the expression "orgaizacións políticas da colectividade" Antón Castro was primarily talking about the Federación de Sociedades Galegas (FSG). The institution held a position far-removed from pro-Galician ideology.

119. Conversation between Uxío-Breogán Diéguez and Bernardo Souto, Mar de Plata, August 7, 2008.

120. As told to me by Bernaldo Souto and as can be seen in the pages of *A Fouce*. See Fungueiro, "Cousas da Nosa Coleitividade" *A Fouce* 1 (back page), II Xeira, August 15, 1941.

121. As will be seen, the Consello de Galiza (= Council of Galiza) would be the unofficial Galician government in exile.

122. It has been estimated that the Galician community in all of Argentina at that time was some 600,000 people.

123. As his daughter, Rosa Puente, told me. Puente provided Castelao and Pereira with a centrally-located apartment in the Argentine capital, on the seventh floor of Rúa Belgrano, no. 2605.

124. See Daniel Rodríguez Castelao, *Sempre en Galiza* (Vigo: Galaxia, 1994), 139 and 436–37.

125. "Irmandade Galega" *A Nosa Terra* 425, June 1942, 2.

126. Moreover, the unsuccessful Antón Alonso Ríos was, from the founding of the Consello de Galiza, a member of this entity. After the death of Castelao—a period I do not analyze in this study—he assumed the leadership of the group.

127. "Irmandade Galega."

128. Blanco Amor returned to Argentina in 1935, where he had lived between 1919 and 1928. Despite participating in the creation of the Irmandade Galega, he stopped being a member shortly thereafter, surrounded by various controversies that dogged him during his complex time in exile; he was attacked primarily for his almost complete use of Castilian in his works from that time on.

129. Blanco Amor was editor of this publication, printed by the Federación de Sociedades Galegas Agrarias e Culturais da Arxentina, from July 26, 1936 on. Although it was published in Spanish, it had an antifascist and pro-republican stance, compared to the *Correo de Galicia*, which, within the Galician collective, would side with the insurgents from September 1936 on. See Claudio Rodríguez Fer, "Emigración, Exilio e Guerra Civil," in *Jornadas de la Emigración gallega a Puerto Rico* (Sada: Ediciós do Castro, 1997), 70–71.

130. So much so that many groups of exiles called themselves Partido Galeguista/ Irmandade Galega or Irmandade Galeguista. The most outstanding example of these groups was in Mexico.

131. Ibid.
132. Ibid., 4. The event is today known as "Día da Galiza Mártir" (Galician Martyrs Day).
133. This tribute was only performed by the Galician exiled community until 1976. It was performed mainly by Galician nationalists and leftists.
134. Typified as *regions*.
135. With the participation of representatives, as well as political parties and nationalist syndicates, from the three countries, specifically, and in the following order: Comunitat Catalana, Partido Nacionalista Vasco, Solidaridad de Trabajadores Vascos, Partido Galeguista, Esquerra Republicana de Catalunya, Estat Catalá, Acció Catalana, Partido Socialista Catalán, and Unió de Catalans Independentistes, which had been founded two years prior.
136. "Pacto de Galeuzca firmado en México," *A Nosa Terra* (front page), January 1945.
137. The formal launch of the Consello de Galiza took place in the Ateneo in the Uruguayan capital on June 30, 1945.
138. Euzkadi National Council.
139. National Council of Catalonia.
140. Javier Alvajar López, "Apuntes sobre la Delegación del Consejo de Galicia en Europa" *Anuario Brigantino* 11 (Betanzos: Concello de Betanzos, 1988), 125–36
141. "Creación do Consello de Galiza," *A Nosa Terra* (front page), December 1944.
142. Interview with Lois Tobío by Xan Leira as part of the *Memoria da Galiza* project, at http://www.culturagalega.org/TV/video_detalle.php?id=722&lyr=1600.
143. *Always in Galicia.*
144. It was distributed clandestinely in Galicia, after being shipped in by sea.
145. Castelao wrote the first book of *Sempre en Galiza* between Valencia and Barcelona, publishing parts of it as articles in the previously mentioned journals *Nova Galicia* and *Nueva Galicia*. The second book covers Castelao and Virxinia Pereira's time in New York, together with their voyage to Buenos Aires in the summer of 1940. The third book was written entirely in Buenos Aires between 1942 and 1943, with previous notes and memoirs. Lastly, there is a fourth book that does not appear in the original publication, made up of Castelao's writings from 1947 and 1948, a period in which he was minister without portfolio in the Giral government. The work starts with *Adro*, which collates Castelao's texts and musings sent to *A Nosa Terra* from Badajoz in 1935, during the exile imposed by the CEDA government.
146. In which, in contrast to Castelao, the Basque president, Agirre, was not so involved. Agirre was focused on his relations with the United States State Department, which trusted him to reconstruct the republican institutional framework with the aim of counting on the presence of a republican government at the San Francisco Conference of June 28, 1945. For Agirre, this meant the removal of the Francoist dictatorship and the explicit recognition of not just a Spanish, but also a Basque government.
147. See Xosé Estévez, *Castelao e o Galeuzca* (Compostela: Laiovento, 2002), 68.

148. "Adhesión de Don Manuel Portela Valladares ao Consello de Galiza," *A Nosa Terra* (front page), July 1945.
149. Held between April 25 and June 26, 1945 in the US city that gave its name to the meeting.
150. "Antes la Conferencia de San Francisco," *A Nosa Terra* (front page), April 1945.
151. And the conversion from the League of Nations to the United Nations (UN).
152. In any case, his integration in the Consello de Galiza did not lead to Portela becoming a member.
153. Specifically, it was approved in the session of November 9, 1945. See Diéguez Cequiel, *Nacionalismo galego aquén e alén mar*, 130–38.
154. See Antom Santos and Uxío-Breogán Diéguez, *Antón Moreda. Memoria do exilio* (Santiago de Compostela: Instituto Galego de Historia, 2011).

Contributors

Eduardo J. Alonso Olea (Bilbao, 1962) has a Master's Degree (1988) and PhD (1993) in History and Geography from the University of the Basque Country (Universidad del País Vasco/Euskal Herriko Unibertsitatea—UPV/EHU). He was a permanent researcher in the Department of Contemporary History at the University of the Basque Country between 2011 and 2018 and is currently a tenured professor in the same department where he does most of his teaching. The subject of his doctoral thesis was the Basque Economic Agreement up until the civil war. Since completing that work, he has continued a line of research related to that question and participated in different projects to spread knowledge about the Economic Agreement.

He has also published monographs (28) and articles and book chapters (145) on: the history of the administration (*Historia de la Diputación Foral de Bizkaia*), company histories (Santa Ana de Bolueta, 1841–2016; Historia de la Mutua Vizcaya Industrial, KUPSA), and biographies (those of Víctor Chávarri and Casilda de Iturrizar). He has also participated in different projects and research contracts (Ministry of Science and Innovation; Basque Government; Foral Deputation of Bizkaia; Bilbao City Council, among others).

He forms part of the consolidated research group "Biography & Parliament," created in 1989 and is recognized as such by the Basque Government in successive calls since the year 2002. Over the years, this research group has focused its lines of research on the biography of parliamentarians and members of the Representative Assemblies (Juntas Generales) of the Basque Country.

He is editor of the journal *Historia Contemporánea* and deputy director of the Documentation Center of the Economic Agreement and Foral Treasuries (Centro de Documentación del Concierto Económico y Haciendas Forales).

Giovanni C. Cattini (Mantova, 1972) has a Master's Degree in Contemporary History from the University of Bolonia (1998) and a PhD in History from the University of Barcelona (2006). He was a lecturer in the Department of Contemporary History of the University of Barcelona between 2006 and 2016, and is currently an Associate Professor (Serra Húnter Programme) in the Contemporary History & Current World Unit of the History & Archaeology Department (University of Barcelona).

His field of study is the nationalist movement between the eighteenth and nineteenth centuries; however, he specializes in contemporary Catalan Nationalism and intellectual movements of this time. He's the author of several publications regarding the history of intellectuals, cultural identities, and the Spanish Civil War. He has also collaborated with many reviews of contemporary history. Among his many publications are: *Historiografia i catalanisme. Josep Coroleu i Inglada (1839–1895)*, Barcelona-Catarroja, Afers, 2007; *Prat de la Riba i la historiografia catalana*, Barcelona-Catarroja, Afers, 2008; *El Gran Complot*, Barcelona, Arallibres, 2009—italian edition; *Nel nome di Garibaldi. I rivoluzionari catalani, i nipoti del Generale e la polizia di Mussolini (1923–1926)*, Pisa, BFS 2010-; *Joaquim de Camps i Arboix. Un intel·lectual en temps convulsos*, Barcelona, FJI, 2015; (with Xavier Fabrès) *Política i cultura: l'ateneisme en la Catalunya contemporània*, Barcelona, AB—DB, 2017; (with Àngel Casals) *The Catalan Nation and Identity throughout History*, Bern, Peter Lang, 2020; *Storie di antifascismo popolare mantovano. Dalle giornate rosse alla Guerra civile spagnola*, Milano, Franco Angeli, 2020.

As a researcher, he has taken part in six projects of the Ministry (MICIN-MINECO), five at the regional level (Catalan Government), three at the UB level, one Italian project, and two European projects. In addition, he has developed six private contracts with the Ateneu Barcelonès [Barcelona Athenaeum] to carry out the "Almirall project" since 2010. The purpose of this project is to expound upon the importance of the bibliographic resources of the library of the Ateneu Barcelonès, as a tool to understand the reception of European strands of thought, both humanistic and scientific, in Catalan and Spanish society in the late nineteenth century.

Uxio-Breogán Diéguez Cequiel (Madrid, 1978) is Professor at the University of A Coruña. He holds a PhD in Contemporary History from the University of Barcelona and has been the Director of the Chair of Historical Memory of the University of A Coruña since its founding.

In addition, he is a specialist on the history of Galician nationalism and author of many works, including *A Asemblea de Concellos de Galiza Pro-Estatuto* [The Pro-Statute Assembly of Galician Councils] (2001); *Álvaro de las Casas. Biografía e documentos* [Álvaro de las Casas. Biography and Documents] (2003); *Alexandre Bóveda nos seus documentos* [Alexandre Bóveda in His Own Words] (2011); *Nacionalismo galego aquén e alén mar* [Galician Nationalism Here and Overseas] *(1936–1975)* (2015); and *As Irmandades da Fala. Reivindicación identitaria e activismo socio-político-cultural no primeiro terzo do século XX* [Identity claim and socio-political-cultural activism in the first third of the twentieth century] (coord., 2016). He is also the author of numerous articles on the subject of the exile of Galician republicans, such as "The European Exile of Galician Nationalism from 1939. France and the case of Xohán Xosé Plá" (2017), published in *Cahiers de civilisation espagnole contemporaine* from the University of Angers, France. He has participated in various research projects on the national question and the workers' movement and has curated various exhibitions, including *Nunca Máis. A Rebelión do Pobo* [Never Again. The Revolution of the People] (2012), *70 anos do Consello de Galiza. O goberno galego no exilio* [70 Years of the Council of Galicia. The Galician Government in Exile] (2014), and *O Sindicalismo Nacionalista Galego na Transición* [Galician Nationalist Syndicalism during the Transition] (2017).

In 2003, he cofounded *Murguía, Revista Galega de Historia* [Murguia, Review of Galician History], of which he is still director. He is a lecturer and organizer of numerous conferences, workshops, and scientific meetings. Among these, he participated in the launching of the manifesto which, in 2008, gave rise to "Galeuska Historia" (which organizes meetings between Galiza, the Basque Country, and Catalonia).

Index

Note: Tables and associated captions are indicated by *t* following the page number. Notes are indicated by n and note number following the page number.

Made in the USA
Monee, IL
26 May 2022